# MEN
# HEALING
# SHAME

## AN ANTHOLOGY

Roy U. Schenk, PhD
John Everingham, PhD
Editors

with contributions by
Robert Bly and Gershen Kaufman

 Springer Publishing Company

Springer Publishing Company, Inc.
536 Broadway
New York, NY 10012

Cover design by Tom Yabut
Production Editor: Pam Lankas

95 96 97 98 99 / 5 4 3 2 1

---

**Library of Congress Cataloging-in-Publication Data**

Men healing shame : an anthology / Roy U. Schenk, John Everingham, editors.
    p. cm.—(Springer series, focus on men)
    Includes bibliographical references and index.
    ISBN 0-8261-8800-1
    1. Shame.  2. Men—Psychology.  3. Stigma (Social psychology)
4. Masculinity (Psychology)  I. Schenk, Roy U., 1929– .  II. Everingham, John, 1932– .  III. Series: Springer series, focus on men
BF575.S45M46 1994
155.3′32—dc20                                                        94-36330
                                                                          CIP

---

Printed in the United States of America

# Contents

# Preface

Shame is a deflating feeling of personal worthlessness—like when you're suddenly laid off without explanation even though the company is doing well. You're hurting, and feel there's nobody to blame but yourself. Yet *you can't for the life of you figure out what you did wrong.* "There must be something *wrong* with me, but what?" This is Shame. Not guilt, but shame. You just want to disappear, or lie in bed, hoping to wake up and find out that it was only a dream. You have to keep active so you won't get depressed.

Maybe you watch sitcoms on television and feel edgy as the men all act like fools. Shame. Or you get caught peeking in a window at a girl undressing. Shame on you! You write a brilliant story on a friend's computer, and forget to save it. You *know* you can never rewrite it as well. And you think, "Not again! How stupid can I get?" There's a war going on in your guts, and both sides are losing. Shame turns to discouragement, depression, and anger at yourself.

That's where this book comes in. You will learn here how to keep shame from overwhelming you. You won't eliminate all shame from your life; no man can do that. But you *can* learn how to handle it before it breaks your spirit or manifests as a major disease. Healing shame can be an exciting adventure, and it might even get to be fun.

Shame shapes, controls, and limits men's lives. It is our most powerful negative affect. It drives men to violence, to war, to uncaring pollution of our planet. If we men are to become whole human beings, we will have to understand, confront, and surmount the shame that now creates havoc in our lives.

Women also experience shame, and are deeply wounded by it. Both men's and women's lives are restricted by the use of shame to enforce gender roles, and to control and manipulate us. David Ault (Seattle, WA) once pointed out that the shaming epithet "tramp" has been used against both men and women to enforce gender roles.

But from birth, males are also subjected to another devastating shame message. It tells men, with almost hypnotic effect, that we should feel ashamed simply because we are male. Whatever we may call this messages—*the shame of maleness* (Schenk) or *basic male shame* (Gagnon)—it places us in a Catch-22 predicament. We are shamed when we deviate from our traditional gender roles but shamed also when we conform to these same roles. Our book explores the sources of this shaming.

It is no accident that men are greatly outnumbered among therapy and counseling clients. Not only must we surmount the shame of not being able to go it alone, but we also face a therapeutic format and mind-set that is often alien to men's style and mode of feeling, and is sometimes overtly hostile to masculinity.

It appears that socialization of females tends to promote fear in women, who develop more than 90% of clinical phobias. In contrast, many men develop a shame-driven, foolhardy fearlessness. Some may appear to be shameless, both uncaring and careless. We suspect that they really harbor a huge burden of shame inside, which is so painful that they fear to show any of it, even to themselves. Perhaps there is also a "shamelessness" that women manifest in relationships.

For centuries, shame was used in Western culture to coerce both men and women into conformity with sex roles that were limiting at best, and frequently onerous. As women's liberation worked to free women from the shame of breaking long-enculturated taboos, it became almost standard practice to blame men for the origin and maintenance of these constraints. Now, a generation later, men are beginning the same liberation process, albeit in our own style. We too are sorely tempted to blame women for many of our constraints and the shaming that so powerfully maintains them. The editors view such blaming by either sex as profoundly counterproductive. We must all speak up to acknowledge our wounds, but to project blame onto others serves only to keep them festering.

Being human means that we are not perfect. We recognize that we may not always succeed in avoiding blaming.

Roy Schenk recounts that "this book was conceived as a way to examine, confront and heal men's shame. Many techniques arose before their authors had a clear understanding that they were dealing with shame, but others grew out of this understanding and of the internal predicament which underlies shame."

"I came to appreciate the impact of shame on men from a social and theoretical basis, and only with time began to understand the power of shame in my own life. My coeditor, Dr. John Everingham, came first to a recognition of the impact of shame on his own life, which later grew to an understanding of the pervasive role of shame in society." We think these contrasting approaches have contributed breadth, power, and a wider range of insight to this work.

John Everingham says, "I too, am a shame man. I didn't discover this until my middle years, and it dawned on me more slowly than Robert Bly recounts in chapter 4. Like Robert, I felt great relief at the discovery. All my life, I've had a strong sense of being seriously flawed. Despite twenty years of relentlessly exploring psychological and spiritual matters, the nature of this anomaly remained a mystery. It didn't seem to be anything I had done wrong, but like something I was born with—my fate. What a relief to discover that it has a name—shame. And by this time (late 1987), the work of Schneider, Kaufman, Kurtz, Fossum and Mason, and others had revealed the outlines of the modern view of shame and had suggested healing methods. At last!"

"After vowing never again to go to a psychotherapist who didn't understand shame thoroughly, I became a client of Carl Schneider, and later George Lindall. Both these men helped me a great deal, but neither should be blamed for my blind spots. Other input comes from being a member of a 12-step group, from reading and listening to tapes, attending seminars and workshops, discussions with many of the authors cited, and from interacting nonprofessionally with other men concerning personal shame."

We're proud of this book. The contributors share their experience with insight and passion. As editors, we have been moved or enlightened on first reading a manuscript, and we have often felt the sense of relief that comes from new evidence that we are not alone in our wounding or dysfunction. We believe this book contains new approaches of considerable value to most therapists and counselors who wish to enhance their work with men. And to the large majority of readers in other lines of work we say, "Welcome, brothers. Enjoy!"

The chapter authors work in many professions, have a variety of concepts about human growth and change, and represent several "schools" of psychotherapeutic orientation. We come from various positions in the spectrum of men's liberation, including those who see themselves as nonaligned. Half of the chapter authors practice psychotherapy, and others work as a chemist, anatomist, poet, musician, lawyer, and psychologist. We all have advanced formal education, and roughly an equal number of us hold doctorate and master's degrees. Most of us lead experiential workshops for men or for both sexes, and many of us teach and write. We believe our most valid credential is that all of us are working on our personal shame issues, and have made some substantial progress on this journey. Our writing grows out of our lives and experience, enriched by assimilation of the work of others.

We admire also those who contributed to the survey about why men do not seek help in therapy or self-help groups more often (chapter 7). Their breadth and depth is impressive, and so is the wide range of life experience that they share with us. As our book nears completion, the editors feel a deep sense of fulfillment for our part in bringing the voices of these men to a wider audience.

The chapters fall into five broad categories. Chapters 1 to 6 are overviews on the nature of shame, its origins and sources, representations of shame in mythology and the arts, and a broad palette of healing techniques. Chapter 7 is a survey about why men do not make more use of therapy and self-help for emotional and behavior problems, and what might make such help more attractive to most men. In the next chapters, five psychotherapists describe innovations that they have found to be successful.

Chapters 13 to 17 are a collection of special topics relating to shame: the Rescue triangle, forgiveness, "rules" that maintain shaming among men, the goodness of men, and masculine intimacy. The final chapters and the appendix contain our vision of how the world is changing as we heal toxic shame. They deal with men's initiation and the emerging culture of initiated masculinity, with the rise of self-esteem as shame declines, improvements in epistemology, and the vision of a society in which pejorative judgment is out of place.

There are some biases in this book. The chapter authors are mostly heterosexual white men, professional and upper middle class, but diverse in religious affiliation. At one point, we considered including chapters written by a woman and a clearly pro-feminist man, but did not diligently pursue authors with these perspectives. John Giles's chapter on forgiveness and Philip Powell's on the journey from shame to self-esteem were both chosen for the excellence of their contents, not for the sexual orientation or race of the author.

One of our strengths is that we include authors who represent the men's rights, mythopoetic, men's initiation, 12-step, and gay rights arms of contemporary men's liberation. We welcome and respect contributors with different experience, despite occasional disagreement. At first our attitude toward profeminist men was less than welcoming, for we saw them, rightly or wrongly, as committed to blaming and shaming men, themselves included. Recently we have gained respect for the honesty and passion of some of them, especially those who are leaders in the American Men's Studies Association. We welcome all to the joys of combating shame by facing it directly.

Another obvious bias is that our book is about men, and addressed to men. We deem it important to look specifically at the ways men are shamed, and the ways men heal shame. Both editors, and many of our authors, are unabashed advocates of men's liberation. We make little attempt to balance our presentation by including feminine viewpoints, and we are certainly not dispassionate. We aim for honesty, and maintain that passion is compatible with it. It's our belief that the dispassionate stance often conceals a multitude of conscious and unconscious biases, untenable tacit assumptions, and doubtful epistemology.

The standard of validity for information presented in most of this book is not the scientific method of control/measure/reproduce, which is so well suited to the physical sciences. We most commonly communicate our personal experience, and invite readers to choose what they find useful or worthy of testing for themselves. Our experience comes from dealing with both our personal shame and that of clients, and is integrated with intuition, reading, discussion, and the arts. Although we find most of the theory presented herein to be compelling and helpful, it is offered for exploration, not as generally accepted fact. The methods we suggest are designed to facilitate further work. As with most knowledge and theory, validation of these ideas will come from men discovering their value in their own lives. A broader context for evaluating knowledge about shame is presented in the appendix.

The authors use a variety of styles, and we're not always scholarly in the classic sense. Please don't be fooled; we're thoroughly serious about our subject. Most of us use an informal, even conversational style, and some employ vulgarity. We like the emotional honesty promoted by these styles.

Our aim is to speak to the hearts of men. We're not here to prove anything in the formal sense, nor to win arguments. Our model of communication is to awaken a deep longing in the reader. Most of us assume that all men have a lust for healing, wholeness, and completeness, a drive to align with the world axis, the flow of the universe, the grace of God. Our styles are designed to touch this sense in the reader, and to be congruent with our true selves.

In the interests of brevity and directness, we have frequently deleted phrases, such as "in my opinion," "I believe," and "in my experience." Readers may pencil these back in if they wish, and are invited to "translate" what we write into more—or less—formal language, as they choose. Nor should the book be seen as the definitive work on men's shame. It is a kind of progress report, written by men whose lives are in progress. We regard the field of shame as still in flux, unconsolidated; we're well advised to delay codification of concepts and terminology. We see ourselves in the most creative of times.

We invite you to join us in effective action impelled by our common urge for health and magnificence, and a desire to narrow the gap between our true and false selves, and thereby align ourselves with the Divine, however defined. We want to speak to your heart, and convince you that healing shame is not only possible, but well worth the effort. And you don't have to do it alone, for now there are plenty of buddies to join you for the trip.

R.U.S.
J.E.

# Acknowledgment

We express our great appreciation to Maret Thorpe for her expert editorial assistance and copy editing, and to Roan Kaufman for his contribution as editorial assistant, doing so many tasks that no one else was available to do and doing them well. We acknowledge with gratitude those who read and critiqued chapter drafts. They include Dmitri Bilgere, Del Marshall, Rosalie Conner Sutcher, Howard Sutcher, Kathryn Seifert, Bob Everingham, Rich Zubaty, Tom Hytry, and Petra Ressler. We thank Jane DeLong for preparation of audiotape transcripts, Tim Sonder for translating disks from DOS to Mac, Barbara Hennings for proofreading most of the manuscript, Walter Greaves for computer graphics, Ken Everingham for help with duplicating and mailing, and Jill Hayworth for typing assistance at a crucial time.

John Guarnaschelli submitted an excellent chapter on "When Shame Turns to Gold," and Tom McFarlane worked on preparing a chapter based on his studies of fathers' blessing. Unfortunately, space and time prevented their publication here. We thank these men for their effort, and hope to see their work published elsewhere. Special appreciation goes to the Chapter authors and the many contributors to Chapter 7. Together you have helped create a powerful book. We thank Bill Tucker, our Editor at Springer, for his unfailing assistance, and our agent Jane Jordan Browne for her knowledge and skill concerning the promotional, legal, and financial aspects of our project.

John Everingham voices his thanks to Irwin Aloff, Tom Hytry, David Iverson, Steve Jaffe, Jules Kaplan, Harvey Wigdor, Foster de la Houssaye, Bill Power, John Perrin, Dave Lindgren, Mike

Greenwald, and others of the First Chicago Integration Group. You know for what.

Finally Roy Schenk acknowledges the ongoing support and caring of his partner, Kathryn Seifert, whose assistance and critiques were so valuable throughout this project, and also the many people who have contributed by discussing and arguing with him about his developing ideas.

ROY U. SCHENK
JOHN EVERINGHAM

# Contributors

**Robert Adler** is author of the book, *Escaping the Job Rut: Losing the Misery and Finding Your Mission*. He was the first Texas participant in the New Warrior Training Adventure Weekend in June, 1989. Mr. Adler resides with his wife in Houston, Texas.

**Irwin Aloff, MA**. From India to Indiana, from secretaries to CEOs for over 25 years, Irwin has helped enrich the personal and professional lives of hundreds of people. A former professor, he is now a consultant and facilitator.

**Dieter Ammann** is an executive with a large government agency. He has led workshops in communication and management skills, group dynamics, and self-esteem both inside and outside the government. Dieter is a graduate of the New Warrior and ABC training, has staffed New Warrior trainings, and has led integration groups. He is married and has two children, a son, 25, and a daughter, 14.

**Asa Baber** originated the MEN column in *Playboy* in 1982 and has been writing it ever since. He served in the United States Marine Corps, and has been a full-time freelance writer since 1972. He is the father of two sons, Jim and Brendan.

**Francis Baumli, PhD**, is a noted author on men's issues whose works have been published in *American Man, M. The Humanist, Asahi Shimbun*, and other publications. Best known for his work as the Missouri representative for the Coalition of Free Men, for several years he hosted the radio show, *Men Freeing Men*. He has served on the faculties of several colleges and universities and has pursued studies in counseling psychology and neurology. He is married to Abbe Sudvarg, a physician with a specialty in family practice, and has two children, Dacia and Marion.

**Dmitri Bilgere** is a long-time activist in the men's movement. As a writer and seminar leader, Dmitri has come to see that men and women are actually more alike than they are different, and his mission is to heal shame and to facilitate gender reconciliation by teaching the power of the shadow. He has been facilitating the shadow work process and deep emotional work for more than 5 years.

**Robert Bly** is regarded by many as a prophet of men's reawakening. Although he resists affiliation with specific organizations or schools of thought, his writing, conferences, public appearances, and audio/videotapes have been sources of inspiration for over a decade, expecially for mythopoetic and men's initiation work. His prose poem, "Finding the Father," became a metaphor for the task of the movement in its early years, and his best-selling *Iron John* (Bly, 1990) has opened a door to the joys of reclaimed masculinity for many thousands of men.

Born in 1926, Bly was educated at Harvard and the University of Iowa, and received a Fulbright Award for advanced study in Norway. His first book of poems, *Silence in the Snowy Fields*, appeared in 1962. He has since published about 30 books, including more books of poetry, as well as translations of prose and poetry from Norwegian, Spanish, German, and Swedish. His last two books are *The Rag and Bone Shop of the Heart*, a collection of the poems most admired at men's conferences over the last 10 years, edited with James Hillman and Michael Meade, and *What Have I Ever Lost By Dying?*, a book of collected prose poems.

**Michael "Bull Moose"** prefers anonymity. He came to Windsor, ON, in 1964 to learn tool and die making, and now works as a process engineer. Married in 1971, he has two daughters, aged 19 and 21.

**Lawrence J. Diggs** is a writer, producer, and lecturer on sociological, psychological, biological, and legal issues, especially those that uniquely impact men. He has created workshops, seminars, and radio and television programs whose theme is bringing true equality to gender issues. A divorced man, he has three adult children and a new grandson.

**Frank A. DiLallo** has practiced individual, marital, family, and group counseling for the last 15 years. Mr. DiLallo is also the pastoral counselor for Central Catholic High School of Toledo, OH, where he directs a counseling ministry for faculty, students, and their families. He holds a master's degree in counseling and is a licensed professional counselor and a certified chemical dependency counselor in Ohio.

**Patrick Dougherty, MA, LP,** is a licensed psychologist in private practice in St. Paul, MN. He is a storyteller, writer, and adjunct faculty member at St. Mary's College of Minnesota. As an ex-Marine who fought in Vietnam, he uses his storytelling to speak of the complexities and ambiguities of war. He has been published in journals and books, including several essays and professional articles dealing with men's issues. He co-teaches a graduate counseling course entitled, *Working with Men in Psychotherapy*.

**John H. Gagnon, PhD,** is a psychotherapist in private practice with adults, couples, and families. He received his doctorate in psychology from Union Institute in 1982. He teaches at the University of Connecticut, Torrington Branch, and has written several technical articles and edited a book titled, *Wounded Healer*. He lives with his wife, a neonatal nurse practitioner, and has an adult daughter, Isabelle.

**John Giles** holds Bachelor and Master of Music degrees from the University of Illinois, and advanced certification in musicology from the University of Michigan and in voice performance from Northwestern University. He has served as Director of Music at the Unitarian Church of Evanston, IL, since 1981.

**Michael Greenwald, JD,** has been a trial lawyer, counselor, mediator, and facilitator for nearly two decades. He received his BA in sociology and anthropology from Swarthmore College and his JD from George Washington University. He serves the New Warrior Network by leading Training Adventure weekends, in leadership training and certification, and as general counsel of the corporation. He lives in Winnetka, IL with his spouse, Micaela and her two daughters.

**Ian Harris, PhD,** is a Professor of Educational Policy and Community Studies at University of Wisconsin–Milwaukee, where he has taught a course on male identity since 1978. He has been an active participant in the New Warrior Network–Milwaukee, and a counselor at Batterers Anonymous. Dr. Harris is the author of the upcoming book, *Messages Men Hear: Constructing Masculinities*.

**Andre Heuer, MS,** develops and teaches curricula in men's life skills and human sexuality. He also teaches in county adult correctional facilities. A psychotherapist in private practice in Minneapolis, MN, he is known for his workshops for men in the Twin Cities and other locations. He is involved in professional, educational, and pastoral ministry and conducts workshops and retreats for churches in spirituality, family life, and men's issues.

**John Higgins, MS,** is a sales representative (independent contractor) in a publishing-related field. He holds Bachelor and Masters degrees in secondary education and library science, respectively. He first met his biological father at age 37—a very positive and fulfilling decision/experience. He regrets not doing it sooner. He has been happily married to his wife, Norma, for 18 years.

**Jack Kammer** has been active in activities related to men's issues for many years. He was Executive Director of the National Congress for Men for 16 months. He conducted a talk show called *Men, Sex, and Power* at a Baltimore radio station for several years. He is the author of *Good Will Toward Men: Women Talk Candidly About the Balance of Power Between the Sexes*.

**Gershen Kaufman, PhD,** was educated at Columbia University and received his doctorate in clinical psychology from the University of Rochester. He is a professor in the Counseling Center at Michigan State University and also maintains a private practice. A pioneer in the study of shame, he is the author of *The Psychology of Shame: Theory and Treatment of Shame-Based Syndromes* (Springer Publishing Co., 1989); *Shame: The Power of Caring* (1992); and *Journey to the Magic Castle* (1993). He is the co-author with Lev Raphael of *Stick up for Yourself! Every Kid's Guide* to *Personal Power and Positive Self-Esteem* (1990), and *Dynamics of Power: Fighting Shame and Building Self-Esteem* (1991). He has lectured widely on the role of shame in personality, psychopathology, and psychotherapy, as well as its significance for gender, culture, and society.

**Bill Kauth, MA,** is a founder of the New Warrior Network and has been the Wisconsin organizer of the New Warrior Training Adventure Weekend for many years. He recently embarked on the project of taking the New Warrior Network worldwide. His mission is to create a safe planet through empowering men.

**George Lindall** was a college instructor and advisor from 1974–81, helping students with work, career, and personal issues. Since 1983 he has been a psychologist working with addicts, codependents, and families in outpatient, inpatient, and private practice settings. He is a co-author of the unpublished manuscript, *Against the Tide: Why Addicts Aren't Recovering in Today's World*. He lives with his wife and four children in Minneapolis.

**David L. Lindgren, MA,** has been a practicing psychotherapist, author, and workshop leader for the past 20 years. He is co-founder and Executive Director of New Warrior Chicago which presents initiatory trainings for men and adolescents. For the past year he has directed a mentoring program at an inner-city, all-Black male high school and has completed a leader-training curriculum for men's work.

**Jim Lovestar** has lived in Minneapolis, MN for many years, where he is an outstanding massage therapist. His mission is to touch the divine essence in all beings. Coming from a history of fear and mistrust towards men, he is committed to heal that within himself and to assist every man he encounters to trust himself and other men.

**Christopher Miller** earned his BA degree in psychology at Northwestern University, and his Master of Divinity and Doctor of Ministry degrees at the Chicago Theological Seminary. He has extensive training in individual, marital, and family therapy, and has been an adjunct faculty member at the Chicago Theological Seminary. He is currently the director of a pastoral counseling center in Evanston, IL, where he lives with his wife and two daughters.

**Bob Porter, MSW,** has been an individual, marital, family, and group therapist since 1981, and is an instructor at the University of Wisconsin–Milwaukee. He has been facilitating men's groups and workshops since 1982.

**Buddy T. Portugal** is a psychotherapist in private practice and organizational consultant to corporations and businesses. He is co-creator of the Men's Room Weekends, and co-author of a book on the Men's Room, published in 1994.

**Philip M. Powell, PhD,** grew up in tough surroundings and has tried to help others who grew up in similar or even better circumstances. He earned his PhD from the Committee on Human Development at the University of Chicago in 1981. He has taught at Yale University in the Department of Psychology for 5 years and is currently an Associate Professor in the Department of Educational Psychology, University of Texas, Austin.

**Al Ring, MD,** is a Clinical Professor of Pathology at the University of Illinois College of Medicine. He received his MD from the University of Michigan Medical School in 1958. He has conducted research in physiology, embryology, chemistry, and clinical pathology, has published over 40 articles and books on a variety of medical subjects including anatomic and clinical pathology, and has received extensive honors and appointments in the medical field.

**Rich Tosi** is the father of two sons, married to Char, and now lives in Michigan. He was an officer in the Marine Corps, and worked for many years as an engineer with General Motors. He is a co-founder of the New Warrior Training Adventure, and is currently President of the New Warrior Network.

**Tom Williamson, MA,** has worked with the Nassau County Department of Health, Office of Social work. He conducted a private inquiry for the New York Center for Men into why battered men do not seek help. He is the long-time President of the National Coalition of Free Men. Currently Mr. Williamson is employed in the computer industry as a technical writer.

# 1

## Some Basics About Shame

*John Everingham*

This chapter presents an overview of the editors' current views on shame.[1] Part of our purpose is to answer the natural question, "Why another book on shame?" And authors differ in the way terms are defined and in some of the basic concepts, as might be expected in an emerging field of inquiry. These basics may help to organize your comprehension. Should we disagree, the point of our divergence may be more accurately charted.

And disagree we will. It has been only a few years since the modern understanding of shame came busting out of the closet into public consciousness. New awareness swirls about us like floodwater suddenly released from a century of impoundment behind the high dam of denial and mislabeling. We can expect things to be topsy-turvy for a while.

Students of shame often resemble the proverbial blind men describing an elephant. Accurate portrayal of some parts may overlook other vital regions. Lacking universal answers, we aim to share our experience and thought honestly, in masculine voice and viewpoint. Let's all keep a certain sense of freshness and wonder, being wary of overly cherished dogmas or the voices of "authority," old and new.

We see considerable reason to hope that a new synthesis—indeed a planet-saving synthesis—will emerge from our collective effort to understand and heal shame. Until then, take what you can use, and leave the rest.

1. *Shame is the "Invisible Dragon."* Shame is a powerful but often overlooked emotional force, whose widespread and pervasive effects have not been widely recognized until recently (my personal breakthrough came from Fossum & Mason, 1986). Shame is still seriously misunderstood by many psychotherapists, psychologists, professors, and mental health professionals. But thanks to the work of Schneider (1977), Kaufman (1980), Kurtz (1981), Fossum and Mason (1986), Bradshaw (1988), Miller (1981), Bly (1995), and many others, there are now thousands of us who *do* understand the basics, are working fruitfully to heal our own shame, and applying what we're learning to the upgrading of our personal and social environment.

2. *Healing our shame offers hope for healing our world.* Men have for centuries been willing to die to maintain their honor—to avoid public and permanent shame. Behind our cool facade, we don't say "honor" or "shame" much these days, but we'll still do almost anything to avoid public humiliation, personal or national (Kaufman, 1992, pp. 227–241). "Anything" can mean vengeance, blaming, violence, war, struggle for control, compulsive overachievement, and denial in many forms. These tactics lessen the awful feeling of shame for a while, but drive it underground and make things worse in the long run. Such tactics cannot heal, and are as futile as giving a pacifier to a hungry baby.

   Shame is a natural emotion. There is no danger in openly feeling ashamed and saying so. The trouble comes when we're fiercely determined to *avoid* feeling shame, by burying or denying it. It's this buried, internalized shame that leads to violence, war, addiction, child abuse, emotional dishonesty, protracted feuds, a narrow "bottom line" mentality, and other evils. Mastering the simple relationship between shame, honor and violence offers new hope for a peaceful and cherished planet.

3. *Understanding shame clarifies issues in the ongoing battle of the sexes.* Kaufman and Raphael (1991) argue cogently that interpersonal shame cannot be healed until power is shared. We support equality and shared power, which are the birthright of us all. Underestimation of the "shame factor," by men and

women alike, unfortunately has led to serious miscalculation of power equations. Much confusion arises from the false assumption that sexual asymmetry is the equivalent of inequality (Moore & Gillette, 1993b, pp. 21–30). The goal for us all is to feel pride in our own sex and profound respect for the other.

It is still true, as Schenk (1991) says, that men have more control in the world of work, money, and politics outside home and family—in the areas of "doing." But women wield more power in the arena of sex, nurturing, child rearing, and comfort—and in the "being" areas. The considerable power of beauty, the breast, and the hearth are frequently overlooked today.

American men are particularly vulnerable to shaming, and almost oblivious to its pervasive presence and effects. Both sexes engage in habitual shaming practices, unconsciously or regarding them as justifiable parlor games or 'little white sins.' Then we wonder at the rage and violence increasing in our land. Shaming men is never a "freebie," but rather a serious violation of both our honor and our inner spirituality.

We present this book primarily to raise men's consciousness, not to plead with women for understanding. Though rarely admitted, liberation movements usually harbor plenty of anger, insensitivity, intolerance, or outright contempt for outgroups. Our liberation strategy is to strengthen men, not "civilize" women. As men experience bonding and initiation, and learn to resist shaming personally—eyeball to eyeball, I predict that habitual shaming and semiconscious oppression will wither. Together we'll create safety for both sexes to heal and grow.

4. *Why deal only with men's shame, when much that we offer may apply to women as well?* We wanted to tell it like it is, for us, without being concerned with applicability or acceptability to women. We desire to speak in male voice, with the male mode of feeling (Bly & Meade, n.d.). When men separate from women and begin to talk of matters close to our heart, the tone changes. As we let go of trying to be sensitive, reasonable "nice guys," our language gets coarse and powerful—more congruent with our bodies. It sounds honest and authentic. Even when the talk is gentle or vulnerable, there's a tone that I've never heard when women are around (Perry, 1985). We speak to men in this masculine tone.

Part of the atmosphere of shaming that envelops men today is the disparagement of our strong language. It's not only vulgarity, but also bluntness, directness, forcefulness, lack of euphemism, emotional congruence, telling it like it is, and greater concern for the honesty of the speaker than the hurt feelings of the hearer. When a man hears that this kind of talk is "inappropriate" to his present setting (classroom, mixed discussion group, talk show), the subvocal message is: "Don't be *truly* honest; adopt a false persona, because the real you is 'out of place' here." We choose to make a book where mantalk is not out of place.

I suspect that something is quite different about the way men and women experience, process, and seek to avoid shame. It's difficult to say what this supposed difference might be. The only distinction that seems clear is that women tend to be ashamed of their bodies, whereas we men are more ashamed of our feelings. I sense that I don't understand women's shame in some essential quality. When one relies so much on experience and intuition, he's well advised to stick close to matters of personal knowledge. Remember those *male* psychotherapists who wrote about women's supposed penis envy and Electra complexes (Gilligan, 1981). In addition to the wrongheadedness of drawing conclusions from a faulty epistemological paradigm about matters outside their own experience, these men played key roles in the longtime cover-up of mountains of sexual abuse and attendant internalized shame (Masson, 1984). Women's shame deserves its own specific treatment, and we hope that savvy and compassionate women are writing it even now.

5. *In its primary form, shame is an emotion with well-defined facial and other physical characteristics.* These include head down, eyes averted, blushing (Kaufman, 1989), and a sinking feeling; "Sartre's shudder" (Sartre, 1955, p. 222); and a compulsion to hide. Shame is one of the nine "primary affects" described by Tompkins (1987), based on findings of similar "faces" of shame in many cultures. Internally, the feeling of primary shame is distinctive, once we allow ourselves the time to really experience it. Recognition may be aided by permission to call it by name, and by realizing that shame is usually felt and expressed silently.

Primary shame is *not* destructive. It feels *awful*, but it doesn't do us any harm in itself. The trouble comes when we try to avoid this piercingly uncomfortable feeling, or make it go away—quick. Typically, we allow ourselves to feel primary shame for only a few milliseconds, before shifting automatically to some other emotion, often fear or anger. This practice confuses recognition and tends to internalize the shame. It's a habit we need to break, because the resulting internalized shame is both destructive and dangerous (Kaufman, 1989).

6. *Internalized shame is a reaction to the* prospect *or fear of feeling ashamed—of feeling the primary emotion.* Internalized shame often has a frozen or hollow feeling, with eyes glazed, brain numb, and face immobile. I may become inarticulate (Baumli, 1995) or have a desperate desire to hide, while being afraid (ashamed) to admit it. A man may act like a puppet, moving jerkily through the day with a mechanical smile, hoping that nobody will ask if something is wrong. We usually feel deeply ashamed of feeling ashamed, and try to hide *that*. Like primary shame, internalized shame is felt and expressed in silence, but with our bodies more rigid and "playing possum."

As with primary shame, most of us develop strategies to try to avoid feeling, or showing, internalized shame as well as primary. Suppressed emotions, workaholism, being overcompetitive, taking anabolic steroids, unnecessary violence, and stylized tough talk (e.g., "Read my lips!") are some examples. This cover-up is aided both by poor recognition of internalized shame, and by societal pressures to deny or disguise it—pressures *not* to see shame, or to feel or talk about it.

As we continue to avoid experiencing shame directly, we adopt a false self—a "front," a "persona," an "act." In time, we tend to forget that it's an act, and believe it to be who we really are (Miller, 1981; Fossum & Mason, 1986; Bly, 1995). But the disowned parts of the true self make their presence known through addiction, a sense of futility, grandiosity/depression swings, and feeling disconnected from ourselves and others.

Internalized shame is often described as more than an emotion—as a complex experience which involves feeling, behavior, and core beliefs (Potter-Efron & Potter-Efron, 1989). Without realizing it at the time, I came to the conclusion—deep down in my bones—that there was something terribly wrong with me. My head knew that it was irrational, but my body was even more certain of its truth. For some unknown reason, I just don't belong here; I'm an impostor. If only I can be perfect, or merely wonderful, maybe they won't notice and I can stay. This core belief—subconsciously held—reinforces the false self already created, and becomes part of the "experience" of shame internalized. Note that many, even most, emotions tend to be converted to anxiety and fear—fear of exposure.

Internalized shame starves the soul. Patrick Dougherty (1988) says, "Where shame is, God is not."

7. *Long-standing internalized shame develops into a shame-based identity (Kaufman, 1989).* This identity is a life pattern or "script" in which hidden shame is the central feature. It usually arises in childhood, when abuse, neglect, and shaming rules pile on more and more internalized shame. Synonyms for a shame-based identity are "addiction to shame," (Bly, 1995), a "shame-bound" person or syndrome (Kaufman, 1989), tertiary shame, or a shame "racket."

The concept of a "racket" comes from Transactional Analysis (James & Jongeward, 1971, p. 189), and refers to a series of interactions that culminate in a man receiving his favorite emotional "payoff." The payoff is a painful but familiar feeling, which is preferred because it's somehow more acceptable than other emotions. By a combination of excessive people pleasing, withdrawal, grandiosity/depression swings, incompleteness and passive-aggressive behavior, I managed to feel ashamed most of the time. Projects were unfinished, commitments unkept, and despite lots of television and escape reading, I was usually "too busy" to spend much time nurturing or being nurtured, or just having fun. I felt chronic internalized shame—my favorite payoff. Shame rackets deserve to be recognized and named.

Shame may be an important element in *all* rackets, because of the feature of substituting emotions. The painful excitement of constant turmoil is a favorite payoff for some men who would be too ashamed to become depressed, or can't afford it (i.e., won't face the shame of being an inadequate provider). Some may develop serious illness in order to quit the rat race and be cared for, finding a way out that preserves their honor.

"Simply making up a false personality to please our parents can generate shame for a lifetime" (Bly, 1990, p. 167). As internalized shame became a life pattern, I forgot that I ever *had* a true self, and saw it as a sign of my basic defectiveness that I even *wanted* anything other than what my parents or peers wanted. The Invisible Dragon feeds on himself, and reproduces.

8. *Internalized shame is maintained by a set of rules (blame, denial, incompleteness, perfectionism, etc.).* These rules govern

our behavior by dictating habitual patterns of shaming actions (Fossum & Mason, 1986; Everingham, 1995d). To "kick" the bad habit of reinforcing shame in ourselves and others, we can learn to *break* the rules.

Shaming rules were first described by family therapists and referred to as "family rules." To keep families mired in internalized shame from generation to generation, they act like the inertia we studied in high school physics, in that the shame keeps going until some force stops it or alters its course. This was a breakthrough concept for me, for I saw that neither I nor my parents had done anything especially heinous; we had only followed unquestioningly the shaming patterns handed down to us as normal, correct behavior.

Shaming rules may be found in force in all human interactions, not only inside families. As we move to break the bad habit of shaming each other without really meaning to, major bottlenecks are failure to recognize these rules or underestimating their effect on our friendships. Like the Invisible Dragon himself, shaming rules lose much of their power in the light of understanding.

9. *The Rescue Triangle is another way of clarifying interactions that maintain internalized shame* (James & Jongeward, 1971; Karpman, 1968). As players, we adopt one of three *manipulative* roles: Persecutor, Rescuer, or Victim.[2] As the "play" unfolds, the actors switch roles in dramatic fashion. Rescuers "help" by putting more energy into a Victim's problems than he does, then become the Victims of frustration and lack of appreciation, and, finally, Persecutors by kissing off the ingrate with a vengeance. In the modern sociopolitical "scene," we see those who struggle to maintain their superior Victim position, so as to gain license to Persecute by blaming and shaming others with impunity. The Rescue triangle is the subject of chapter 13, and discussed also in chapters 14 and 15.

10. *Poisonous Pedagogy.* Alice Miller (1984, 1986) introduced this concept to cover several coordinated rules, prevalent in our culture, that come from the presumption that adults are right and children wrong. Poisonous pedagogy assumes that children should serve adults' emotional needs, and that children's impulses are bad and must be trained[3] out of them early—so that they "dare not notice" that a false self has been substituted for the true self. Once "trained," they become adults who perpetu-

ate both poisonous pedagogy and their own deeply internalized shame, which they see as normal.

One result of poisonous pedagogy is a core belief that I need reforming in some way, or am dominated by disruptive or dangerous qualities that must somehow be held in check. Schoenbeck (1992) illuminates the important distinction between reformation and transformation. Transformation requires that a man accept himself as he is now, whereas reformation assumes that he needs to be altered in order to become acceptable. I feel a cleansing breath of fresh air whenever I contemplate this difference.

11. *Good news! It now appears that internalized shame can be healed substantially by laymen using simple techniques.* We encourage readers to begin healing this easy part on their own. It's not so complicated or mysterious, because much of shame's destructive power depends on its remaining hidden or disguised. Now that the basic form of the Invisible Dragon is discerned by thousands of us, many new healing methods are being developed by laymen and professionals alike.

Some of these methods are tried and true, such as the 12 step program pioneered by Alcoholics Anonymous (AA). Others are being invented and tested even as we write. We hope our book will be useful to ordinary men, as well as professional psychotherapists. In a sense, it can be seen as a collection of recipes for healing internalized shame. Like any good cook, you'll undoubtedly want to add a dash of your own flavoring. We welcome diversity, because it's unlikely that any one recipe will suit all tastes.

Bringing primary shame out of the closet is a basic technique useful for defanging internalized shame. We learn to see the shaming rules in operation (Everingham, 1995d), and stop playing our habitual "shame game." We can start to recognize primary shame and allow ourselves time to really feel it, rather than bailing out immediately into some other emotion. We can learn to avert our gaze, hang our head, blush, shudder, remain when we desire to flee, and then look a man in the eyes and say, "I feel ashamed."

But technique isn't everything. Healing even the easy part of shame requires commitment. And your personal healing will operate on its own timetable, difficult to predict and impossible to control. We bless your effort.

12. *For men with a big burden of internalized shame, healing the*

*difficult part is likely to take several years, and require plenty of guts and persistence, as well as the help of a psychothera-pist.* Don't try to work on shame with a therapist who doesn't grasp the modern concept and hasn't done substantial work on his own shame. I've had this experience, and it only added more confusion, internalized shame, and self-doubt.

Schneider (1977) has shown that philosophers (especially Nietzsche and Sartre) understood shame clearly when the psychologists and therapists did not. Nathanson (1987) gives a candid account of one psychiatrist's "awakening" to shame issues after 20 years of practice. Although many psychotherapists now see the light, there are still many others who remain unawakened. Ask a prospective therapist what he's doing to heal his own shame, and look into his eyes as he answers. For the man with a shame-based identity or other deep shame issues, a male therapist is strongly recommended.

13. *It's often beneficial to say "shame" and "I feel ashamed"— right out loud.* The sound of the word (perhaps the "shh" sound) somehow evokes the feeling for many of us, accurately and powerfully. The word itself lifts the emotion from its hiding places deep inside my body, in a way that "guilt," "low self-esteem" or "narcissism" cannot. At last, I've found a true name for my invisible, formless deformity!

We have enough trouble experiencing primary shame, without burying it again in euphemism. "Humiliated" feels strong and evocative also, but not quite so fundamentally naked and exposed as "shamed."

14. *Let's draw from a variety of sources to deal with shame.* Books and tapes by the modern "shame authors" offer a great deal, and many are included in our references. Oral tradition, anthropology, mythology, and the arts have much to teach us about our basic emotional and spiritual issues. The mythopoetic and men's-initiation arms of Men's Lib make extensive use of these approaches, and draw from them much that is innovative and valuable in healing shame.

It's wise to make use of our intuition, our experience, and *both* our cerebral hemispheres, despite the subtle shaming that their use has sometimes received from the health establishment. The 12 step program of Alcoholics Anonymous, which emerged in the 1930s largely from the intuition and experience of desperate men and women, is now credited with employing technique effective for healing shame (Fossum & Mason, 1986), and with reflecting a sophisticated existentialist philosophy (Kurtz, 1982). The AA founders hadn't read Sartre or Nietzsche, but were guided by their own intuition and honesty.

The best source of knowledge comes from the experience of healing one's own internalized shame. For understanding shame, there is no adequate substitute for immersion in that process.

All of us have blind spots. Here's a common occurrence: I approach a subject that contains unhealed personal shame. My discomfort grows, and my subconscious fear of exposure and shame propels me into some form of "approved" bullshit. I abandon the enlightenment and join the cover-up. Nobody's completely immune, so you're advised again to take whatever reinforces your own best instincts, and leave the rest.

15. *Is shame innate, or is it learned?* Most writers imply that it's learned, but I propose that it's *both*. Biology governs the primary emotion—the response to voice tone, shaming eyes, and other nonverbal signals—as well as the natural reaction to shaming acts based on the 'family rules' which maintain shame. I regard these responses as deeply instinctual and embedded in our biopsychological "hard-wiring."[4] Kaufman (1989, p. 35) portrays the infant's fundamental need to gaze into a smiling face and eyes, and the shame that arises from the absence of such contact. Shame has been recognized in mammalian behavior since the time of Darwin (1872).

The *capacity* or *propensity* to internalize shame is also instinctual, in my view. Dogs slink away, tail between legs, in response to coded shaming behavior from both canine social superiors and human masters ("Bad dog!"). Young baboons cringe in response to a fierce look from an elder. It's not difficult to see that among social mammals, shaming is more efficient than beating the kids, especially in situations in which survival depends on timely social control. And some internalization (i.e., anticipating being shamed for certain acts) would make the social control more effective.

The learned part is what to be ashamed *of* or *about*. Shaming techniques and our response to them are seen as universal, but the specific acts or attitudes that bring down shaming upon us—these vary considerably in different families, ethnic groups, and cultures, and are certainly different for men and women. Kaufman (1995) reminds us how males are systematically shamed in contemporary America for some natural emotions and actions, and how boys learn the risk of being shamed by peers for things not shamed in the family.

Learned shame can be unlearned. In the safety of our support groups, we discover how to express our natural feelings without being shamed again. We learn to be emotionally authentic—to rage and love, hug and confront, curse and cry, and to sit silent and ashamed without being urged to stop feeling this basic emotion. We are regaining a vital element of our masculine heritage, however we may choose to contain these feelings in other settings.

Let the unlearning continue. It's time for us "enlightened, sensitive" men to resist further shaming of our natural aggressiveness, our powerful language, our masculine spirituality, and our rampant, thrusting sexuality. It's time to celebrate and bless our masculinity.

16. *Most European languages have 2 to 7 nouns for shame (Schneider, 1977), but English has only one.* We have to use compounds, such as "internalized shame," "shame-bound," or "the shame of maleness," when we want to make important distinctions (Bly, 1995b). We take this to be a reflection of our blindness to the magnitude and complexity of shame, which, in turn, makes us more vulnerable to its effects. Imagine what it would be like if we had 10 short, strong nouns that accurately connoted the concepts discussed previously.

Meanwhile, we struggle along with the language we have. I consider toxic versus healthy shame (Bradshaw, 1988) and disgrace versus discretion shame (Schneider, 1977) to be useful conceptually, but they don't seem to fit easily into either primary or internalized shame, although they often require that the primary emotion be considered or visualized in advance.

17. *Shame is not all unhealthy.* Schneider (1977) points out the value of discretion in protecting our privacy and reducing social chaos. Bly (1995b) extols *aidos* shame, which might be translated as "awe" or "proper respect." Sociopaths may appear to be shameless, but I think they bury overwhelming shame down deep, beneath the "frozen over" surface. A few others, clearly not sociopaths, have a "shameless" demeanor that I find unsettling, perhaps because they don't show any of the body language of primary shame. I regard such people as dangerous to my emotional health, and avoid them.

18. *What's the relation of shame to guilt?* There are several views about this, with no one of them being clearly superior. If it be-

comes bothersome, I don't think the distinction is worth the trouble. There's general agreement that guilt is about the perception of *doing* something wrong, whereas shame is about the perception of *being* flawed and worthless. In this respect, shame is completely irrational or founded on a defective premise (albeit no less powerful, as an emotional reality), whereas guilt may have elements of reasonableness. To some, guilt generates activity to restore the situation, whereas shame makes us frozen and withdrawn.

Kaufman contends that shame and guilt have the same facial characteristics, so they shouldn't be regarded as different primary affects. I agree. Because Kaufman believes that it's important to match emotions with their verbal labels, he sees guilt as a subdivision of shame—the shame felt in response to violating some agreed-on value.

Bradshaw, Fossum and Mason, and most other authors consider that the being/doing distinction is important in helping people to grasp an essential feature of shame—that irrational sense that somehow I am incurably unworthy. Their books list distinctions between shame and guilt; readers may find them helpful. To face shame, I think it's important to get a body "read" on that irrational feeling/assumption of unworthiness; any construct which facilitates this deserves to be honored for its teaching value.

Here are some additional considerations. Guilt may convert to shame when, publicly or privately, my actions are considered to reveal my essentially flawed nature. I may feel guilty when I've violated my own values but ashamed when I've publicly violated someone else's values (even though I may pretend that they're my own). And feeling guilty may cover other emotions which are more difficult to own or discuss (Perls, 1969, pp. 182–183).

Middleton-Moz (1990, pp. 53–65) uses "debilitating guilt" to name what sounds to me like "internalized shame." Redundant and inconsistent terminology often occurs in a new and growing field, and it helps to understand which terms are being used as synonyms. Above all, let's resist substituting a word or concept for the experience itself.

19. *Many of our authors use the term "Shadow" in its Jungian meaning*. The term may be capitalized or not, and used either as noun or adjective. It refers to that part of ourselves that we try to keep hidden from our own awareness or public view.

Thus the shadow "contains the hidden, repressed, and unfavorable (or nefarious) aspects of the personality" (Henderson, 1964, p. 118). When a man is unwilling to "own" his shadow, he usually projects it onto others, where it becomes "those qualities and impulses he denies in himself but can plainly see in other people—such things as egotism, mental laziness, and sloppiness; unreal fantasies, schemes, and plots; carelessness and cowardice, inordinate love of money and possessions" (von Franz, 1964, p. 168). The idea is that we all act out shadow parts daily, so we might as well start by giving up perfectionism, and seeking to balance shadow and virtues "good enough." Robert Moore is fond of saying that the question is never *if* but *how* I'm acting out my shadow.

There is in me, as in every human, a killer, a self-righteous asshole, a liar, etc. These characters become much more troublesome when their existence is denied or projected. American political history for the last half-century seems to have been dominated by a desperate search for external "demons" on which to project our negative shadows (Bernstein, 1991; Keen, 1991).

The shadow may represent positive qualities that are disowned and projected. A man may keep his tenderness secreted in the shadow, and we often sadly keep our magnificence locked away as well, thus becoming tempted to excess hero worship. Little-used abilities are here too. I was in middle age before I discovered the poet in my shadow, and now welcome him into my internal circle of honor in the same way that I welcome the killer. Chapter 6 contains more about the necessary process of owning, welcoming, integrating, "eating" the shadow (Bly, 1988, pp. 27–43). This process is an important antidote to internalized shame because the true self is both recognized and blessed.

20. *"Until a man becomes secure in his masculine identity, he will remain a sadomasochist in his relationships with women."* Thus Moore and Gillette (1993b, p. 231) identify an important element in gender reconciliation, which we assume to be equally true for women in their relationships with men. Greenwald (1995) sees the ability to claim the shadow as a distinguishing characteristic of masculine maturity. In recent decades, we have been advised repeatedly to acknowledge our "feminine" qualities, which are sometimes called the contrasexual, or the *anima*. Moore and Gillette (1993b, p. 223) warn that

"integration of the personal Shadow solidifies the integrity of the Ego, and its achievement of a healthy psychosexual identity. Without a cohesive nuclear self, work with inner contrasexual structures can be confusing at best, and dangerous at worst." Thus, it appears that healing internalized shame is a necessary component of integrating one's Shadow, and that substantial experience in both are prerequisite to "forming a mature relationship with his inner feminine energies" (Moore & Gillette, 1993b, p. 224). Sadly, many men have tried to do it backwards, with unhappy results, considerable confusion, and additional shame. Self-doubt is the running mate of internalized shame (Erikson, 1963, pp. 251–254).

21. *With Jung (1983) and many others, I believe the restoration of balance to be the overall strategy for emotional/behavioral/ spiritual healing.* Healthy balance may involve holding the tension of paradox (see chapter 6). This means that we honor as valid, each in its own right, matters usually seen as opposed to each other, such as love and hate. Dialectical processes have considerable value because they can heighten our awareness of precisely what it is that needs to be balanced. In this light, shame is both a dragon to be slain and a child to be embraced.

## NOTES

1. Where opinion or a statement of value is in the "we" form, Schenk agrees with me; when they are in first person singular, Schenk disagrees or has no opinion. Both editors enjoy the dialectical tension of respectful disagreement, and hope that readers will join us in this.

2. By convention, *manipulative* roles are capitalized; *legitimate* roles printed in lower case. See chapter 13, note 1.

3. Miller's ironic use of the German, *Erziehung*, suggests the kind of pedagogy that dogs receive at obedience school.

4. For evidence that many of our symbols and emotional/behavioral patterns are rooted in our biology, see Stevens (1983), and Moore and Gillette (1990).

# 2

## Shame in Men's Lives

*Roy U. Schenk*

### WHY ARE MEN LOCKED INTO SELF-DESTRUCTIVE ROLES?

For many years I have struggled to understand why men seem so locked in to self-destructive gender roles. For example, men are disabled and killed on the job 12 times as often as women are. Men experience far more violent assaults than women do: 1.7 times as many reported assaults, and who knows how many times more unreported assaults, because men generally consider it unmanly to report being assaulted. Men are killed violently 3.55 times as often as women are (U.S. Department of Justice, 1993). The list could go on and on. Why do men continue to accept such violence to themselves?

The behavior of male feminists leaves no doubt that these men have intense feelings of guilt. But it is not guilt associated with any specific behavior. Instead, it appears to be a feeling of guilt merely because one is male. I believe that this guilt is felt by most if not all men. In my book, *The Other Side of the Coin* (Schenk, 1982), I called this phenomenon *"male existential guilt."* Shortly later, a workshop participant pointed out to me that this "guilt for being male" is another name for shame. The literature on shame confirms that "guilt for being male" is a type of shame. I then changed the name of the phenomenon to "Shame of *Maleness*" (Schenk, 1989).

This sense of shame that men experience simply because of being male is an intense and powerful force in men's lives. I now realize that this sense of shame for being male is the driving force that locks men in to their destructive and self-destructive roles. This shame may be as universal among men as having a cock.

Where does this shame come from? Shame is a consequence of believing that one is defective and unlovable. It is manifested both by men and women, although men get an added shaming message that women do not experience. It is probably the dominant negative affect, particularly for men. In this chapter, we examine how this shame develops.

Let's start at the beginning. When an infant is born, the first question that is asked is: "Is it a boy or a girl?" This is no accident. We simply do not know how to treat a child until we know what its sex is. Once we know the sex of the newborn infant, we immediately expect that a boy will show behavior that favors achievement, such as toughness, strength, ability to take abuse, insensitivity to pain, and all the other features of the male gender role. We immediately expect the girl to behave well, to be sensitive and caring and all the other features of the female gender role. If we divide life into doing and being, we find that boys are expected to excel in doing, whereas girls are expected to excel in being.

We then enforce these expectations through the differing ways we treat children. For example, we treat boys more roughly and with less attention, and we tend to interpret boys' pain as anger. Although it is most often done unconsciously by enforcing gender roles, for both boys and girls, it is one of the most powerful activities we pursue as adults. Through a wide spectrum of shaming actions, attitudes, words, and expressions, we make our disapproval very clear to growing children when they deviate from gender role expectations. The word "tramp" exemplifies this shaming process. In one sense, the word means the same thing whether it is applied to a male or to a female: It means a person who deviates from the expected gender role. For a man, it involves failing to be an achiever; for a woman, it means failing to maintain moral superiority. The roles are different for men and women, but the shaming message is the same.

I have heard many men say that they have never felt safe in their lives. When I ask them to explain, I find that the lack of safety has a moderate physical aspect, but the more important component is fear of being criticized, put down, disapproved, ignored, or otherwise told that they are disapproved of because of their behavior. These shaming messages are experienced as so painful that children learn to inhibit and repress their behavior to avoid further shaming. It appears to me that the pain of shame and the fear of experiencing more shame are the primary causes of inhibitions and repression of our natural abilities. For example, when I am singing a solo while other people are present, I may be so fearful of making a mistake, and thereby being subjected to criticism, that I may make mistakes that I would not make if I were alone.

## MEN'S SECOND SOURCE OF SHAMING

In addition to the shame used to enforce gender role expectations, males experience a second source of shaming. This involves shaming simply because we are male. This creates a Catch–22 situation for men: We are damned if we do and damned if we don't. Some background will help us perceive how this shaming occurs.

Because males are expected to excel in achievement, men have been perceived as the authority on achievements. Naturally, they define their own achievements as the norm or the standard. When women's achievements are compared with this standard, they often do not measure up and are found to be inferior. As a result, women have long been perceived as inferior in achievement. In recent decades, feminists have at least partially succeeded in successfully challenging this perception of inferior female achievement. Unfortunately, feminists have tended to explain every difference between men and women as an expression of supposed female inferiority, and they have therefore promoted women as victims. Later, we will discuss this point and its implications for male shame.

Conversely, because females are expected to excel in being, as distinguished from doing, women are perceived as the authority on behavior. Morality is the definition of proper behavior, so women are seen as the authorities on morality. Women's moral authority extends to aesthetics, nurturing, relationships, attitudes, motives, spirituality, feelings, and values. Naturally, women define their own behavior as the norm or the standard. When men's behavior is compared with this standard, it doesn't measure up and is found to be inferior. As a result, men are perceived as morally inferior to women.

The perceived moral superiority of women is not a new phenomenon. It was clearly articulated in the feminist Seneca Falls Declaration of 1848 (Schneir, 1972). Because superiorities and inferiorities develop together, female moral superiority has presumably existed as long as the belief in male achievement superiority. When a person or group is seen as inferior, it is treated as not deserving fair treatment in the area in which it is seen as inferior. This happens to racial minorities. It has happened to women in the area of achievement. And it happens to men in the area of morality and behavior.

Any group perceived as being superior is given special favored treatment. For example, men open doors for women, women go first into lifeboats, women expect men to put the toilet seat down, men stand and offer chairs for women—these are all examples of women being accorded special favored treatment because of their presumed behavioral superiority. The imperial behavior of royalty, the expectations by bosses that workers will defer to them, and the racial biases against blacks all result from the expectation that presumably superior people deserve special privilege and presumably inferior people do not deserve fair treatment.

One of the ways men's presumed behavioral inferiority is expressed socially is by greater criminalization and punishment of men's behavior. For example, men are arrested 4.6 times as often as women. Men are convicted of crimes 5.8 times as often as women. Men are sentenced to prison 13.2 times as often as women, and a man is 20 times more likely than a woman to occupy a prison cell. A black man, experiencing the double whammy of sexism and racism, is 140 times more likely to be imprisoned than a white woman. For identical crimes, men typically receive a sentence 1.5 times as long as women receive. Although women are convicted of 14% of murders, less than 0.7% of persons executed for murder are women. This biased treatment occurs because of the societal belief that men do not deserve fair treatment in the behavior areas, whereas women deserve special favored treatment.

Women's presumed superiority in behavior also results in women generally receiving favored treatment in divorce and custody, as most men are well aware. Still another result of women's presumed superiority in behavior and motives is that when a man hits a woman he is seen as the bad guy, and when a woman hits a man he is also seen as the bad guy. The same attitude is evident in domestic homicide. The man is generally seen as the bad guy whether he kills or is killed. This is a result of seeing women as victims. Seeing women as victims is another expression of the belief that men are morally inferior, because victims are seen as morally superior to perpetrators. This is why a woman who has self-doubts may use becoming a victim as a way to reaffirm her belief that she is morally superior.

Whenever we define a person by some specific attribute, whether it be as rapist, perpetrator, victim, murderer, welfare mother, angel, or hunk, we are dehumanizing that person. Dehumanizing is another way of shaming that person. The "male bashing" so prevalent in the media serves, whether consciously or not, to dehumanize all males.

It is sometimes argued that men control morality because in most religions men are the preachers of morality. But morality is largely learned by the time a child is 3 to 5 years old, when children are typically under the tutelage of their mothers. Men generally preach the morality they learned from their mothers. Interestingly, typically a man puts on a robe, which is a kind of dress, and symbolically becomes a woman before he begins preaching. In addition, when one partner takes another to church, it is usually the woman who drags the man to church so he can get the "proper" morality preached to him. Most of the sins preached against are male activities. If you doubt that women are favored by traditional religions, count the numbers of men and women attending the services. Generally, women far outnumber men.

If we are to heal shame and attain equality between men and women, it is important for men to identify and honor their own morality. In our society today, men's morality is more likely to be articulated in taverns than in churches, which is probably one reason why churches rail so persistently against taverns. In the past, male morality could be articulated in the workplace, but sexual harassment laws are displacing it with female morality. If sexual harassment laws were truly designed to combat sexual harassment, they would equally ban the activities by which women sexually harass men. Instead the laws ignore the ways men are generally sexually harassed.

Men typically live in a sexual desert (Schenk, 1982). That is, they find sex about as available as is water in a desert. And men act toward sex much like a person acts toward water when in a desert. It becomes very important. It is sought for and protected. Even if one momentarily has enough one doesn't stop searching. In contrast, women typically behave toward sex like a person in a sexual rainforest behaves toward water. The different behaviors seem to occur mostly because men are expected to initiate sexual encounter.

Because of this sexual unavailabilty for men, whenever a woman calls attention to her sexuality on the job, she is sexually harassing every man around her. This ubiquitous harassment is legally ignored because the fundamental purpose of sexual harassment laws is not to eliminate sexual harassment but to enforce the presumably superior morality of women and to punish men.

As a result of allowing women to define morality and to define women's behavior as good and right, men learn that their own behavior is perceived as bad particularly when it is different from women's behavior or does not benefit women. Even when men's behavior is the same as women's behavior, men's behavior can still be seen as bad because men's motives are presumed to be bad.

Male children quickly learn the message that they are presumed to be bad. Typical of this belief, my third grandson's sweatshirt proclaims in bold letters: "I'm BAD!" Although the term "bad" is sometimes used by young people to mean its opposite, one rarely sees a woman proclaiming such messages. For a more global example, 90% of punishments doled out in schools are experienced by boys. Boys are into overachievement by the time they are 3 years old; and overachievement is a shame response. Boys learn that they are defective because they are male, and if they are defective they are unlovable. The sense of being defective and unlovable is what triggers shame in anyone. Shame just for being male, however, is the added shaming message that males learn from a young age. This is what I call *shame* of *maleness*. Dr. John Gagnon (1995), who discovered this phenomenon independently, calls it *primary male shame*."

It may not be immediately apparent why this extensive discussion about male-female superiority-inferiority is so important when discussing men's shame. The reason is this: To heal shame, just as to heal any physical disease, it is helpful to understand the source or cause of the disease. The source of the shame of maleness is the societal belief learned early by male children that because they are male they are inferior to women in behavior and morality. What this means is that healing shame requires equality: equality between men and women, between races, and between all groups of people.

## A LOOK AT THE DARK SIDE

Because of the importance of male/female inferiority feelings, we need to understand the dynamic that creates and perpetuates the beliefs on which these feelings are based. Basically, these beliefs come about because of the societal expectation that women will excel and set the standards in being or behavior while men will excel in doing or achievement. As noted earlier, when men define their own achievement as the standard, women are found wanting; when women define their own behavior as the standard, men are found wanting. This sets up a vicious circle which I call "The Dark Side of Male-Female Interactions." This is shown in Figure 2.1.

This is a circle, so one could start anywhere on it. But because feminists have alerted us to half of the circle, it seems reasonable to start there, specifically with men's presumed doing or achievement superiority. This sometimes induces us to perceive women as inferior in doing or achievement. Along with these feelings of inferiority, women may develop self doubts, excessive fears, and feelings of inadequacy. Alfred Adler pointed out in the early part of this century that when we believe a message that we are inferior, we experience a drive or psychological need to compensate for those inferiority feelings in some way (Ansbacher & Ansbacher, 1956) A person can compensate in many ways. One way is to go to an extreme in behavior. For an "achievement inferior" woman, going to the extreme involves becoming a totally helpless, superfeminine woman.

A second response is to develop one's own area of perceived superiority. For women this means developing a belief in women's being or behavior/morality superiority. Women teach this to their children, boys and girls alike. This lesson need not be taught explicitly or consciously because it is an inherent belief of our culture. Infant boys learn this message and compensate for these inferiority feelings. One response of boys (and men) to feeling morally inferior is to feel defective, unlovable, and ashamed of being male. A second response is to go to an extreme, such as the machismo

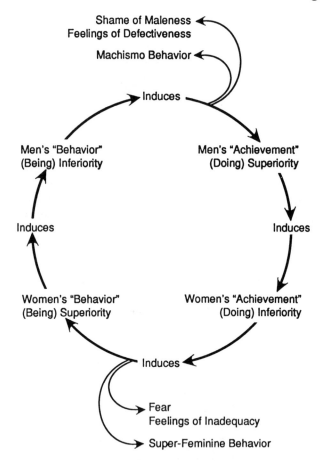

Reprinted from Schenk (1991)

**FIGURE 2.1**   The dark side of male–female interactions.

response. In effect, the machismo male says: "You think I'm bad? You haven't seen anything yet! I'll destroy the world." Indeed, war and mindless pollution are in large measure responses to men's sense of inferiority and their resulting shame. Another possible male response to feelings of behavior inferiority is to develop their designated area of perceived superiority, doing or achievement. This completes the vicious circle.

Unfortunately, because women are so regularly seen as superior in morality and because women's behavior is defined as good behavior, the tendency is simply to blame men rather than realizing that what actually happens is a dance or symbiotic interplay between men and women, with members of both genders wounding members of the other gender in an ongoing cycle. Actually, it is more like a spiral than a circle. The superiorities, particularly our belief in women's moral superiority, have increased to the point of threatening all life on earth.

Men are often defined as bad, blameworthy, and the cause of all evil. A striking example of this belief is the near-unanimous passage by the U.S. Congress of the Violence Against Women Act (S-11, HR 1133, 1993). This act defines violence against women as more deserving of punishment than violence against men and declares that stopping violence against women is a higher priority than stopping violence against men even though men experience 1.6 times as much criminal violence as women do. The Violence Against Women Act creates a beautiful example of the Rescue triangle (see Everingham, 1995c) with women officially being declared Victims, men being declared Persecutors, and the U.S. government being appointed the Rescuer.

This legislation might better be titled the Sexist Bigotry Act. It represents the most bigoted legislation passed by Congress since before the Civil War. If we mentally substitute white people for women, the bigotry becomes readily apparent. A Violence Against White People Act would provide safe streets, campuses, and homes for white people (even though racial minorities experience 1.4 times as much criminal violence as whites do), and would provide protection and assistance for white runaway children but not for minority children. Such a proposal would immediately be recognized as racist bigotry and would not be enacted into law. Yet few people recognize the bigotry against males in the law as it is now written and a great many people, both men and women, seem to believe that a Violence Against Women Act is appropriate. Why is this so?

Joseph Campbell (1988) had a great deal to say about the power of societal myths. He pointed out that a myth is a societal belief that is accepted as the truth. Because it is accepted as true, no one questions it. Many people insist that our society lacks myths, but in actuality we have had two myths regarding men and women. One of these myths has been challenged in recent years; the other has grown stronger. The challenged myth is the belief that men are the achievers. The unchallenged myth is the belief that women are the humanizers, the definers of behavior and morality. Because this myth is accepted without question, Congress is afraid to vote against any legislation proposed by feminists.

Because men have been the appointed achievers, men have been encouraged and even pushed to achieve, whereas women have been impeded and shamed when they strove to achieve. Not surprisingly, when men's achievement was defined as the standard, women did not achieve as well as men did. This has been challenged in recent years, and women are gaining in the achievement area. In the same way, because women are the appointed experts on behavior and morality, women have been pushed to conform to "higher" standards of behavior, sometimes called double standards, whereas men have been impeded and shamed when they strove to develop skills in relationships and nurturing. As long as women's behavior is the standard, it should not be surprising that men do not seem to behave as well as women do.

At this point it seems appropriate to point out that there are no absolute superiorities or inferiorities. Superiorities and inferiorities are simply expressions of a society's choices and definitions. For example, if two runners run a mile and one completes the mile in 4 minutes, whereas the other takes six minutes but runs far more gracefully, a decision as to which is the superior runner would be determined by whether the society places a higher value on speed or gracefulness. It is important to recognize that if we can choose to assign superiorities and inferiorities, we can also choose not to assign superiorities and inferiorities. Indeed, this is an essential key to the healing of shame. We can simply accept people as different and even celebrate those differences.

Shame is based on judging people on the basis of superiority-inferiority, better or worse, good or bad. Even if I am judged as better in a specific experience, behavior, or characteristic, I still receive the message that I am at risk and that at another time I may well be judged to be inferior, defective, or bad. This judging, blaming and shaming, and the fear of experiencing these are at the root of our shame-based society.

Inferiority feelings and the resulting shame and fear of being shamed are also the root cause of war, mindless pollution, viciousness between men and women, and conflicts between different (i.e., "better/worse") groups, whether ethnic, religious, or national. Some religions speak of an original sin, a defect that fundamentally damages human beings. I am convinced that inferiority feelings, and the resulting shame and fear of being shamed constitute that original sin.

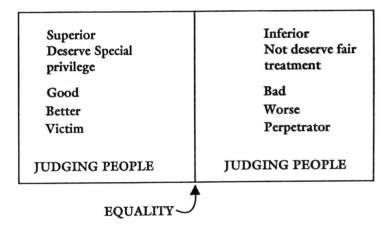

**FIGURE 2.2** Our current plane of existence.

## OUR CURRENT PLANE OF EXISTENCE

My mission in life is to achieve world peace by creating sexual equality. In a recent discussion about this objective, Carl Larson remarked to me that he visualized equality as a fine line. This made immediate sense to me. If we choose to judge people and so divide them between good and bad, superior and inferior, then we have superior, and good on one side and inferior, and bad, on the other side; separating them is a thin line of equality (see Figure 2.2). There is no way for everybody to stand on that line of equality. Even if we tried, we would be overlapping into one or both sides of the line. Consequently, we cannot achieve equality as long as we insist on judging people. We need to develop a new belief system or world view (see chapter 20).

## MANIFESTATIONS OF MEN'S SHAME

The shame of maleness can be seen as a response to what John Everingham (1995d) calls the 10th shaming rule: moral intimidation. This shame is a result of the dominance of women's input into the socialization process, and of women's claiming the moral high ground as a result of their control of socialization. It is not surprising that women would generally teach children that women's behavior, attitudes, values, motives, and style of nurturing are correct or good. Inevitably, boys' behavior deviates from women's behavior, and they learn that as males they are defective and bad.

Other manifestations of men's shame include homophobia, concealment of one's financial worth and income, capitulation to women's manipulation, inability to criticize women's negative behaviors (and panic whenever another man does criticize such behavior), acceptance of societal abuse, treatment of women as "ladies" (i.e., as morally superior), physical battering of women, machismo strutting, avoidance of intimacy, inability to defend boundaries from invasion by women, and withdrawal when attacked by women.

## VIOLENCE: SHAME IN ACTION

Violence is a manifestation of the belief that another person is inferior or subhuman in some way, and is thereby not worthy of dignity, respect, and fair treatment. Violence is shaming in action. Whenever a person has violence done to him or her, that violence is demeaning. It conveys the message that he or she is defective and unlovable, and this induces shame feelings.

Not all violence is physical. Indeed, some of the most intense expressions of violence are verbal and psychological. Murray Straus (1993), a world authority on domestic abuse, asserts that "verbal aggression may be even more damaging than being the victim of physical attacks. One can hurt a partner deeply—even drive them to suicide—without ever lifting a finger." In this important sense, any demeaning word, expression, or action is a form of violence. This includes any judgment that a person or group is inferior.

Theologian Langdon Gilkey (1966) wrote of "that sharpest of all hostilities of one human being to another—that nonacceptance which springs from moral disapproval and so from a feeling of moral superiority." Gilkey is saying that *an attitude of moral superiority*, of seeing others as morally inferior, *is the most intense form of violence one person can do to another*. I suspect that he is correct. I once visited a woman whose physically abusive husband had just left her. She used a steady stream of put-downs of her husband and repeatedly depicted herself as so superior that she would not condescend to discuss issues with him. I experienced her continual put-downs as verbal and psychological violence; and I understood how he could become physically violent just to shut her up and stop her violence to him.

It is important to recognize the violence in seeing others as inferior and therefore undeserving of fair treatment. It is particularly important to recognize the intensity of the violence created by seeing others as morally inferior.

It is often claimed that men are more violent than women, and are, therefore, inferior, less human, and more deserving of punishment. This claim sounds plausible if we limit our concern to physical violence, because men are typically stronger than women and so generally can do more damage with their hands and feet. However, women compensate for this by resorting more quickly to using weapons. Men are also taught that it is more shameful to hit a woman than to hit another man. Women have permission to be more violent, because our society is relatively accepting of women's violence against men. When we understand that emotional and psychological abuse and particularly attitudes of moral superiority, are severe forms of violence, and that women regularly inflict these kinds of violence on men, we realize that there is a likely balance in the violence done between men and women. When we understand this, men can begin to abandon the *shame of maleness*. As we heal this shame, we can begin to confront the shaming messages we have been given for failing to live up to our gender roles, and all of the other shaming messages associated with our imperfect behavior.

## IS SHAMING NECESSARY?

Gershen Kaufman (1995), Carl Schneider (1977), and other authorities on shame contend that some forms of shame are good or at least potentially beneficial. I believe their argument is that we all need to learn that we are fallible and imperfect; discovering our imperfection creates in us the belief that we are defective, which breeds feelings of shame. It feels risky to challenge those who are more knowledgeable than I am. Nonetheless, I firmly believe that shame is not a necessary part of this process. If we start from birth to teach children that as human beings we are fallible and that we all make mistakes, and that making mistakes does not in any way mean we are defective or unlovable, then it seems to me that shame need not develop. To the extent that we are able to accept people's mistakes as part of their essential being, and to the extent that we accept people along with (not despite) their mistakes, I see no reason why shame should develop.

The argument is made that shameless people are dangerous because they are not repressed by the fear of feeling ashamed. But I believe the kind of person described is a person who has experienced so much intense shaming that he or she has repressed shame feelings as a survival response. I propose the possibility of a truly shameless person at the other end of the spectrum, one who has not been repressed by shaming messages and who still retains the excitement, enthusiasm, and joy of childhood. Perhaps this is an idealized vision, but it seems worthy of pursuit.

The disintegration of social inhibitions and the increasing violence in our culture certainly call on us to teach our children what is appropriate behavior. Yet I sense that the apparent decline in the acquisition of social values has been accompanied by an increase in shaming and a decrease in self-esteem. This is the opposite of what we would expect if shaming were necessary to instill social values. It seems more likely that shaming contributes to violence and disintegrating social values.

In our shame-based culture, we tend to reject people because they make mistakes and are not perfect. The more imperfection by our standards, the more rejection we project. What we currently see in our society is more shaming and blaming as the social fabric unravels. I believe that shaming and blaming are causing the disintegration. I believe this is the force that is filling our prisons, with a tripling of the number of men in prison in the past 20 years. We already have close to twice as many men in prison as any other civilized nation, and the incarceration rate shows no sign of slowing down.

## THE MEN'S MOVEMENT

Men experience intense abuse in our society but because of the *shame of maleness*, they tend to feel that they deserve the abuse. It is difficult to fight against what you think you deserve, and men generally have not put up much of a fight. This is why there has never been an effective movement of men as men.

The past several decades have seen a tentative and sporadic men's rights movement, composed of men who have experienced such severe abuse from the social system that they have finally rebelled. Most of these groups are concerned with fathering issues, because it is in divorce that many men finally become conscious of society's intense bias against men. These men's rights groups attract other men who are being similarly abused by the system. But most of these men drop out of the groups when they resolve or learn to live with the abuses. This is a result of the shame-induced belief that we deserve the bad things that happen to us because as males we are defective human beings. The men who do not drop out are generally motivated by rage at the abuse that they and other men experience from society.

Another shame-induced behavior is a need to control. This need has resulted in hundreds of little men's rights groups, generally focused around the efforts of one outraged man. It seems that every time a man becomes outraged at how the system abuses him as a male, he sets up another "national" men's organization. Even Evansville, Wisconsin, population 2,800, had its own national men's organization for a few years. Evidently, men's shame-based need to control prevents these small groups from uniting into a powerful national organization, despite regular attempts to achieve unity.

In the 1980s, Robert Bly triggered a new component of the men's movement, which Shepherd Bliss has named the mythopoetic men's movement. Bly contends that the absence of men's fathers from the home since the industrial revolution has denied men the role models they need to learn how to be men, and this has seriously wounded them. In addition, the absence of older men in the lives of younger men has denied adolescent males any meaningful initiation ritual into manhood. Acquisition of a driver's license may be the closest thing to an initiation ritual in our society today. (Adolescent girls have menstruation as a form of natural initiation, which males lack.) I believe that the industrial revolution only made worse the disease I call *shame of Maleness*. This disease has been around for many thousands of years.

In response to Bly's identification of the father loss, many "wildman weekends" have sprung up. These weekends try to provide some form of initiation. In addition, they help men feel better about themselves, see that they are lovable, and recognize that they deserve to be loved. Men do need to feel better about themselves as a result of all the shaming messages that tell men they are defective and unlovable.

Generally, these weekends do not consciously focus on the shame that men learn. The one clear exception is the New Warrior Adventure Training Weekend which was founded in Milwaukee in 1985 and has since become available nationwide. In part because of the influence of Dr. Everingham and me as active participants, the New Warrior Training has consciously focused on the effects of shame on men. The shame of maleness is confronted along with other shaming messages that men receive. The initiation ritual of the new warriors is different from traditional initiations in that it strives to initiate men into a transformed world rather than into the traditional culture.

Most "male initiation" groups tend to be apolitical; they seem overly reluctant to criticize women's negative behaviors. Most of the focus of the groups and their publications is on individual betterment and self-love.

However, this self-focus cannot last forever. As men become more healthy, and more able to love themselves and other men, it is inevitable that they will become increasingly aware of the unfair treatment that men experience in divorce, draft registration, insurance premiums, sexual harassment, incarceration, and assault laws, to name a few areas. They will become aware that domestic abuse experienced by men is ignored whereas that of women is vigorously prosecuted. The list could go on and on. With only a little education, men will understand that they are treated unfairly in their very being because men are seen as inferior in this area. As this happens, efforts to achieve real equality between men and women will become more viable.

# 3
## Men's Shame*

*Gershen Kaufman*

Our topic is shame. We're going to attempt an understanding of the nature of shame: what it is, where it comes from, and how to heal it, particularly as it affects men. Let me begin by talking about what shame is, what it feels like on the inside, what it looks like. Then we'll look at how men are socialized in this society around shame.

### WHAT SHAME IS

Understanding the inner experience of shame is critical to understanding shame's significance and impact. To feel shame is to feel *seen* in a painfully diminished sense. What happens is that our eyes turn inward, and we're suddenly watching ourselves. Shame can be generated in an instant. It can last for 5 seconds, 5 minutes, or 5 hours. When we're young children, shame is generally a wordless, nonverbal experience. It flashes through our awareness, and often passes just as quickly. The characteristic facial signs of shame are: eyes and head down, or we blush or look away.

Shame causes an interruption; it disturbs us. We feel momen-

*Based on the audiotape, "Men's Shame," of a joint presentation sponsored by the Alfred Adler Institute of Minnesota, Minneapolis, April 23, 1989.

tarily transparent. It's as if everybody can see into us. Everybody can see how stupid, foolish, awkward, and dumb we are. Shame feels like exposure. In the moment of shame our eyes turn inward, and because we're watching ourselves, we feel like everybody else can see through us as well. We feel defenseless against their scrutiny and critical appraisal.

Shame is a wordless emotion; only much later do we attach meanings to it. In the midst of shame, we feel an urge to hide. We want to cover ourselves, retreat, disappear, turn off all those watching eyes—most of all, our own.

These are the *critical* effects of shame. The self is paralyzed momentarily. Speech is interrupted; we can't talk and can't even think clearly. Sometimes we feel paralyzed physically, and stand still, or sit still, and can't move. I can remember countless times when, in the midst of shame, I couldn't will my body to move. It was frozen.

Following shame are several *secondary* reactions. Anyone who has experienced deep shame does not look quickly for a repetition. We escape and avoid it, and feel fearful of further shaming. We learn to see shame coming from afar and try to dodge it before it overtakes us.

We also respond secondarily with another emotion—the "distress affect" of Tomkins's affect theory. We may feel sad and cry. Children display it—a momentary hanging of the head in shame, and then they begin to cry. What gets recognized and attended to by parents (teachers, etc.) is the crying part of the sequence, and what gets systematically *ignored* is shame.

It's missed in this culture because shame is under taboo, but that taboo is now beginning to lift. There has been a cultural shift. In the last 6 years shame has been surfacing more, and people are beginning to pay attention to it, particularly in the mental health field. This shift has been fueled by the recovery movement and its concern with addictions. These are disorders in which shame plays a central, organizing role. So now we're beginning to rediscover shame.

## CULTURAL INJUNCTIONS ON MEN

There are cultural injunctions in our society to compete, be successful, achieve, and perform. That's especially true for men: We are supposed to be successful, and failure for men is shameful. Failing at anything is tantamount to being cursed. Another injunction is to be independent and self-sufficient. I know many men who will never ask for directions when they're lost. If they are lost they're in shame, and announcing it is like saying, "I don't know where I am, I don't know how to get there." That's too shameful. I've also known men who won't ask a waiter or waitress to bring something to the table because asking is too shameful.

Our society has tried to bury shame. In our refusal even to talk about it, we have reversed our language system. Think about all the times we say, "I'm too proud to do that." An Appalachian father might say, "I'm too proud to take a handout." It's not pride that stops him, it's shame, because taking a handout would mean announcing, "I'm no good! I can't provide for my family!"

The same thing happens when a man loses his job or is laid off. Because of the overvaluation of work for men as the principal route to self-esteem, any impediment to our achieving what we are all "supposed" to achieve produces shame. The American dream—you can be anything you want to be if you only try hard enough—has really become a pathway into shame for us.

## FORMS OF SHAME

In our culture we lose the experience of shame because shame itself is under such tight control and strict taboo. Shame goes underground and instead we talk about guilt. It's easier to say, "Well, I did something I shouldn't have done and I feel guilty" than to experience shame about oneself.

*Discouragement, shyness, embarrassment, self-consciousness, inferiority,* and *guilt* are simply different forms of shame. But we give them different names and, therefore, experience them as distinctly different experiences.

Shame is expressed in many different forms, and the face of shame changes depending on the context. If I approach a stranger and feel inhibited, self-conscious, or like I'm going to make a fool of myself, we call it shyness. The emotion present is still shame. If I am presenting to a group and discover my pants are open, or if somebody comes up to me whose name I can't remember and I'm supposed to, we call it embarrassment. Even though we give it different names, the same underlying emotion is present. And when it's the self that feels inherently flawed we call it inferiority, though it's still the emotion of shame that's present. Guilt is immorality shame at having transgressed.

Guilt poses some additional problems concerning its perception. In response to wrongdoing, we may also experience other emotions that we mislabel, or fail to label precisely, and so ambiguously refer to them all as guilt. If I've done something wrong, instead of hanging my head in shame I might feel *angry* at myself for having done something wrong. I might turn the finger of blame inward and angrily accuse myself repeatedly for misconduct or wrongdoing. We also call that guilt. Instead, I might feel *fear*, as when people worry, "Will my name be in the paper?" or "Will there be some punishment?" The fear we feel about having done something wrong we also include under the general heading of guilt. Instead, I might become *sad*, and cry or grieve at having done something wrong. We call that remorse. Our judicial system is predicated on the appropriate and genuine display of remorse in response to wrongdoing. Many children learn that if they show remorse, then punishment is mitigated—but not always. We can also turn *disgust* against ourselves and begin to experience ourselves as loathsome, without dignity, as something to be squashed into the ground. When it's in response to transgression, we call that guilt as well. These constitute different affective states. But when the ethical judgment of transgression is added to any of these, then they take on the distinctive feel of *guilt* states. And guilt can be either about the self or about acts, just as shame can be either about the self or about acts.

The important distinction here is not between shame and guilt, but between shame as an emotion, a feeling that is activated and then passes, and shame that becomes internalized and magnified. Then shame becomes potentially crippling.

## POSITIVE SHAME

Shame is inherently healthy, and we would not evolve as a human species without shame. First of all, shame alerts us to any violation of human dignity. It has served the centuries-old function of alerting people to indignity. Second, without appropriate doses of shame, we would not develop a conscience, a sense of right and wrong. Finally, our identity would be completely blocked from developing, because who we are as human beings evolves directly out of experiences of shame. When encounters with shame are appropriately graded and effectively neutralized, they do not become internalized, magnified, or crippling.

## STRATEGIES AGAINST SHAME

I want to mention some of the strategies that we develop to cope with or protect ourselves against shame. When shame becomes inordinate and excessive, we have to survive somehow, and we always survive the very best ways we're able. We need to honor the person we are and the ways we've had to function to get to this point in time, because if we don't, then we continue to undermine ourselves.

*Rage* against other people is one strategy, whether in the form of chronic, rageful eruptions as in an alcoholic family, or quieter hostility that's transmitted and communicated, perhaps every time the family gets together. Or it may become directed specifically toward one child or another. Rage is a way of protecting ourselves against shame. A father who has experienced considerable shame may reenact analogous scenes of shame toward his son by means of rage. Anyone may learn and adopt such a strategy and thereby keep people away with rage.

*Contempt* is a different strategy in which we elevate ourselves above others and experience other people as lesser. Now they're beneath us. If you're beneath me and I'm superior to you, then your ability to shame me is lessened. It's a strategy that enters subtly into many of our interpersonal relationships through judgmental, faultfinding, or condescending attitudes. Anytime we look down on another, the strategy of contempt is operating at some level of intensity.

*Perfectionism* is a strategy designed to perfect the self, erase every blemish, and escape from or avoid shame by excelling in an ever-widening circle of activities.

*Power* strategies are designed to maximize power as a way of life. One way to protect myself from shame is to always be in control. If I'm always in power, whether as head of a household, in a company, or in a relationship, then I am likely to generate shame in others and also protect myself against shame.

Another strategy is the *transfer of blame*, which is a way of transferring shame away from me to other people. In the moment of shame I'm faced with the dilemma, what do I do with it? One strategy is to transfer it outside; it's not me who has failed. I haven't done anything wrong, I'm not to blame; it belongs out there.

## FEELINGS SHAMED IN MEN

What happens developmentally is that different parts of our personalities become associated with shame. And what happens for men is specific and powerful, in terms of the parts of us that become systematically shamed—in the family, in the school setting, and in the emerging and continuously evolving peer group of early adolescence (which I'm convinced now has almost equal power with the family to shape personality).

Let's look at the specific parts of us that become associated with shame. One of the most profoundly shameful experiences for men has been crying. Men have been systematically shamed in American culture for crying. The degree to which this has been true in other cultures is an open question, and there are certainly variations on the theme, but men in American society are made to feel there's something wrong with feeling sad, crying, or openly displaying that particular emotion. It can happen when men are told: "Don't be a crybaby." "Take it like a man, with a stiff upper lip." "You should be ashamed of yourself." "Boys don't cry." "Real men don't cry." To be psychologically healthy, we need to have access to crying, to be able to feel and freely express sorrow, or we'll never deal effectively with loss, death, relationship failure or breakup, with all of the disappointments life throws at us. Crying, which is a natural human emotion, becomes bound by shame in this way.

Following sufficient repetitions of the pairing, or linkage, of expressions of distress (crying) with being shamed for crying, shame becomes internalized: "Don't cry," "Don't express that," "You're stupid," or "You're a crybaby."

I can remember times when I would cry, and peers would stand around, laughing, ridiculing, mercilessly shaming me. I have repeatedly met individuals—generally men—who are subjected to the severest sanctions when observed to cry, and I know of one individual for whom the humiliation, shaming, and ridicule continued for 3 or 4 years as he progressively went through school. The *history* of his being observed to cry publicly stayed with him.

When this happens, what is created is an *internalized shame bind*. Now the emotion of distress—crying, sadness—spontaneously activates shame, without anybody else ever having to shame us again. Think of somebody who begins to cry (think of yourself). Immediately, what's the first thing we do? We look around to see if anybody's watching. We may apologize, if somebody's there. Or perhaps we'll say, "I'm sorry for *breaking down in front of you.*"

There's nothing inherent to crying, or sadness, to cause us to feel like we're "breaking down in front of" someone. The "breaking down in front of" is the shame part of this sequence. Whenever those words are expressed, you're observing a *distress-shame bind* operating. What happens is that progressively we feel not only like *hiding* tears, but that there's something wrong with us for *feeling* sad in the first place.

We feel lesser; we feel deficient. Somebody immediately offers us a Kleenex, and we try to dry the tears. Or we pretend they're not there and ignore them. Other people get visibly agitated. We have a lot of difficulty simply tolerating distress, which is often displayed through crying, or sadness. We're not supposed to cry, and when somebody does, thereby violating that cultural taboo, we immediately become agitated. That's one reason we have so much difficulty dealing with death and dying in this society, because feeling sadness and distress spontaneously trigger shame. We run and hide from sorrow; we disappear and don't acknowledge pain.

Distress is not the only emotion that's heavily shamed for men. Fear is another. An analogous process occurs here. Men are not supposed to be afraid and are, in fact, systematically shamed whenever they express fear.

It may be in the family, when young boys begin to wake up frightened from a nightmare and are told, "That's stupid; don't be ridiculous." Or they imagine monsters in the basement and are ridiculed for being frightened of such silly things.

It progresses from ages 2 to 3 when young boys display cowardice before others, and the shaming comes from peers who will gather round and ridicule whoever is not being appropriately fearless. You can imagine the difficulty for a young boy who may not be as inclined to be aggressive, who is perhaps more fearful, when forced into that contradiction.

I remember when I was growing up, I wouldn't fight back when I was picked on or hit. When my father observed that, he was so enraged that he started beating me to get me to fight back. As I look back on it, I think it triggered too much shame for *him* to allow me to deal with it myself, or for him even to be comforting or reassuring.

Instead, he attempted to humiliate me and force me to fight back. It didn't work; I ended up not fighting back *and* not giving in to his power, because either way I turned I was going to experience shame. At that point, it was a hopeless, insoluble dilemma. Whatever I did, there was shame. If I went ahead and fought back at that point, I was giving in to his power and letting him dominate me; so there was shame no matter what I did.

Expressing fear becomes associated with shame for many men in this society. We're not supposed to be afraid or show our fear. When we *feel* fear, at whatever level, we think there's something wrong with us. Feeling afraid translates into, "I am deficient. There's something wrong with me."

That's the key to understanding shame—realizing how we learn, how we are taught, how we are made to feel deficient for having natural human emotions. So fear and crying are two important feelings that are heavily shamed in males.

Also heavily shamed is any expression of shame itself. I can remember hanging my head in shame, and teachers saying, "Keep your head up. Don't look down, don't hang your head." In effect they were saying, "Don't display shame."

## PRIMARY INTERPERSONAL NEEDS

I have formulated a group of primary interpersonal needs that I consider to be innate in the sense that they constitute the requirements for optimal development. One need is to be in a relationship with parents and anyone else significant. Another is the central need for touching and holding. The need for identification—for fusion, merging, and a sense of belonging—is yet another crucial need for human beings. This need alternates with the need to be separate and different, to differentiate. They oscillate. On some days my son would look up and say, "Daddy, I want to *be* you." The next day he would look up and say, "I'm *not* you; I'm different from you." Both needs have to be responded to appropriately. The challenge for parents is to provide for the child's emerging needs and the oscillating pattern of needs as they unfold.

Another need is a need to nurture, to give. I believe children need to give—whether it is gifts, love, or affection. It may be an arm around the parent's shoulder, saying, "It's gonna be okay, Dad," when Father is upset. How many fathers have been so ashamed to appear "weak" in front of their own sons that they have pushed the boy away? Or they may shame him verbally, or respond with a facial look that is sufficient to create shame in the boy.

We all have needs for affirmation, valuing, recognition, and admiration. And, finally, there is a need for power—power in the positive sense of being able to predict and control. To experience a degree of power is important to human beings. We never have all the power, but we do need to experience sufficient power in any area of life essential to us. This is crucial for human beings.

Now let us consider how these basic needs become shamed for men.

## Shaming of Interpersonal Needs

There are particular interpersonal needs that, for men especially, become heavily imbued with shame. The first is the need to be in a genuine *relationship*. Every child needs to be in relationship with each parent and subsequently with anyone who becomes central in his developing world. The need for relationship is the need to feel wanted, to feel special to another, and to feel that this other person truly wants a relationship with me. Men in particular feel deeply ashamed of needing a relationship.

A related need is for *touching and holding*. We need physical contact. Touching is required by every infant if it is to thrive. We know that beyond question. The skin has to be touched, to be stimulated. Infants have to be picked up and rocked. They need to be held, talked to, sung to, and smiled at. All of these are *vital*.

And yet, ours is a touch-phobic culture. We don't touch each other. And we are made to feel an inordinate degree of shame about our fundamental human need to touch and to be touched. It happens in multiple ways in this society. At some point boys are greeted with a handshake instead of a hug. Or when a parent, particularly a father, begins to feel uncomfortable and looks embarrassed or ashamed when his son reaches for a hug. Usually the change occurs somewhere between childhood and adolescence. Boys aren't supposed to hug each other. I can remember being told, "Boys don't hug each other. Boys don't *kiss* each other." And we begin to shut off these natural dimensions of our personality, all of which are readily observable when we're quite young so long as we're allowed freedom to express them.

There are times when touching is simply a desire for bodily contact. Watch young children around ages 3, 4, or 5. They touch everybody, even strangers sometimes. Touching is simply a way to connect with others. Put together adults who are stoic and don't touch, bring them into a room with pets or little kids, and suddenly they start touching. But generally they won't touch other adults.

Men certainly don't touch each other, unless it's in the context of adversarial contests. If we're fighting, or if we are engaged in sporting contests together, suddenly touching becomes okay, because then it's the congratulation of triumph. We can be close to each other only after we've vanquished somebody. That's a clear, narrow, and powerful script for living life. If that's what it takes to be close, then we're going to have to engage continually in adversarial contests.

Touching and holding are also ways of communicating affection, tenderness, and intimacy. Sometimes it's a need for bodily contact, and at other times what's needed is the restoration of security—a sense of protection.

There are times in our adult lives when we truly need protection and support to be communicated bodily. Sometimes—for children, adolescents, and adults—verbal comfort is not sufficient. This is true in response to deep emotional pain, as well as deep shame.

Touching and holding are crucial to healing shame. That is true for children, and it is equally true for adults. The conditions for growth don't change, and the conditions for healing don't change when we become adult. But our culture and socialization lead us to presume *mistakenly* that they *do* change after we're grown up. And also much of our science, in the mental health field, has been similarly infected with this false idea.

Touching and holding have also become unfortunately equated with sexuality. Certainly the two overlap, but not all touching is sexually motivated. Many people confuse the two because they have been confused for us. Our culture and our science both tell us that the *only* reasons to want to touch another adult are sexual. We know in our hearts that's not true. There are times when it's sexual, but there are times when it's simply an expression of closeness. But we men usually deprive ourselves of closeness, especially with each other.

The only times it's okay for men to touch are on the gridiron, in the midst of contest, or at the bar after a few drinks. Then anyone can touch, and it doesn't count, because we're not responsible. Or maybe at the airport, where you can hug or touch anybody, so long as it's brief.

Much of my work has been aimed at constructing a general map of how human beings function, so that we can understand ourselves and begin to distinguish what is happening inside. The Eskimos have 32 words for snow. We have maybe a half-dozen for all that happens inside of us. I want to develop a common language for how we feel, function, and operate. Then we will have increasing knowledge of ourselves and be able to communicate our feelings and needs to one another.

Men have been much more limited in that vein because we've been denied access to so many parts of our personality. So many feelings have been too shameful to express. It's okay to be angry, but it's not okay to be sad. It's okay to feel contempt for others, but it's not okay to feel shame or fear. We've inherited a warrior script aimed mainly at vanquishing others, and we still operate from it to varying degrees. This script has lost contemporary meaning in the sense that it no longer has the survival value it once had.

The *identification* need is simply the need to feel identified with someone else, to feel a part of another person. We all yearn to feel *one* with another, to feel connected or bonded together.

Think of the earliest universal scene. An infant is cradled in his mother's or father's arms during breast or bottle feeding. I experienced this, because I participated actively in parenting both my sons from an early age. When I held my infant son and gave him a bottle, I would gaze directly into my son's eyes, and he would look up into mine. And well after he was done feeding, we would continue to look into each other's eyes. It's as if we were locked in a *facial embrace*. I believe it's through the eyes that we become *one* with another, that we merge with another person momentarily, and feel temporarily fused. In this way, we come to experience identification.

This experience is so powerful that it is taboo in all cultures to some degree. The most intense experience that we can have is mutually gazing into each other's face and directly into each other's eyes, and holding that gaze for an extended period. What usually happens is that we immediately begin to look away, look down, break the contact. We look instead at the forehead or the nose because we're not supposed to gaze too directly into each other's eyes. Only mother and child, or father and child, freely experience that unashamedly.

The other time we recapture the experience of facial gazing is when we fall in love. You meet another person whose face you gaze into and with whom you enjoy that unashamed mutual facial gazing. That's how we know we're two people in love: we look into each other's eyes—seemingly forever. Even in the supermarket line, anyone can tell two lovers by the way they look endlessly into each other's eyes. That's the experience of fusion, merging, or oneness.

Men rarely do that with each other, though I am convinced that it's possible. When my younger son was 3 or 4 years old and I was putting him to bed, there were times when he would look up into my face and eyes and say, "Daddy, when I grow up I want to be you; I want to be just like you." And we would gaze into each other's face and into each other's eyes.

Other children sometimes come up to me and look into my eyes, and hold the gaze for a long period. We have been made to feel ashamed of that; it's systematically shamed in men particularly. Men are supposed to be separate, independent, self-sufficient; we're not supposed to be intimate and close, certainly not with each other. Instead we should fight each other. We're adversaries or warriors—certainly not intimates. Increasingly, particular dimensions of our nature become partitioned and stratified, cut off, and blocked from expression.

This identification phenomenon is so important because it is systematically devalued in the West. In the East, everyone is socialized to feel identified with each other, to feel a part of the group, and thereby a part of the same culture. That is particularly true in Japan and China, where identification with the group is the modal pattern. In the West it's just the opposite: we're encouraged to individuate, to differentiate from one another, to go our separate ways, not to be communally close. We can only experience identification briefly, if at all.

In the East, the culture is openly organized around shame.

Traditional Japanese society has always been a shame-honor society, just as Mediterranean cultures are shame-honor societies. And in some parts of the United States, particularly the southern states, shame-honor cultures are present as well.

Everything in the East is geared to avoid causing shame, not triggering shame. In traditional Japanese culture the only antidote to bringing shame on oneself—which also brings shame on one's family and ancestors—was ritual suicide. I don't think they have more shame, though they are certainly more aware of it. It's simply a more conscious experience for them. Asians are more likely to display shame openly when they behave in a way that dishonors them or others.

I do not want to idealize the East but simply to look at the contrast between our two cultures. I don't see either as having the complete answer. I think we need to have access to all aspects of our being. I don't think either culture is better than the other; they're simply different.

We need to be able to express all emotions freely and comfortably when we feel them—whether it's fear or sadness. We need to be able to identify and feel connected. We need to be able to feel close, and that's particularly true for men with each other, because we do have needs for close male friends, for other men we can feel connected to. And, of course, there are times when we need to be separate and independent. So the goal, the path of development, is to reclaim all of our misplaced parts.

## DISCUSSION WITH AUDIENCE

*Audience member:* When I was a kid my dad used to make us look into his eyes, and then I knew that I was in trouble. I remember I was about 6 or 8 and my dad said, "You look into my eyes." It was like a shock.

*Kaufman:* Well, you've internalized almost the opposite of the taboo against identification, being *required* to look into his eyes. In a sense, it's dominance-submission; he was dominating you at that moment.

There was a fellow in one of my workshops who discovered the opposite.

When he was 6 years old he realized he could stop his parents from shaming him by staring into their eyes. He stared directly into their eyes, and they became so uncomfortable that they stopped shaming him. So your dad was using that strategy on you; it's a way to dominate by humiliating the other person.

There are two ways in which people in all cultures are placed under taboo for gazing into each other's eyes. In one instance, we're shamed for looking too directly into the face of a stranger; every child has been made aware of this. On the other hand, we are also shamed for being shy in the presence of others.

It's a twin strategy: Someone comes to the door, the boy is hiding behind mother or father, and the child is made to feel ashamed for being shy. He comes out and looks, actually stares into the stranger's face, and then he is shamed for staring. Those are the twin strategies that usually produce this particular taboo.

*Audience member:* In my particular situation my father used face gazing as a boundary invasion; it was his way of gaining power over me. In fact he even put a double bind on me by saying, "You look at me when I talk to you," and "Don't you look at me that way." "Look at me when I talk to you"—and we all get that from our fathers—and then, "Don't look at me that way." And half the time, if I think back, I didn't know which one I was doing when.

*Kaufman:* There is a tremendous power in our eyes. There are times when I'm driving and have stopped at a light. I'll stare at the head of the person in the car beside me who's a little bit in front of me, and within 10 or 15 seconds that person starts looking around. And I've also had experiences of either being or sitting somewhere and suddenly feeling as though I'm being looked at, and somebody *was* indeed staring at me when I looked around. I think there is a very powerful nonverbal communication that we are somehow able to transmit and receive through the eyes. I don't understand it fully, but I think it's primarily a process of imagery.

*Audience member:* My view of this is simply that the eyes are a way of getting past boundaries. When I wish to set my boundaries aside and be intimate with you, I can do that with my eyes. If I force you, I'm zipping your boundaries open from the outside, invading you against your will. At the same time, I think there can be a powerful healing of shame in eye contact.

*Kaufman:* I think you're right. We're dealing with boundaries, what's okay and what's not okay, where you can enter and where you can't tread. The eyes hold tremendous power. I've witnessed this over and over when I've asked people to look into my eyes. I've not forced them, but invited them; there can be tremendously powerful healing through that experience. There have been times I've done this with clients who've experienced a lot of shame. I move my chair closer and say, "I want you to look into my face." I wouldn't force my client to do it, but I'll make a very direct invitation and I'll lean a bit. I don't think I'd force it on kids, because it does trigger tremendous discomfort unless it's open, free and mutual—that's the key.

I had a very powerful experience which resolved some of the internalized shame that I carried from childhood. It happened with the man who was my mentor until

1973—Bill Kell, to whom I dedicated my first book.

This experience was triggered by working with a client who was dealing with what he had never experienced with his own father. He came in one day and said that he had just been home, and had been able to tell his father how important he had always been to him. As soon as he said those words, a voice went off inside me saying, "I've never been able to do that."

He proceeded to relate a few more experiences, and then said, "I'm done with therapy now. I've done what I needed to do." I was shocked and surprised and said, "Okay, I guess if you feel you're done, then you're done."

After that session I raced down the hall and knocked on Bill Kell's door, because I knew something powerful was opening inside of me. He was busy, but I interrupted him and said, "I need to talk to you." We arranged to talk the next morning.

When I related what had happened with my client, I said to Bill, "I have never been able to say to my own dad how important he has been to me." We conversed about that for a while, and by then I was able to tell Bill how important *he* was to me. Bill just turned and looked out the window and said matter-of-factly, "I've known that." We went on, and later I said, "I don't feel done, I don't feel resolved, something is still not finished." Then he looked directly into my eyes and said, "You haven't said the words." At that moment my heart sank; I just caved in and went into an acute shame experience.

I sat there, paralyzed. I couldn't move. I couldn't speak. Finally, I was able to say something that let him know I was feeling shame. At that moment he came closer, and I think he put his hand on my knee. We had already realized how important it is to reestablish touch and physical connection when shame is surfacing.

It's one thing to talk about shame, but it's quite another to experience an acute shame attack. It was agony. Bill just waited, while I sat in paralyzing shame for some 20 minutes. There was a knock on the door; we were well past whatever time had been allotted, but Bill advised the visitor that we needed more. Then he sat down again and waited. That was Bill's style. When I finally looked up at him, I remember looking into his face, looking directly into his eyes, and he looked back into mine. We continued that way for an extended period of time. Finally, I said to him, "I love you."

That was the hardest thing I ever had to say. Tears were streaming from my eyes, and I was crying. And all Bill did was smile at me, look into my eyes and say, "Good." That experience resolved and healed something in me that had been so powerfully bound by shame. This is the healing process.

## PATH TO HEALING

When I was growing up I thought that when you got to be a man you never had any more problems. You knew all the answers, you always figured things out on your own, and you certainly never needed anything. And since I never was able to feel that way, I never thought I was grown up. I never felt I was a man. Finally, I realized that it's okay to have problems, it's okay to need, it's okay not to know something, it's okay to have difficulty. The challenge is simply to start where we are, accept *who* we are, and build relationships with people who foster our health and growth.

It's going to mean risking. Nothing could make it easier to face that shame with Bill Kell and finally say to him what I needed to say. I agonized over it. Two years before that incident, I would not have even asked him for the time. It's taken me well into my 40s to feel essentially free, as free as any human being can be, of all the shame binds that I grew up with. And they still sneak up unexpectedly.

We are never going to escape shame binds completely; we're never going to erase our history. We can't eliminate it because there is no delete key to consciousness. We can't reprogram ourselves like a computer, but we can go through that process and learn to tolerate the shame that may be evoked. And we will need to continue to go through it; that's how to dissolve shame.

We all need people with whom to do that inner work. You have to build into your lives people whom you trust, who will assist you in that process, whatever the context. But it's not easy. It does mean tolerating some awful feelings and persevering on through. I think it's a process we have to stay with for the rest of our lives.

Knowing what is happening helps. Knowing that the feelings we're struggling with are inevitable and natural, given our socialization, means that we cannot only tolerate but endure shame. And every time we do so, even a little bit, we increase our ability to tolerate shame further the next time.

If we allow ourselves to just sit there and feel it, shame will rise to a peak, but then it will start to burn off. It will implode and begin to reduce itself. Progressively, each time you go through this process more of it is healed.

I've also taught people a strategy for reducing shame when it's being generated in the present. Whenever you are feeling shame in the moment, whatever the context or situation, refocus your eyes back outside. The essence of shame involves our eyes becoming fixed on ourselves. In our shame, our eyes turn inward, and we're watching ourselves. What we need to do is turn the watching eyes back outside.

I have been experimenting with this technique for 20 years. I've taught anyone willing to experiment with it how to successfully release shame. The way to implement it is by becoming immersed in external sensory experience, particularly visual and physical. Even if you talk to yourself about what you are seeing and hearing around you, all of your attention is getting progressively refocused into the external environment. When that happens, shame is released; it becomes immediately interrupted.

If you're in a room, you can count the number of people in the room. You can ask yourself, "Is there anyone here who interests me?" "Is there anyone here I want to get to know?" You can also go outside for a walk and become immersed in the environment, in the sights and sounds surrounding you. Music can do this, and there are other ways of completely refocusing attention back outside. As long as the eyes remain focused outward, directly onto the external environment, shame is interrupted.

Another way I've accomplished this is by closing my eyes. If I'm walking somewhere or if I have to function, then this is not going to be effective. But if I'm sitting in a room, I can close my eyes. I taught this to a man who felt acute shame whenever he went into the steam room at his gym, where there were other men. He would feel paralyzed with shame. I taught him the strategy and said, "Next time you go in there, focus your eyes back outside." He said, "That's not going to help, actually looking at the other men." I laughed and said, "Okay, when you go in, just sit down and close your eyes." He came back the next week and said, "It worked!" As soon as he closed his eyes he felt completely relaxed and comfortable; when our eyes are closed we are not watching ourselves.

This is one tool for releasing shame in the moment. It does not deal with internalized shame binds, and it does not work with the early shame that needs to be healed. Resolving internalized shame binds or early scenes of shame involves a process that first consciously recovers those scenes. Next, the scenes are reexperienced with all of the original emotion present, and, finally, they are transformed by infusing them with new affect. We'll explore this further in chapter 5.

## CONCLUSION

In the last 20 years it has become less valuable and respectable to be male in our society. That's unfortunate. But I consider it part of the profound transition that we are going through. We will come out of it, begin to reclaim ourselves and eventually be perceived as true coequals. It's an inevitable part of the process of exploding the gender scripts that have controlled us all.

We are faced with a culture in transition. We are moving toward the emergence of new ways of being, of thinking and feeling, as men. And we are in the grip of a profound transformation. Where the future will take us remains open. But we ourselves will create it—that is the hope for the next century.

# 4

## Seven Sources of Men's Shame

### Robert Bly

RB: It's a great honor for me to be here with Gershen Kaufman. About four years ago in a friend's house, I saw his book called *Shame*. When I read it, I was astounded, because it was obvious that shame was a taboo subject, and that he had entered into it. I realized also that it had been taboo in my own family.

Psychologists talk about *affect* a lot. An emotion the body strongly participates in can be called an affect. There are people whose primary affect is surprise. Some people know fear as their primary affect. Others have joy, and the spectrum ranges from vague delight all the way up to intense joy. And anger is a very strong affect, with a wide range. Michael Meade, for example—he can go all the way up and down the scale in 2 or 3 seconds.

I knew that I wasn't an anger person. I wasn't a fear person. I wasn't a joy person, even though joy appears in some of my poems, but (hesitating for ironic effect) that's just to fool people (laughter). I realized that I was a shame person by the time I had gotten 20 pages into Gershen's

*Based on the audiotape, "Men's Shame," of a joint presentation sponsored by the Alfred Adler Institute of Minnesota, Minneapolis, April 23, 1989.

†"Fifty Males Sitting Together" may be found in somewhat different versions in Bly's books, *The Man in the Black Coat Turns* (1981) and *Selected Poems* (1986).

**50**

book. It was a *wonderful* homecoming; I was really glad to know that.

And it helped explain an incident I had never understood. My family lived out in Western Minnesota, on a farm. When I was very small, my mother arrived home with two bottles of milk, the sort with little paper or cardboard tops. I reached for one, in that way of trying to be helpful—dropped it—all the milk spilled out.

And what I did was to run into the grove, and I hid far back in a corner there, by a tree. Gershen pointed out that many of us deal with shame by withdrawing into isolation. I probably remembered this incident because it made clear to me that withdrawing was my maneuver.

I remember hiding and hearing my parents calling for me. And not answering. Because shame has it's *own* power. By not answering I shamed *them*. Isn't that right?

I wouldn't give them the satisfaction of answering. But eventually they did *not* come to look for me (with playful plaintiveness). I mean, it was a small grove (audience laughter). (Continues mock plaintiveness): They could have *come*! (more laughter, continuing through next two sentences). And they didn't come. So in the end they won; I didn't. I came creeping out around twilight.

So then I understood why I remembered this incident out of all the other possible memories. It was at that moment that I acted on shame as a primary emotion. And not only that, but I also set a certain way of responding to it, by withdrawal into isolation.

Gershen has set down a wonderful list of seven responses to shame. I have used all seven (laughter). Of course, I specialized in withdrawal. And then I think I found a couple of others that Gershen doesn't mention . . . (laughter) . . . that I also use.

So, I'm really grateful to Gershen Kaufman. His work made a profound change in me, and grounded . . . grounded me in shame is what it did (ironically). Thanks a lot! (much laughter).

I thought I'd begin my talk with a poem. My father was an alcoholic. That is in the background of the poem. And, of course, that's a very fruitful ground . . . for the little bushes of shame to spring up, isn't it? One might say that alcoholism is the favorite way that American and Russian families have to be dysfunctional. There are many other ways. Anne Wilson Schaef, you know, took a poll and found out that the percentage of dysfunctional families in the United States is 102% (audience laughter). So if your family is not alcoholic, just translate into your own mode.

I am very interested in the idea that shame is an enchantment. The original enchantment makes you drop your eyes. To overcome or reverse the enchantment, you can reverse this act—that is, lift the eyes and focus them. For perhaps 15 years, I have been focusing my eyes as a sort of discipline—on a pine cone, a bird's wing, a piece of amethyst. It is a writing exercise.

One afternoon I was walking in the woods in northern Minnesota, near Kabekona Lake. When I came down to the lake, it was dusk. There were some hills in the west whose shadows had fallen about halfway over the lake. But the eastern half of the lake was still lit. Near shore I saw some reeds, and a *third* little band of water between the reeds and the shore. You see that sequence?

I decided to describe that scene. Images came, and I noticed that all the images of the dark were male, and all the images of the lighted part of the lake were female. And this doesn't fit with the Jungian view *at all*. Jungians associate darkness with the feminine, and solar light with the masculine.

I realized that I was describing my father with the dark part, and my mother with the light part. The band of protected water near shore was probably me. But when you're writing you don't know what you're doing. You just write. I'll read you the poem that I eventually worked out of that. It's called


### Fifty Males Sitting Together

After a long walk in the woods clear cut for lumber,
lit up by a few young pines,
I turn home,
drawn to water. A coffinlike band
softens half the lake,
draws the shadow
down from westward hills.

It is a massive
masculine shadow,
fifty males sitting together
in hall or crowded room,
lifting something indistinct
up into the resonating night.

I had in mind a group of Tibetan monks I once heard singing.

After a long walk in the woods clear cut for lumber,
lit up by a few young pines,
I turn home,
drawn to water. A coffinlike band
softens half the lake,
pulls the shadow
down from westward hills.
It is a massive
masculine shadow,
fifty males sitting together
in hall or crowded room,
lifting something indistinct
up into the resonating night

Sunlight kindles the water still free of shadow,
kindles it till it glows with the high
pink of wounds.
Reeds stand about in groups
unevenly as if they might
finally ascend
to the sky all together!

Reeds protect
the band near shore.
Each reed has its own thin
thread of darkness inside;
so it is relaxed and rooted in the black
mud and snail shells under the sand.

The woman stays in the kitchen, and does not want
to waste fuel by lighting a lamp,

as she waits
for the drunk husband to come home.
And then she serves him
food in silence.
What does the son do?
He turns away,
loses courage,
goes outdoors to feed with wild
things, lives among dens
and huts, eats distance and silence;
he grows long wings, enters the spiral, ascends.

I must have been 48 or so before I began to think, "What was
all that like? What did I do as a son?" A man said to me: "When
my father and mother were fighting, I'd walk out on the railroad
track for miles."

The mother's silence would be a good strong *shaming* silence, wouldn't it? The husband has to eat his food in silence—the
woman won't say a word to him.

What does the son do?
He turns away,
loses courage,
goes outdoors to feed with wild animals

Do you think you could stay in the house and deal with those
two? Often I couldn't. I just lost courage and *left*.

goes outdoors to feed with wild
things, lives among dens
and huts, eats distance and silence;
he grows long wings, enters the spiral, ascends.

Such a young man has a tendency to ascend, get above it all,
transcend it. Men of this sort are called "swans" in folk tales, for
example in "The Six Swans" that the Grimm brothers collected.
Some New Age people are like that in their flightiness. "If I eat
enough yogurt, I'll never be shamed again" (laughter from
audience).

eats distance and silence;
he grows long wings, enters the spiral, ascends.

(pause)
How far he is from working men when he is 40!
From all men! The males singing
chant far out
on the water grounded in downward shadow.

I like to hear Tibetan men singing together. They enjoy each
other's voices, and they enjoy the shadowy masculine ground
they're sitting on. The young man with long wings finds it difficult to be on that ground.

He cannot go there because
he has not grieved
as humans grieve.

At that point I had to ask a question about my family:

If someone's
head was cut
off, whose was it?
The mother's? (that's right)
Or the father's? (that's right!)
Or mine?

How far he is from working men when he is 40!
From all men! The males singing
chant far out
on the water grounded in downward shadow.
He cannot go there because
he has not grieved
as humans grieve. If someone's
head was cut
off, whose was it?
The father's? Or the mother's? Or his?
The dark comes down slowly, the way
snow falls, or herds pass a cave mouth.
I look up at the other shore; it is night.†

RB:          It occurred to me that one reason many American
             men don't grieve is shame. Perhaps we are too

ashamed to grieve. We imagine that if our own head was cut off, it was our fault.

In the United States, men are only allowed to grieve when they go to a funeral. The part of us that we have never grieved for is the part Gershen has been talking about. I mean the small boy who receives so much shame early on that he just can't take it any more, just can't live anymore.

I'd guess my little shame boy died long ago. What we need to mourn for are those little children inside of us who died. We don't mourn for them. Is that right? We just go "mmmmmmm, I'll make it through. I'll get a PhD."

*Audience*:    Will you clarify? In what sense does this shamed boy die?

*RB:*    Well, you know fairy stories say that witches or giants die, but they're not really dead. The next year you throw a log on the fire, and they jump back out again. So in the psyche nothing dies, but it goes dormant and cannot grow any further. If a little boy or girl gets completely blocked in there, they stop taking in anything from the outer world. And when you're 30, neither are very good in conversations or arguments, because they don't know anything. They're naive and very hurt. And blaming—they also blame a lot, these little ones. Why not?

So as an adult, one can stand there and watch them ruin a whole conversation (laughter). Moreover, if you're talking with a woman then, when your little shamed boy contributes a few words, you'll probably evoke in her the little shamed girl. . . . When the two of them control the conversation, it's hopeless! (laughter). They'll make a mess that won't be solved for 6 days. When those two get going, blame gets added onto shame. Jung remarked that the clichés spoken in such arguments haven't changed since the Egyptians. "You always do this to me (laughter); you never hear what I'm saying." To say the shamed boy or girl "dies" is a kind of metaphor. But I like it because it implies that "a death" is something we need to mourn for.

*Audience*:    That process for me is just a little different. I find that I'm getting back *in touch* now with my little boy, and he's been reborn.

*RB*:    That's lovely; that's the next step we want to talk about. How does that feel? Or how did it happen?

*Audience*:    Well, for me it started with getting in touch with the fact my father was extremely abusive on many levels. I was never in touch with that before, and I realized that I was talking to my little boy. I didn't know those words at the time; the process has taken me there. I am realizing that the little boy never died. He's just under water and trying to swim up. And 30 years later he got to the surface.

*RB:*    That's beautiful. Let's say he *was* under the water trying to swim up. But we never gave him a chance to swim all the way up, because we never got back to those times when he was so deeply shamed. We lived in denial, as they say in AA. The shame we felt was deeper than we were able to handle at the time.

As we get older and a little stronger, we can begin to relive the experience. Every man can choose at some time to dive down into the water, where he'll find the boy under the surface.

One has to choose to dive. And one must say that if you don't choose, the psyche may give you an accident, an illness, or a serious addiction. That acts as a way to get you down.

You know, in my mother's generation, a parent might die suddenly—say in a flu epidemic—and no provision was given to the child to mourn. No one would say, "Are you angry about your mother dying?" Relatives would say, "Well, you'll live with Aunt Margaret now; it will be all right." And no one asked: "Do you think your mother abandoned you? How do you feel about that?" No one asked any of these good psychological questions. And sometimes the development of the child stopped right there. It's a great blessing the work that psychologists have been doing recently in helping with mourning. But most of us in our 50s and 60s didn't get much of that help early on.

*Audience*:   You got me thinking of my story. I had a real significant experience. There's a process called Rebirthing, which I've been involved in for about a year. In the middle of one of my sessions, an image came to me from the movie, *Wings of Desire*. I cried during the whole thing because of this image of an angel coming down and setting his hand on the shoulder. That really struck me.

*RB*:         Was that connected with your rebirthing experience?

*Audience*:   Yeah. I became that angel that went back to the little boy, that little 4-year-old lying in his bed all alone in his room crying. Something awful had happened, and I was alone. All I wanted was for somebody to just sit there with me and put their hand on my shoulder, and say it was okay. I know that sounds kind of mystical, but it works.

*RB*:         It's just common sense actually.

*Audience*:   I got to be the man who went back and said, "Michael, it's okay."

*RB*:         Wonderful! If you're working with that boy, you might ask him if there's a place in your current house that he likes. Ask him where he wants to be. And then for a month or so you bring him a flower every day to that place. And don't let anyone know what you are doing either. If they ask, "Who's that flower for?" say "It's for my dead Grandmother." You lie all the time . . . (laughter).

              Because this little boy wants to be able to establish a connection with you in which he doesn't have to be overly adult, and yet you're not going to beat him up either. You are just going to honor him. And you need to have a real container for just the two of you, one that is secret and protected. Then I think he'll change, become in life again, and grow.

              It's a long process, isn't it? Two or three years at least. But give him gifts. Do you know how much little boys want gifts? They want whistles. They want little bits of candy. You could eat them later yourself (laughter). But he'd appreciate it. He'll eat the smoke from the candy.

*Audience*:   You mentioned some type of force that can bring one back to that little boy, and alluded to an addiction or a car accident. Please explain.

*RB:*    We don't know about all of that, but there's some force in the psyche that wants us to move forward. According to the old Gnostic tradition, a twin was born with you. And at the moment of birth, the twin separates from you. He remains invisible and lives elsewhere on the planet. And he knows everything that you knew in the other world before you came. He's aware of all the steps that you need to take, but you can't locate him. The deep longing that we have is partly a longing for this missing twin. Does this make any sense to you?

I spoke about this once for some 20 minutes, and then a man of about 35 said, "I had a sort of vision one day, and I told it to my therapist, but he just ignored it and went on." I said, "What was it?" He replied, "At the end of a corridor, I saw a 9-foot man who was luminous. He approached me carrying a spear, and said, 'Either change your life, or I'll take it from you.'" Now that's a serious message! It would appear that this man has to live seriously, or he's going to be in trouble. The visitor is 9 feet tall, and *luminous*!

So, one could say that there is someone interested in how you live. And that 9-foot luminous being can easily cause you a car accident; no problem. He just says, "Look over there." And then you end up lying on your back for 3 months, which is what he has wanted you to do for a long time. So you can think over some things. James Hillman mentioned that an overly active American man ordinarily can go into soul only when he's lying on his back in a bed, defeated by bacteria. He's no longer victorious; the bacteria won, the man lost; finally he's a human being. When a person is in defeat then the soul is able to come forward and speak to him. I like that very much. I think it was Woody Allen who said, "Death is nature's way of telling you to slow down."

## INTENTIONAL SHAMING

We might talk about sources of shame. I love what Gershen Kaufman has said here; I'll add some ideas of my own.

How do we get shamed as a child? Gershen writes that, first of all, your parents could just say to you, "You ought to be ashamed of yourself." We tend to believe what grown-ups say. And immediately the whole shame affect is evoked. We could say that we store our shame in *shame tanks*, which are very small when we are young.

When we get heavily shamed, our shame tanks start to flood over. Whenever my parents would say, "You should be ashamed of yourself," my shame tanks would start to run over. In school, I'll get more shame from teachers or other students. I'll have to get rid of some of the excess, by shaming other kids. Remember that? Playgrounds are not really playgrounds—they're shame grounds! They're places where shame is passed on to the smaller kids. Finally, one little guy over in the corner with pimples gets it all by 4 o'clock. He goes home and gets rid of it with his still younger brothers.

We could carry this image a little further. Let's say that we don't have big enough tanks when we are small to contain all the shame that we receive. One advantage then of growing older is that, if you work on it, you can hold more in your shame tank without passing it on to others immediately.

As Gershen says, "You can tolerate more shame if you practice tolerating it." Practice doing absurd things in front of square people, and let them shame you. And as soon as they've shamed you, dance! It will blow their minds. And in addition, you are increasing your own ability to hold shame. If you do certain odd things in front of your teenage children, they'll start to shame you right away (laughter). That's nice and that's okay. Just hold it.

One can play with being shamed. Suppose you're with a couple of very proper church women, just say, "Is it true that Presbyterians have hair between their third and fourth toes?" (laughter). Watch what they'll do. They'll put the kibosh on you. Since you evoked the shaming, you can handle it. I am off the subject, I think; we'd better get back (much laughter).

## SHAME THROUGH SILENT RESPONSE

A second way we get shamed—Gershen is brilliant here—is this: *The child asks his or her parents for a response and does not get it.* For example, you bring a little drawing or a joke to your father and you say, "What do you think of this?" And he does not reply. Then two thoughts appear: "If I were an adequate person, I would not have had to ask for this response." And second, "If I were an adequate person, he would have given it." The logic is irrefutable.

Shame has to do with perceiving, "I am an inadequate person." I've had that feeling since I was very small. So I know that logic. Once I asked my father to come to a spelling contest at my country school, because I knew I was going to win. But he didn't come.

I'm sure I went through both those two steps. "If I were an adequate human being, I wouldn't have had to ask him to come. And if I were an adequate son, he would have come." So that's that.

On this planet I am not adequate, that's all. So, I'll have to live with that. And I don't know what I'll do, but I'll do something. So the words adequate and inadequate are very deeply connected with shame.

All of this debate goes on inside. Did you think I mentioned these doubts to my father? Not at all. I withdrew. It wasn't inside me to confront my father and say, "Why didn't you come?" That would be out of my style. Is it clear what I'm saying? That would break the shame. And my family didn't know how to break it.

I'll tell you a story. About 3 years ago I went out West to give a poetry reading. And to my delight, my wife came with me. We were staying in a cabin near the ocean, and she had work of her own that she was doing. When the night came for the reading, I asked her, "Would you like to come to the poetry reading?" And she said, "Do you want me to come?" Now when you're well into shame, you often are not aware of what you really want. So I said something like, "Well you've been to so many of my poetry readings—maybe you should just stay here and study." I didn't say what I wanted.

I went off to the poetry reading. About half way through, unexpectedly, I missed her being there; I felt abandoned. Tears came to my eyes, and it was hard for me to finish what I had intended to do. When I arrived back at our room, I told her about it. As I talked, I suddenly remembered that detail of my father not appearing at the spelling contest. In one of those exchanges of gender which take place so easily in the psyche, she had become my father—my unreliable father, should we say?

The boy disappointed long ago woke up and was perfectly

present in his sadness when I was 48, 49, 50 years old. I can never predict when that boy is going to appear. So I learned a lesson that night: It's all right to say, "I want you to be there. Do come. Just sit in the second row, and smile." Then it's up to her to decide.

This is a story about a son asking a father for a response and not getting it. A father or mother can't give all the responses asked for. His typical refusal was clear, sharp edged, so to speak. My mother was quite different. If I said to her, "Would you protect me today?" her reply might be, "Well, gee, Margaret is coming this afternoon." Her responses were so confused or fragmented that I didn't know which country we were living in. What she said seemed so foggy to me, that I couldn't tell if she had answered or not. That was her style of shaming.

Being a woman she was much more alert, I would guess, to the fact that an answer was needed. But the response didn't meet the request; even though her feeling was charming and feminine, the answer didn't make sense. But in general I think that women shame boys less in this area of responding or not responding. I think it is mainly the fathers—who don't talk much in the United States—who do most of this second kind of shaming. Do you think so, Gershen?

GK:     Yes.

RB:     Well, we're pioneer people. Immigrants in North Dakota, who were chasing cattle and hogs . . . might not talk for four years (laughter). And that's the way it is. So the immigrant men became culturally adapted to fixing broken fences and that's about it. I never realized that a man who spent his life fixing fences might cause unintentional shame in his sons and daughters. Of course my father's father, who was born in Illinois, must have shamed him the same way. Isn't that right? And his father shamed him; it's probably in the family.

I'd like to lay out five other sources of present shame. We talked about two sources so far. These might be called intentional or deliberate shaming, and shaming by nonresponse. The second one leaves the shamer looking clean, because he or she doesn't appear to have done anything.

## INHERITED SHAME

The third source is *inherited shame* from the far past. Shame of that sort is connected with certain secrets that your grandparents kept. For example, an uncle embezzled money; an aunt had a mental breakdown and was in an institution for a while; a child was retarded. People used to encapsulate an event like that in silence. They put a skin of silence around it, as the body sometimes encapsulates foreign germs. And when so encapsulated, it passes down through the bloodstream of the generations. Eventually that silence will open or blossom in you as shame.

For example, there's more shame in my psyche than is justified by anything I've done. Where is it coming from? It's coming right down the genetic line. If my ancestors had spoken about the shameful event openly, the shame would not have been encapsulated. They might have said, "You know, Margaret went completely crazy; she's been crazy for a long time. We hid her for a while; then we couldn't do it any more (laughter). Would you like to go and see her?" That would have been a part of the family history, which is very interesting. But since these nontalkers encapsulated it, the shame comes down with its original energy and appears in each of us as a puzzling shame. We don't know the source of it. We just feel ashamed. It is a subtle shame.

In our generation, we can interrupt this sequence by not hiding shameful things from our sons and daughters, by talking about everything. Embarrass them deeply at all family meetings (laughter). Say, "Let's invite cousin George for Thanksgiving." "Wasn't George in prison?" "Yes, he knows a lot of stories (laughter). I think he knows some Etheridge Knight poems too; let's invite him." Say all you can about the crazy and failed people in your family. And your kids will hate it, but that's all right; they'll bless you later.

And then we could talk with the children about our own errors and our own disasters, and we could decide not to hide all that. Tell them details about your high school time.

I had to find out some details about my father from relatives. Once they said, "Your father used to play the trumpet; did you know that?" I said, "I didn't know that." "Yes, he played the trumpet during his time at high school, or Normal School, as they called it then." I said, "What happened?" "Well, he was courting your mother at the time. She lived in town, and one night he fell off the horse he was riding to meet her. He knocked out his front teeth and never played the trumpet again."

This is an important story, and I want to know it. He must have felt ashamed that he got his teeth knocked out because he fell off a horse. Is that right? Why didn't he tell about that? I played the saxophone in high school. Why didn't he say, "It's lucky you don't need teeth to play the saxophone" (delighted laughter).

Robert Frost is wonderful on encapsulated shame. He knows a lot about how secrets are kept in New England. "A Servant to Servants" is a long monologue by a woman in *North of Boston*. She mentions that her father's brother went mad quite young, and the family eventually built a sort of cage for him, made out of hickory, on the upper floor. Her mother came into the house as a bride, and had to help take care of him.

> That was what marrying father meant to her.
> She had to lie and hear love things made dreadful
> By his shouts in the night. He'd shout and shout
> Until the strength was shouted out of him,
> And his voice died down slowly from exhaustion.
>
> —Robert Frost, 1939

Frost didn't fool around. He put all of them right in the house at the same moment. One could say that in every family there's someone caged in the attic that nobody knows about. That's why your honeymoon doesn't go well (laughter).

## SHAMING THROUGH EVENTS

*[handwritten annotations: Cut from team during senior year / Expelled from school Senior (review)]*

As the fourth one, we'll name external *shaming events in one's own life*. For example, a boy can get caught shoplifting. I did—very shaming. Some children fail a grade, or don't read well. You don't get chosen in the ball game, remember that one? The captains deliberately avoid looking at you, and after everyone else is chosen, one of them finally says, "We'll pick you" (laughter). When we are small, as I've said, our shame tanks are small; and that scene in softball is enough to keep them filled all month.

Or you may fail to achieve some complicated task that you've been given. *Hamlet* is a shame play. Hamlet's father appears and says, "I'm your father. I want you to kill the new king and settle the whole thing, good-bye" (laughter). And Hamlet can't do it. He feels shame *all through the play* because he can't do this thing, which his father sets him to do. Of course, he's Danish (laughter). Maybe if he had been Norwegian he could have gotten it done. In his shame, he keeps checking it out: "Was that ghost my father?

Did it look like him." It was a genuine task, and he wasn't up to it.

How does Hamlet die? Got pierced with a poisoned sword. And after he had shamed Ophelia so much that *she* died. There's much else in the story, but it's true that when we're in shame, we shame others. There's no other way!

One more detail. For a child, seeing grown-ups naked can be a shaming experience. I visited a commune recently in which the parents practiced nudity triumphantly in front of the children, and required the children to be nude also. That was a favorite thing in the 60s. But children have a great sense of modesty, especially as they get a bit older. They do not want that. The parents imagine that they can get rid of their parents' repressive shame by doing the opposite. I said to the grown-ups, "You know you're crazy; you're shaming these children." "Oh they like it." "How do you know?" "They don't object." I said, "It's a form of child abuse; don't come to me with that shit" (tense and thoughtful silence).

Suppose you're in high school, and your mother comes to you without any clothes on. Isn't that shaming? Deeply shaming. Perhaps she was drunk. It's still a shaming event. And as children we're not responsible for it. Events happen to children. Incest between mother and son can happen that way, or between father and daughter. Sexual abuse of any kind leaves a trail of shame as deep as dinosaur tracks.

If anybody disagrees with me on these points, please interrupt.

## AN IMPERFECT BODY

As the fifth source, we'll take *inadequacies of body shape*. Body shapes are taken as a kind of excuse to feel shame. In high school, I was so skinny that I couldn't bear to be seen on the basketball court. I didn't go out even for intramural basketball, because I *knew* that the girls would burst into laughter as soon as I ran out there in my jersey. Actually they wouldn't have. They might have said, "There's that skinny Bly kid; he's kind of bright." That's what they would have said. I didn't know that then. And so the whole thing wiped me out.

And everybody is too thin, or they're too fat, or one shoulder is wrong, or their ankles are big, or they've got a birthmark, or they're too short. Can you feel the shame deepening in you now, looking back at all that stuff in childhood, how unfair it is? Some women feel deeply ashamed by every minor inadequacy in their own bodies; it's just incredible. Marion Woodman told me recently: "I've never had a female client in the last 7 years that didn't flagellate her body." I said, "What do you *mean*?" She said, "The women I see are not satisfied with the body they've been given." Incredible! This sort of shaming seems deeper for women than for us. But still it's enough, even for us, to fill our shame tanks.

## MAINTAINED SHAME

Let's go on to the sixth source. I'll call this one *maintained shame*. It's really routine maintenance of our shame vehicle. Gershen calls it *internalized shame*. The idea is that if by 14 say, you've been shamed well enough by other people, you won't need an external person to shame you anymore. You'll do it yourself.

Why is it that men who are well shamed, let's say by an angry mother, will pick a woman as their girlfriend or wife who will do exactly the same thing to them? Now why *is* that? Maintained shame implies comparison with all forms of maintenance, such as the 40,000-mile checkup on a new car. You've reached a certain level of shame performance as a child, and your job is to maintain that level. If you live with a woman who doesn't shame you enough, life doesn't seem real to you. Something is missing. "I want a female friend who can replace my father and my mother as a shame maintainer." And all over the United States there are women saying, "Let me try" (much laughter).

I recall an afternoon 3 or 4 years ago, when I was at a men's conference trying to teach some of this. A young man said to me, "Robert, we know how destructive shame is to our feelings, to our self image, to our masculinity. Why would anyone want it?"

I think the *intensity of* shame is the answer. Some people don't like Mozart; they want a rock band because it's more intense. We're hooked on intensity. Just because shame makes you drop your eyes and lose eye contact with another, that doesn't mean you aren't having an intense emotional experience. You are!

It's an intensity of isolation. I think Gershen says something like, "Shame is inward, and not revealed; but it's very intense." Can we call it a cognac? It's more intense than wine.

We do a great deal to make sure that every once in a while we have this incredible cognac of shame. Do you know that some people only feel alive when they're in deep shame? Just a few days ago, I shamed an old friend on the telephone by something I said to him. And he, knowing me well, recognized just what he could say that would put me in shame. And he said it. A few days later, I traveled within a few miles of his house, but I didn't call him to get it settled. Why not? Because I wanted to keep the shame going, including my own. I was a shame addict on that day. This is a serious idea, don't you think so?

There's a recent book that treats maintained shame in a superb way. It's by Fossum and Mason (1986), two family therapists in St. Paul, and it's called *Facing Shame: Families in Recovery*. I recommend it. These authors have dealt with shame issues in therapy for a number of years, and they've seen something which they call *shame cycles*. We know that menstrual cycles average about 28 days, and that there are emotional and creative cycles usually described under the term, "biorhythms." Fossum and Mason propose a shame cycle.

Suppose one person has a 38-day shame cycle, but another person's cycle may last 48 days. Suppose they are married to each other. Each spouse knows intuitively, with ingenious accuracy, how to kick off the other's shame cycle at the right moment to keep it going.

The man may be, for example, an alcoholic. He stops and starts drinking. During the sober part of his cycle, his rebellious crew gets tied up down in the hold. He as captain walks on the deck; he is in control. He walks into the wind and says, "Don't worry, I'm in charge of this ship." This may go on for 21 days.

Then a certain moment arrives. The crew breaks loose, comes up from below, and takes over the ship. Now the captain loses control, the husband gets drunk, disappears for 3 days, and often feels thoroughly ashamed. Everyone in the family shames him. He gets a full dose of it. The idea is that he's not addicted only to alcohol; he's addicted to shame.

Did you hear that one? He probably has a fundamental addiction to shame, and he uses alcohol to get to that place of intense shame. Perhaps one could say that in my family system, my father became addicted to shame early on; that's why he didn't want AA later. His Norwegian Lutheran mother provided it first; she gave him a certain sanitary form of shame: Add water, and serve. She made him ashamed of his sexuality, and of his wildness, I would guess. Perhaps she made him ashamed of his "masculine coarseness"; I'm not sure of that. This "high-toned old Christian woman," as Wallace Stevens calls such a person, made him ashamed basically of being a man.

In my father's case, he found later that the only way he could maintain the appropriate level of shame was to use alcohol. That's my guess. He was still able to work as a farmer and actually functioned very well for years. And everybody thinks that the reason such a man is in the bar is that he loves drinking and telling stories. And he does.

And how about my mother? Well, I would guess that she also became habituated to shame as a young girl. Her mother died in an epidemic when she was only 12, and that abandonment probably produced tremendous interior shame, hidden, invisibly experienced. She lived out some of her shame vicariously from my father's shame cycle. He would kick hers off at the right moment. He did the active part; she got it by picking up the pieces. She looked cleaner; she looked the more respectable of the two, but both were addicted to a repeating shame. It was he who was chosen to act it out.

*Audience*:  Isn't it also possible that shame is a way not to change, not to confront things?

*RB*:  Yes, that's lovely.

*Audience*:  It takes a lot of courage to change the things we do. And shame blocks change.

*RB*:  Perhaps we adopt shame as a way for us not to grow, not to go through the confrontation with the habit that's necessary if we are to grow. Is that right? That would mean that a man has to ignore the 9-foot luminous figure at the end of the corridor. Shame in fact helps us to ignore him. "I can't live my life; I feel terrible."

*Audience*:  I think that one reason we sometimes choose partners who resemble our parents is because certain parts of our unconscious are trying to recreate the parental situation, as a way of trying to solve it this time.

*RB:*        That's right. Many people feel that theory is correct. Suppose as a child, you received a lot of shaming, which weakened you so that you couldn't hold your own against your parents. Then as an adult you reestablish the situation to see if you're strong enough this time, to see if now you can hold your own. But often the new shame is so strong that the old outcome repeats itself. Is that right?

*Audience:*   With most solutions, it never works.

*Audience:*   I like that idea about cognac—as if shame makes you feel alive. I think that shame is the central complex, or central neurosis, of the human endeavor. Shame becomes very safe and familiar. People become passive. Most families work inside shame because it is safe. In order to experience life you've got to kick [back]. . . . And shame keeps you down.

*RB:*        Wow! He says shame is safe and known. Whether intense, or passive, or low, or dopey—it's a known position. And we can always return to it. Everybody prefers the known to the unknown. It's why you keep wanting to go back to your hometown—because it's familiar, and you'll get shamed again (laughter).

*Audience:*   Adult men who molest children were often themselves sexually molested as children. Please address this relationship.

*RB:*        Well, many people have done work on that. Let's say that you have been deeply shamed at the moment an adult invaded your body space. The shame is so huge, and your shame tanks are so small that you try to get rid of it by passing it on to another person. In sexual abuse, the shame is so immense that you've *got* to get rid of it and make another person deeply shameful. Is that sensible? I am sure there are many other solutions and answers to it. But that's a depressing one, don't you think so?

*Audience:*   I address the question of molested people who choose to repeat shaming experiences. Some of the work with abused kids shows that when they have been removed from an abusive family, they will sometimes behave in ways that invite abuse from their subsequent family. One worker said that children growing up need intimacy so badly that shaming or abuse may be the only form of intimacy they know. The only intimacy they become programmed to understand is the intimacy of abuse.

*RB:*      Most abusers do say, "I wanted to give this child something." And, of course, they're giving the boy or girl some kind of touch—touch that they were longing for as children. It happens the touching is contaminated with sexual abuse, but they give it anyway. That's good, thank you for that. Yes, please.

*Audience:*      A somewhat different way of looking at it—this comes from Fossum and Mason—is the idea that families perpetuate shame as a matter of inertia. And for me, unless I break the shame cycle, unless I get fierce, it's going to *just keep going on* the same old way.

*RB:*      Let me read you a sentence here by Fossum and Mason, which is a little bit like what you are saying : "For some, loyalty to the shame leads to such strongly established defense structures, that the only vulnerability known to the person is the vulnerability of the shame."

Suppose that one hasn't ever experienced the normal vulnerability of being with another human being and saying, "Let me tell you what I thought today. It was really terrible." They haven't experienced being psychically open in the presence of another person who can reply to you with feelings, or even with a hug. The *only* vulnerability they *know* is the vulnerability of being shamed. That's hard, isn't it? . . .

To sum up maintained shame, or internalized shame, we could say that at a certain point, we don't need other people to shame us; we can do it ourselves. A friend of mine spent several years in an adulterous love affair when he was 35 and I thought it was one of the best things he'd ever done (laughter). But recently he has been shaming himself over and over about that. Wow! That's maintained shame for you! Choose one event of your past, adopt some

Freudian term such as "Oedipal," and then you can shame yourself for the rest of your life (laughter).

## SHAME OF THE FALSE SELF

The seventh source of shame that I'll mention is the shame that comes from the creation of a false self. Alice Miller (1981) lays this out in *The Drama of the Gifted Child*. She says, in effect, that when you were born, you brought to your parents a fantastic gift. You brought a vibrant, extravagant, excitable, noisy, many-sided nature with you from eons of vegetable life, reptile life, mammal life, lion life, hunter life, aboriginal life—all of it lived before your human birth. You brought it all and gave it to your parents as a gift, and they didn't want it. Instead, they wanted a nice boy (muffled groans).

This rejection was deep. It happens to both boys and girls. Before you were two, it became clear to you that your parents did *not* want the wide range of energy that you were so proud of. They said, "Can't you be quiet? Why won't you be a nice boy like the others?"

Alice Miller remarks that, given our helplessness, we decided to compromise. Using our inborn radar set, we figured out what kind of child they wanted and we created a false self to please them. She said, "You betrayed yourself at that time." And we receive deep shame every day from that betrayal. That false self which each of us made up certainly lasted all the way through high school, and probably for 10 or 20 years more. It helped some. But each of us was also feeling shame all that time in the soul, in the eyes, in the finger nails, because we were no longer the wild person who came whole from the universe.

If you want to get a taste of that shame in a poem, read T. S. Eliot's "The Love Song of J. Alfred Prufrock."* Eliot (1952) realized when he was about 25 that he was living out a fundamentally false self. Prufrock says:

Shall I part my hair behind? Do I dare to eat a peach?
I shall wear white flannel trousers, and walk upon the beach.
I have heard the mermaids singing, each to each.
I do not think that they will sing to me.

*From T. S. Eliot (1952), "The Love Song of J. Alfred Prufrock, in *Complete Poems and Plays*. New York: Harcourt Brace. Reprinted with permission.

You betrayed your deepest nature by creating a false self when you were a child. Alice Miller adds that you must now forgive yourself for doing that, because you did the right thing. And the proof of it is that you are inside this room alive right now. The infant somehow remembers all those children who insisted on their original personality, and they got put out in the snow (laughter, oohs and aahs). So your survival instinct did the right thing. It made up a false self and you survived.

You have to forgive yourself for doing that. And the second thing would be to recognize that you don't need that false self now. One has to go through the grief of abandoning it, or letting it die, or releasing it. There's a lot of shame about this grief. Can you feel it (murmurs of assent)?

How to release it, and let the false self die, has a lot to do with helping your "shadow" rejoin you, or "eating the shadow." We could talk for a long time about that. But our time is up.

I'm sure there are more sources of shame than those I've spoken of, but those are the seven that I have noticed (much applause).

# 5

# Healing Internalized Shame*

## Gershen Kaufman and Robert Bly

*Gershen Kaufman:.* I've already written of tools for releasing shame in the moment [chapter 3]. Now we move on to dealing with internalized shame, the shame that we carry within us, inside. One way we can heal this shame is to redefine the present relationships that perpetuate our shame binds. Another way is reparenting imagery, a process by which we visualize and heal our childhood scenes.

## REDEFINING RELATIONSHIPS

I don't believe we have to stay in relationships that maintain our shame. No amount of therapy can help us overcome shame if it continues to be reinforced in a relationship. But too often we *do* remain in these relationships, particularly in the family of origin. And there are times when it's the relationships we created ourselves—either at home or at work—that we need to change or leave behind.

When we choose to behave differently in a relationship, then the dynamics of that relationship must change significantly. And that may include terminating a relationship that is too damaging to

*Based on the audiotape, "Men's Shame," of a joint presentation sponsored by the Alfred Adler Institute of Minnesota, Minneapolis, April 23, 1989.

us, because we have an inalienable human right to protect ourselves, first and foremost.

People develop expectations and predictions about us. If we
begin to violate these expectations, it's very unsettling to them. It
creates surprise and shock, because we're no longer following the
familiar script, and suddenly *they* don't know how to act. So we
have tremendous difficulty breaking these expected, habitual patterns of behavior, both in the family and in the culture.

We all know the cultural injunctions we've inherited in our
society. Breaking these rules is heresy in every civilization on the
planet. In Western culture it was handed down to us on tablets of
stone: "Honor thy father and mother." It was never to be questioned. There is a parallel principle in the East. It's not written on
tablets of stone, but it's equally enjoined by the culture: Obey
your family.

I believe we need to examine these principles and reconsider
them consciously. A very powerful exercise is to ask yourself what
you believe you *owe* each of the people in your life. Begin with
your parents. What do you consider you owe each of them, given
what each of them gave you? And once we know what we owe,
then we know what we can *freely* give. I know that if a family
member were dying, I would go home. That's what I feel I owe.
The rest is up to me, and in this I do with my family what I would
do with any other adult. But it took me 3 years to consider consciously whether I owed them every vacation, every opportunity
to visit.

Take a psychological inventory, and base your actions on
what the relationship is *now*. A simple example: For years, whenever my Dad would visit, he would always ask what I paid for
things, and then invariably he would criticize me. I either got
taken and paid too much, or I paid too little. I finally decided I
was not going to answer that question any more, because it always
left me feeling ashamed. The next time, I had added a room to my
house, and I was prepared for him. When he visited, he said,
"Well, let's see, I bet you paid $2,000 for it." And I watched the
little smile on his face. You can't build anything for $2,000, let
alone add a room to a house.

So I said, "Oh, somewhere between $1 million and $2 mil-
lion!" He looked at me like, "What?" He was completely dumb-
founded. Then I behaved the message—I walked out of the room.
The next time, he said, "Well, it was probably $10,000 or $20,000,
wasn't it?" He had to find out! He could not tolerate not knowing.

And I never told him. I finally had to say, "You know, I think we'll get along better it you don't keep asking me what I pay for things."

| | |
|---|---|
| *RB:* | He wasn't sure he wanted to get along better, either. |
| *Audience:* | I'm feeling a little uncomfortable with what you are saying. . . . |
| *GK:* | Good (laughter)! |
| *Audience:* | . . . I have an emotional program, but I also have a spiritual program. If I choose what you're suggesting here, it's going to get in the way of my spiritual program. Choosing to have nothing to do with somebody—that's not a Christian way in my personal philosophy. How do you deal with that? |
| *GK:* | Well, about all I can say is you are going to have to live with the conflict. You have to come to terms with how you are going to live your life. There's no right answer! I know what I have done for myself. |
| | I decided there's no reason to be in a relationship with anyone who does not like me or respect me. I don't think it's healthy for me to remain in that kind of position, even when I happen to be born into a certain family or work in a particular place. |
| *RB:* | That's a wild idea you just expressed there! Radical! Even though you're born into a family, you still have to choose whether you are going to live with people who don't like you and have relationships with people who don't respect you. That's heavy. |
| *GK:* | About 10 years ago, I decided I wasn't going home for my niece's wedding. I considered this carefully for a year. And I kept thinking, "I do not want to be around people who do not like and respect me." After I made that message crystal clear to my family, I got a call from my Dad raking me over the coals: "Why aren't you coming home? It's a small family. What will people think?" I got all those shaming messages, but all I said was "I will not be able to." I didn't back down. And from that day forward, I was never afraid of them. They had no more power over me. |
| | The relationship changed because I had changed, |

because I had behaved differently. It was cool and distant for a long time, but now they have a lot more respect for me. Our relationship now is the best it's been in 46 years. But my brother hasn't spoken to me since then—it was his daughter. Frankly, that's fine. I have no need to talk to him, because he never liked me anyway. My dad still tries to get us to talk, but I say, "Hey, you can't fix it. We don't have to like each other, and he has never liked *me*."

*Audience:*  You said that you didn't have to stay in a relationship in which you felt humiliated. If you do want to try to salvage such a relationship, what can you do?

*GK:*  Begin to change the relationship. Identify behaviors that produce shame in you, that trigger your shame. Once you name these clearly and specifically, then you look for ways to change the relationship so these things don't happen.

That's what I did when I stopped telling my dad how much money I spent, or when I decided that I don't have to go home unless I choose to. The others are going to be disappointed. During a phone call from my dad, I finally said—and this is the only thing you can say—"Well, I guess I'm a disappointment to you." He said, "You're right, you *are* a disappointment to me, a big one," and hung up on me.

*RB:*  Great! He played his part well!

*GK:*  But I named it, so I didn't have to feel ashamed because I was disappointing him. I was acknowledging it. And I expect to disappoint people—daily. He was trying to shame me, but he wasn't admitting it. He didn't acknowledge it directly, but I did. I called him on it. I've learned to steal somebody's thunder when they try to shame me. You can pull the rug right out from under them by saying, "Well, I guess I must not be behaving the way you want me to."

*disarming*

*RB:*  There is another way. I talked to a man at a little college in Kansas. He was a sweet man, a Mexican American, and he said that his father had always been furious and would never have anything to do with him. Finally, he called when his father was dying. His dad still didn't want to come to the phone, but the son insisted. So his father said, "What do you want?" and he said, "I want to tell you how much I appreciate everything that you did working in the auto shop so that I could go to college. I have a good job now at this college, and I really want to tell you how much I appreciate that." His father said, "You been drinking?" But the man wasn't going to accept that. He said, "Listen, I have *not* been drinking, and I want to tell you I appreciate what you did, and I love you."

He pushed it a little further. That's a way of changing a relationship, not obeying the hints to back off. "You been drinking?" is a hint to stop the conversation. But you can overpower that negative stuff and make the interaction go a positive way. It has to be genuine—he really felt thankful to his father. But once it's genuine, you can push it to any length. You are a grown-up. If you want to keep going and repeat it 5 times, you can do that.

## WITHDRAWAL, HUMOR, DENIAL, AND ACKNOWLEDGMENT

*GK:* There are other ways of dealing with shame, and they can be healthy or unhealthy. One is internal withdrawal—withdrawing from shame by withdrawing deeper inside, until the self becomes shut in. Lots of people are shut-in personalities, and what they display outwardly is a superficial social mask. But the real self—the needing, feeling, hurting part of the self—is hidden deep inside.

Another strategy is humor, which can be positive and adaptive, because humor reduces shame. But there are some people who seem compelled to joke about everything and continually make light of serious matters. And when humor combines with contempt, we have sarcasm, ridicule, and mockery. These are very powerful vehicles for generating shame in others and creating an atmosphere where shame is threatened.

The final strategy, if all others fail, is denial.

*RB:*      Denial is "I don't have any shame?"

*GK:*      Right, denial of shame! If every attempt to escape from shame fails, the last defense is to deny it.

*Audience:*      Can internal withdrawal reach a point where I'm not consciously aware of my emotions and feelings?

*GK:*      Sure, it can. Whatever becomes bound by shame becomes constricted, inhibited, and finally, suppressed. We stop expressing it outwardly. The effects of shame may then spread inward. Take anger. If expression of anger gets shamed, we may inhibit experiencing our anger to the point where we lose conscious awareness of it. If we defend ourselves by withdrawing, we may isolate parts of ourselves so much that we lose conscious awareness of them.

*Audience:*      It's my opinion that humor is always a defense. You can use it for a variety of purposes, but it's still just a defense.

*RB:*      Maybe you don't have a sense of humor (laughter)! I said *maybe*. . . .

*GK:*      I don't agree. We thrive on humor. It's a way of experiencing communion with each other.

*RB:*      Sometimes, it reveals a common shame.

*GK:*      Sometimes it does. And sometimes it functions as a defense, but there's nothing inherently defensive in humor.

*Audience:*      What about other responses when we're feeling ashamed? How can you respond verbally to the person who is shaming you instead of taking on one of the defensive strategies?

*GK:*      A very important way is *to acknowledge the shaming directly*. Do this especially when the person shaming you is important in your life, and you want to work it through together. Acknowledge the shame. Start looking together at the reactions shame sets off in you and how you evoke shame in the other person.

I've done this with my sons. I try to help them see that the reason one of them is insulting the other is that he's been shamed by the other. I think that's exactly what's needed: To say, "Boy, I just felt ashamed." We must be able to express and release the emotion with people we care about. Naming our shame won't be possible everywhere, but we can do it in relationships where it can be received, and acknowledged and understood.

## REPARENTING OURSELVES

*GK:*  Let me shift here. Another part of resolving internalized shame binds is getting back to our early scenes of shame and healing them. I've been developing a process that I call "reparenting imagery."

This process involves learning to care for and reparent the little boy still inside; we reexperience him in a way that's loving, comforting, and protective. When we can become a good father to the little boy inside, we actually reclaim him. Then we can give ourselves new words, new messages, new ways of thinking and feeling and being, new scripts for living life. We can begin to recreate who we are.

Within each of us, there is an early-child self, and an adolescent self, and perhaps other parts of ourselves that are locked away or hidden. But these parts can intrude into interpersonal relations, parenting relationships, etc., without our conscious awareness. So if we are in tune with ourselves, if we accurately communicate with ourselves, we can embrace those parts and create a whole integrated self. This is the optimal path of development, as I view it.

I want to guide you through this reparenting imagery process. So get comfortable in your chairs, and uncross your arms and legs. Put away your paper and pens—it'll be hard to write with your eyes closed (laughter). Now, close your eyes. I will close mine, and I won't peek. Breathe slowly, in and out. Take a deep, relaxing breath, and as you exhale feel the tension in your body draining into the chair, into the floor. One more deep, relaxing breath. As we proceed, I will suggest images. If you have different images, follow yours. Whatever you experience will be good, and you will experience only what you are ready to have happen.

Imagine you are descending a staircase. It's dark, it's quiet. As you take each step down, feel the sensation of walking, the pressure of the floor, the feel of the banister. When you reach the bottom, you're in a hallway. At the far end of the hallway, you see a light. Walk toward the light. When you reach it, you find yourself in a doorway looking into a room.

Walk into the room. Let it surround you. It's your bedroom, when you were 5 years old, or 10, or whatever age comes readily to mind. If you did not have a bedroom, visualize a room where you went to be alone or to feel safe. Walk around the room. Touch everything. Remember how the furniture was placed? The color of the walls? Run your fingers along the nooks and crannies in the walls. Is there a window? Is there light coming in? Is there a closet? A bed? A chest? Remember what it smelled like in this room?.

This is the room you grew up in as a young boy. This is the room you laughed in and played in and cried in. Look at everything. Touch everything. Remember how you used to play peek-a-boo or hide 'n seek games in this room? Did you hide under the covers or in the closet? What was it like when you woke up on Sunday morning? Did you have favorite clothes? A favorite song? Or story? What was it like being a boy in this room? Where did you draw pictures, or just doodle? Pick up a toy or a book. Hold it. Play with it. Be the child you were back then.

Now lie down on your back on the floor, and look up and take it all in. Remember how huge everything was when you were little? You were tiny. The world was gigantic. The dresser was so tall, the ceiling so high. And you felt small in that world. You are the boy who felt little in this room.

Stand back up again and look around the room,

one more time. Go to the doorway. You're standing there, and your adult self is looking in on your childhood through the door that you have opened. But now you sense you're not alone. There's a figure in the corner, on the floor. It's a little boy. Walk over so you can see him better. It's that little boy you were back then. He's sitting right there on the floor in this familiar room. Picture your little boy as vividly as you can. To deepen the contact, think of an old photograph from back then.

Sit down beside your little boy. Say hello. Hold his hand. Put an arm around him. Say, "I'm here now." Ask him what he's feeling inside. Ask him what he needs from you right at this moment, and freely give it. Say the words to him that *you* wanted to hear back then. Be a loving father to the little boy inside you.

Now pick him up in your arms and give him a great big hug, because he's been lonely a long time. Hold him on your lap, hold him close. Say, "You're a good son and I am proud of you."

Take him out of the room, into the light of day, into the sunshine. Sit together in the grass for a moment, where it's warm and bright. It's a new day beginning. Now imagine taking him to a new, safe place inside of you, a kind of kangaroo pouch just beside your heart. Imagine a warm, soft bed, and tuck him into bed, right inside of you. Pull the covers up tight. And sit down on the edge of the bed. Look into his eyes, and smile, and say the words you need to say to each other.

Now give him one last kiss, one last hug. You'll be back whenever he needs you, whenever he calls for you, because it's safe now. Time to sleep. Say, "I'll be with you always." Tiptoe from your little boy and walk back down the hallway and up the staircase. Come back to this room at your own pace. Whenever you're ready, open your eyes and join us.

There's a lot of pain in the room. What was the experience like for you?

*Audience:*  I've been in rebirthing therapy for 5 years and have done this kind of meditation a number of times. What always comes up for me is my son, who is now 19. I keep coming back to him, to how I treated him in the first 10 years of his life, and then the family disintegrated when he was about 14. I think about how I passed along a lot of my own shame. The challenge I have is trying to reparent him, to undo the damage. But the frustrating part of this meditation is that I keep going to *him*. I can't seem to be able to do it with myself.

*GK:* That's not so surprising. Your son may have to do that part. We need to make peace with the fact that we weren't better or healthier with those we love. You may need to grieve for the ideal father you couldn't be back then. And talking to your own image of your son may be a way of doing this.

*Audience:* Whenever I do these visualizations, it's easy to go back to this nice, generic version of myself when I was a baby. I was present at the birth of both of my children, so I can kind of relive that for myself. My parents are both alcoholics, and it's real hard for me to visualize specific things about later years. I can't remember anything from high school.

*GK:* Try getting a photograph of yourself at a later age, one with an open facial view where you can see your eyes. Put it up on the dresser, and look at it every day. If you try the visualization, this will create an entrance. You may not recall specific events, but you may begin to contact the part of you that's still there. It *is* hard. If it was easy, we wouldn't all be here today.

*Audience:* When I got to the room, I tried to pick the little boy up. But he was kicking and scratching, so I had to set him back down. For awhile there, I was trying to talk to him, but I just couldn't get any farther than that. He's still sitting in the room.

I was really angry going through this whole process. I didn't want to do it. I didn't want to deal with it. But the reality is I have to deal with painful things. So I suppose, somehow, if I can recreate this process . . . it might take a few more times. . . . He wouldn't look in my eyes.

*GK:* He was still too mad at you.

*Audience:* Yeah, he's mad as hell! I can't go to him right now. He wouldn't look in my eyes. I couldn't visualize getting past his anger.

*Audience:* It makes me think back about 4 years ago when I did this with Gershen at another workshop. That experience was just as profound as the one I had today. I went into my bedroom where I was abused as a little boy, and I was able to return as an adult and comfort my little boy and take care of him. It was an absolutely freeing experience. Today, I went back to a different room at a younger age, and I was able to go in and deal with the guilt and the shame I experienced at that time. I feel a great sense of relief from that. I'm no longer beating up that little boy.

*GK:* Sounds like it's been a real healing for you.

*RB:* He's making good use of it.

*Audience:* I didn't feel a lot of pain, only a kind of sadness. It was easy to look at the little boy and recognize myself since I have a fairly good picture of what I was like. The most meaningful part was when you asked me to speak to him and I realized that I never heard my own father saying, "I love you, and I'm proud of you."

My father has died, and we were never very close. But now I don't need to hear that from him, because I was able to say to *myself,* "I'm here with you always." Now I can communicate with the loneliness and the fear that I had as a little boy. And it was remarkably comforting to say, "I'm here with you now." I feel we can talk to each other.

## SHAME AND GUILT: SEVERAL POINTS OF VIEW

*Audience:* I am finding I have to rethink my definitions of shame. That's going to be an ongoing process, but I'd like you to help clarify the idea of "healthy" shame. I saw an interview with Joe Namath, and I heard him speaking candidly about his failure to make it as a sportscaster on a major network. His voice carried his disappointment. What struck me was Namath's openness and honesty. As I see it, he was expressing healthy shame. He seemed totally aware that despite his many achievements, he had some real limitations. Is this really shame? Can we call it healthy shame?

*GK:* I don't know whether it's shame or not. He may have been experiencing some shame. But I can feel disappointed and not necessarily respond with shame. If somebody criticizes me, I could say, "Well, I guess that person is not satisfied with me." I don't necessarily have to respond with shame just because the situation calls for it, or somebody tries to push it on me. Instead, I could be angry. I could feel totally neutral, or disgusted, or I could feel contempt for my critic.

I don't find useful the distinction between healthy shame and unhealthy shame. I don't think it's helpful to set up a judgment that one thing is healthy and another thing is not. We may quickly become pejorative about a natural emotion.

*RB:* I'd say that this was commonsense modesty that Namath was expressing, not shame.

*GK:* Modesty. It's fine to say that modesty or genuine humility is a form of mild, appropriate, normal shame. Shame in moderation is natural, normal, and healthy. The big problem is when shame becomes internalized, and begins to expand until it cripples us. Internalized shame grows like a cancer within us.

*RB:* When I started reading about shame, I must have looked at 20 or 30 articles, and there was almost nothing in them (laughter). But they all made a lot of distinctions between shame and guilt. And I'm hearing you, Gershen, say that these distinctions are not necessary. One thing I did learn was this: There are eight words for shame in ancient Greek, four words for shame in French, five in German, but only one in English. That means we don't want to think about shame. And unlike the Eskimos with their 32 names for snow, we don't make important distinctions about shame.

The Greeks have a word, *aidos*, for holy shame. That's the shame you feel when you go into a great cathedral. We have to put an adjective on it—"holy" shame—but they had a single word to distinguish this feeling from any other shame. This is shame in the presence of the divine, and since we're not divine, we naturally feel it. The latter part of the *Iliad* is connected with this. When Hector was dead, they had no *aidos* for his body—they dragged it around behind a chariot. That was a lack of *aidos*, a lack of proper and divine shame. They got punished a lot for that!

It was the same thing when terrorists held that plane in Cairo last summer. They killed a man and dumped him out, and we all saw his body hit the ground. That's a lack of *aidos*, but those stupid television people couldn't understand. They should not have shown that scene over and over again; once would have been more than enough. Because that's a lack of *aidos*, a lack of holy shame for the divinity of the human body.

So I think about how strange it is that our vocabulary is so crippled in certain areas that we can't make these important distinctions.

*Audience:* The way I see it, shame is when I perceive myself as flawed or unlovable. I like to think that I can motivate some kind of change in my clients through their guilt, through the way they feel about their actions. But I still don't see a positive side to shame.

*GK:* If I am a 4-year-old child, I may want to shoot baskets like my older brother, but I can't even get the ball to hit the backboard. I hang my head in shame at not being able to do it. The shame is not about my whole life, it's localized in that moment and that action. I don't feel defective or worthless, I simply feel shame at not being able to do what my older brother can do. That's shame about actions, not about self. All children experience shame because they can't match their older siblings or parents in skills of various kinds.

Think of the shame we feel when we slip on the ice—you probably have some of that here in Minnesota in the winter (laughter). You fall, you laugh about it, you talk about it as embarrassment. If you watch a toddler learning to walk, you see a lot of shame before that set of skills is mastered. But it's all localized in the action.

The key is for shame to be tempered so it doesn't overwhelm the child. If the parent or some older person responds in a reassuring way, the shame is reduced, neutralized. The child can cope with it effectively. I always had to say to my younger son, "You're not *supposed* to be able to do what your brother can do. You are 4 years younger." It got to the point where he would say, "I'm tired of hearing that!"

*RB:*      I think I agree with you. But I'm still interested in the distinction between guilt and shame. Classically, it is said that you feel guilty for some specific thing you've done wrong. You can atone for it. But shame is a general feeling of being totally inadequate. There's absolutely no way you can atone for it.

If I did a calculated, cruel thing to someone, I can do a ritual to reverse that moment of guilt. There's no ritual that will ever reverse my shame. That's why I find the distinction useful. I don't want to get rid of the word "guilt." We only have two words, "guilt" and "shame," and I don't want to lose one of them (laughter)!

*GK:*      I hear what you're saying, but I'm not convinced yet. I'm not suggesting we get rid of anything, only that we rethink what we're labeling. I use the word "guilt" whenever there is a sense of transgression, a sense of having done something wrong. But beneath the surface of the word, you may actually feel shame, self-blame, or even self-contempt. There can be a whole lot of different emotions underneath what we call guilt.

Guilt is fine to keep and use, but it can be about

the self, too. I have met people who are guilt ridden for things they did 20 or more years ago. One woman was so abusive that she caused the death of her children. She will live with guilt for the rest of her life. She is guilt ridden, and there is nothing that will atone for that.

Guilt can be about acts or about self. Shame can be about acts or about self. That's not the critical distinction for me.

## SHAME IN FOLK TALES

*RB:*       There's a great folktale about men's shame in the Grimm brothers' collection. It's called "Hans, My Hedgehog." The story begins when people say to a man, "Why don't you have any sons? Why don't you have any children?" So he came home angry and said, "I will have a son, even if he is a hedgehog!" But you must be careful about what you say, because soon he had a son who *was* a hedgehog. He was a hedgehog from the waist up and human from the waist down. Because of his quills, his mother couldn't nurse him. So his father said, "Well, what the hell!" and he made him a little bed behind the stove. And he lived behind the stove until he was 12.

Then a beautiful thing happens. One day the son goes to his father and says, "Will you give me a rooster and will you have the blacksmith shoe it?" (Nobody knows what that means—why he wanted iron on the feet of the rooster.) The father says, "Yes." So the son took a bagpipe and some pigs and rode the rooster into the forest. The rooster flew up into a tree, and the boy sat there on the rooster, playing his bagpipe, while pigs were copulating underneath. That's the scene. Nobody knows what that means, either. These stories teach us, in mythological language, about transcending misfortune and avoiding some of life's hazards. This one tells us a lot about how to overcome massive shame. The third time I told it, tears came to my eyes. I realized that in a certain sense, *I* had been left behind the stove. The story says that if you have shame, don't fool around with . . . new age harps. Pick up a bagpipe and really express your grief!

    These happy people are shame killers. . . . Remember that idiot who sang, "Don't Worry, Be Happy!" When I heard that, I said to myself, "This is Ronald Reagan's song. What's a black man doing singing it?" These happy types are dangerous. They try to keep you from feeling your shame, expressing your grief. Buy a bagpipe, that's what this story says.

*Audience:* I'm Irish. I'm Catholic. For an American Irish-Catholic, anything to do with sex is shameful—talking about it, thinking about it. How do you counteract that?

*RB:* Become a Lutheran (laughter)! I mean, at least that would . . . follow history. But that's a serious question. I'd like to hear Gershen's feeling on that.

*GK:* Next question (laughter)!

*RB:* My answer is to try to face that shame without blaming nuns or priests. Try to feel how painful it is to have that divine instinct—sexuality—constantly opposed and humiliated and shamed. Without the blame, I think you'll get at the full grief of it.

*GK:* But in the process you may need to experience your rightful rage at having been humiliated. I think that's crucial.

*RB:* Good point. The anger can't be whitewashed. But can you be enraged by someone without blaming him? I'm not sure . . . it's complicated.

*GK:* It is complicated, incredibly so. There are times when I will roast people in my fireplace . . . slowly!

*Audience:* Is that more reparenting imagery (laughter)?

*RB:* There's a good story in this area of anger—"The Devil's Sooty Brother." A man is discharged from the army and goes looking for a job. A dark man—the Devil—hires him to keep pots boiling for seven years, working underneath the ground. Before he leaves, the dark man says, "Don't look in the pots!" Well of course, that's the way to get him to look in. After a

while, he looks into the first caldron, and he sees his
sergeant. So he puts more wood on the fire
underneath. Three months later he opens the second
pot and sees his lieutenant there, so he puts a lot
more wood on that fire, too.

It says we are to enjoy the boiling of authority
figures who have humiliated us! Isn't that lovely? You
can boil them inside you. It's not necessary to go out
and attack them, you can boil your *fantasy* of them.
These authority figures are images of the shamers that
we have internalized. We have to boil them and boil
them, over and over again, until they're limp and
lifeless. That's what it means, doesn't it?

GK: Yes, we can reexperience our shame-rage until we
release it and kick out the people who caused it. I
think it's possible to literally kick them out. It's not
easy; it takes time. It took me 20 years to undo the
damage of the first 20.

RB: And finding a woman who really enjoys sex can be
helpful, too!

GK: Might help you speed up the process!

## POTPOURRI

Audience: In your list of tactics, I didn't find any place for
sadness, despair, or grief.

GK: Sadness, despair, and grief. . . . Distress is the crying
response; outwardly it takes the form of tears, or
sobbing. Internally, we experience it as sadness.
That's what grief is all about, experiencing the crying,
the distress.

But we also use the word "grief" to refer to the
grief process, which is a reexperiencing and a
reworking of all of the affects. The various stages of
the grief process, which Kubler-Ross and others have
written about so beautifully, are really the sequencing
of these affects over a period of time. So that's grief,
too.

We use the word "hurt" in a curious way.
Sometimes what we call "hurt" is really shame. When

we feel wounded, we're talking about shame. That shame feeling might be accompanied by sadness. But there are other times when we feel hurt, times when it doesn't feel like we've been wounded. Then we may simply be describing sadness or some other form of distress.

*Audience:*  Where do you put sexual response?

*GK:*  Sexuality? Our blackboard's not big enough (Laughter.)!

We've talked of *affects*. There are nine basic affects—surprise, excitement, joy, distress, anger, fear, shame, disgust, and dissmell. We've talked of *needs*, interpersonal needs, which are required for us to develop and maintain psychological health. And we've talked of how internalized shame binds develop whenever any of these affects and needs is subjected to recurring external shaming.

There's a third general category, the physiological *drive* system, which includes the hunger and sexual drives. Drives also can be encumbered by internal shame binds.

A curious thing is that the sex drive is really a paper tiger. It has to be amplified by a positive affect, by excitement. When we are feeling sexually aroused, whether it's during masturbation fantasy or sexual intercourse, we experience sexual excitement not in our genitals, but in our faces, in our nostrils, in our breathing. It's the affect of excitement that we're experiencing. That's the same emotion we might feel at a football game, a party, or a parade. This positive emotion of excitement must become fused with our sexual drive for potency, for integration, for pleasure.

At the first sign of a negative affect—shame, disgust, fear—sexual functioning is completely disrupted. That's a legacy of much of our religious heritage. It's not just one group. I have met many people from varying religions who have been made to feel tremendous shame, guilt, and disgust about sexuality. We're taught that there's something wrong with it. When I go beneath the word guilt, it's shame and disgust that I usually find. Being sexual is *that* dirty, *that* bad, *that* less than human. It's really a disgust response more than anything else.

*RB:* I want to go back to the connection that Gershen made between shame and hurt feelings. If a woman starts to attack the patriarchy, for example, she's got a lot of hurt feelings. You have to notice that shame is there also. It's difficult to hear the hurt feelings—as one should—without starting to feel ashamed. And if you fall into shame, soon you'll be apologizing for things that happened 2,000 years ago. Then you'll find yourself apologizing for all living men. And pretty soon you'll end up saying, "All men are [pigs]." A friend of mine did that; it was the outcome of his shame. From a woman's hurt feelings, he got caught in this trance of shame.

These conversations don't solve anything. You can't make up for 2,000 years of what happened to women. Many of their complaints are justified, but you can't make up for them in 2 or 3 hours. You have to recognize that a trance is starting, and that you don't have to go into that trance any more.

*GK:* Another way to say it is, "Hear the feelings." Recognize that there is hurt and shame beneath the rage. Anybody who has been systematically humiliated for a long time and then finds a release is going to go to rage. This has been true for blacks in this country, or Native Americans, or bearded men. . . . Their experience is analogous to women's. The rage may be an inevitable thing, a natural step in the progression from shame to pride.

My son surprised me several months ago. We have a thing every week where we all sit down together and talk as a family. Everybody gets to share feelings. And my son said, "You don't hear me. You don't listen to me." You could have knocked me over with a feather. I mean, that's my job! Listening is what I do for a living! What I said was, "Boy, I'm really glad you told me how badly you've been feeling."

I listened to his feelings, I cared about them, but I didn't feel ashamed. I had a momentary pang of "Gee, am I really missing something? Am I not paying attention to him?" I considered it, but I didn't *blame* myself. I didn't go into the shame experience that Robert was talking about. I simply listened to my son, and heard his feelings and acknowledged that I'm probably not perfect. I'm human, and I'm going to blow it some of the time. But I cared enough about his feelings to allow him to express them without buying into the shame and taking it inside. That's the hardest thing to do, but learning to do it brings big rewards.

*RB:*       We'll end with a poem by Antonio Machado, a Spanish poet who died in 1939. It's one of my favorite poems, and I think it says a lot about our subject today.


(Playing bouzouki.)
Last night as I was sleeping
I dreamt—marvelous error!—
that I had a spring
here inside my heart.
Along what ancient aqueduct,
Oh water, are you coming to me,
water of a new life
that I have never drunk?

Last night as I was sleeping,
I dreamt—marvelous error!—
that I had a beehive
here inside my chest.
And the golden bees
were making white combs
and sweet honey
from my old failures.

Last night as I was sleeping,
I dreamt—marvelous error!—
that I had a fiery sun
here inside my chest.
It was fiery because it gave
warmth, as from a hearth

and it was sun because it gave light
and brought tears to my eyes.

Last night as I was sleeping,
I dreamt—marvelous error!—
that it was God I had
here inside my heart.

—Antonio Machado, translated by Robert Bly.*

(Sustained applause.)

*Machado poem reprinted from *Times Alone: Selected Poems of Antonio Machado*, translated by Robert Bly. Weslayan University Press, Middletown, CT, 1989. c 1989 by Robert
Bly. Reprinted with permission.

# 6

# Men Facing Shame: A Healing Process

*John Everingham*

I am heartened by today's prospects for significant healing of internalized shame. In the last 10 years, we've cracked open this hard nut, which lay so long buried—misunderstood and ignored—under obscuring psychotherapeutic theory and the unacknowledged shame of many therapists. I honor Schneider (1977), Kaufman (1980), Kurtz (1981), and Fossum and Mason (1986) for their effectiveness in leading us—and me personally—out of the wilderness.

The Invisible Dragon (Shame) recently having become visible in his true form, many are at work zestfully devising arms with which to slay him. New approaches are appearing so fast that it's difficult to keep up with them all, so that the original subtitle of this chapter was changed from "The" to "A Healing Process." Other chapters in this book contain an impressive array of these new discoveries. The present chapter has become something of an overview, as contributions from several authors address in-depth material that is treated here in less detail.

Basic to this approach is the necessity to face shame directly. This is not as obvious as it sounds, for one of the fundamental manifestations of primary shame is to look away, to avert the eyes. Metaphorically speaking, we must look the Dragon full in the face, allowing ourselves to be fearful of his sharp teeth and fiery breath, but steadfastly continuing to look him in the eye.

The metaphor stands for a man allowing himself to feel acutely ashamed for a sufficient time—seconds, and perhaps minutes—to become convinced that he won't die from it. It means that he will learn to recognize the feeling of primary shame and realize that he no longer needs to hide it beneath some other emotion. Facing shame involves calling it by name—"shame," as well as sitting down to make an honest assessment of the destructive effects of internalized shame in my life. As a man continues to practice facing shame, he'll learn to hang his head or look away while he feels it, then lift his head and look someone in the eye, saying "I feel ashamed."

I suggest that a great deal of the dysfunction caused by internalized shame—perhaps as much as half of it—can be reversed by using a set of simple "tools," and that ordinary men can learn to use them effectively without dependence on therapists or other experts. The other half is tougher, and some type of professional help or ongoing program is likely to be necessary for the man carrying a heavy burden of shame. But it's exhilarating to brandish a newly sharpened sword and see the Dragon shrink back in alarm.

The body of this chapter contains discussion of 18 "tools" to help us face and heal shame. In the Dragon metaphor, these tools become the maneuvers of effective swordsmanship, many of which function to render the Invisible Dragon more visible. Some of them are published here for the first time (e.g., Hit the Wall, Integrate It Into Your Body); others are recognized by all the modern authors (e.g., Name It, Talk About It, and Maintain Boundaries). Occasionally, contributions from other authors have been recast into a therapeutic mold (e.g., Break the Rules).

## BREAK THE RULES

Merle Fossum and Marilyn Mason describe the "rules" that maintain shame in families and other human systems.

> The idea of "family rules" is used to describe repeated patterns of interaction that family therapists notice. . . . These rules are descriptive metaphors (Jackson, 1965), unlike the rules and regulations . . . decided on by authority. . . . (They) are descriptive of the forces working within the family which influ-

ence behavior. The eight rules which follow represent a recurrent pattern . . . characteristic of a shame-bound system.
(Fossum & Mason, 1986, p. 86)

The following list of rules that maintain shame is taken from
chapter 15, where I discuss them in further detail, and propose
rule 10. Rule 9 comes from John Bradshaw (1988, p. 39).

1. *Control.* Be in control of all behavior, interactions, and feelings.
   Control is the basic goal of all the shaming rules.
2. *Blame.* If something goes wrong, blame somebody; blame
   yourself if necessary. Don't blame the shame-generating system,
   or these rules.
3. *Perfectionism.* Always be and do right. Feel "right" too. Don't
   try if you might make a mistake. Justify everything.
4. *Incompleteness.* Don't complete or resolve disagreements and
   transactions. Keep feuds and resentments going. Don't
   confront.
5. *Denial.* Deny feelings, needs, and desires—your own and other's especially negative, "bad," or "wrong" ones. Deny even
   the obvious "elephant in the living room."
6. *No Talk.* Hide our secrets with a strict code of silence, among
   ourselves and certainly with others. Hold your breath, look
   away, and shut up.
7. *Disqualification.* Deny by disguising. Spin the shameful episode around; call it something else; distort it; reframe it. Look
   away from the shameful part, and focus attention on the positive or truthful part.
8. *Unreliability.* Don't be reliable or trustworthy, or behave in a
   predictable way. Keep 'em guessing. Watch for others to be
   treacherous and unpredictable toward you.
9. *Not Allowing The Five Freedoms* (Satir, 1974). Don't let others
   perceive, think and interpret, feel, desire, or imagine *in their
   own way.* Especially not children, clients, subordinates, or
   yourself.
10. *Moral Intimidation.* Assume the right to decide what—and
    therefore who—is right, appropriate, humane, enlightened, pro-
    fessional, or politically correct. Enforce authority with shaming
    threats, rhetorical questions, and subtle name-calling.

Fossum and Mason describe each of these rules in some detail, so reading their chapter 5 is recommended. We discover that

shame, powerful though it be, has an Achilles' heel. A decision to break these rules, especially the No Talk rule, is a decision to **break the power of shame**. Good news, indeed!

## RECOGNIZE SHAME

We may be uncertain at first, but we can learn with a little effort, practice, and listening to trusted brothers and our own guts. Also, we may learn to recognize the keys for shame (as a quarterback uses keys—certain positions and movements by his opponents—to read defenses).

Here are some of the keys now known for shame: *emotional* keys include feeling like shrinking, feeling frozen, a sinking feeling, an intense desire to hide, intense emotional discomfort for no apparent reason, feeling like being on the hot seat, or imagining all eyes are on you, and anxious self-surveillance.

The *physical* keys are eyes averted, head down, face flushed, ears burning, involuntary shudders, or throat and chest tight, speech halting or without resonance and power, and gut rigid or churning.

The *mental* and *cognitive* keys involve being inarticulate (Baumli, 1995), the panicky awareness of a mind gone blank, or noticing when someone is using shaming rules on you, or when you're using them on someone else or yourself.

The Recognize Shame tool breaks the rules of Denial, Disqualification, Control, and Perfectionism.

## NAME IT

Whenever I notice one or more of these keys, I've learned to say, "I'll bet this is shame," or "I'm feeling ashamed." Naming shame has a powerful effect, as it brings that which was held in shameful secrecy into the light of self-acceptance. Recently, I felt ashamed when I was refused a hug, when I was talking about inheriting some money, when I realized that part of my feelings for a brother is that I'm ashamed to be too closely identified with him in the minds of others.

Naming shame helps because the word itself is evocative, and perhaps onomatopoetic. "Shame" or "ashamed" evoke feelings in me that "guilty" never does; they seem to resonate with my inner reality. Does the "sh" feel like a sigh of relief, signifying the release and expulsion of a long-held, poisonous secret?

Sometimes Name It and Talk About It can be done simultaneously, but not always, or even usually. The distinction between private self-awareness and public disclosure is often substantial, and I need a kind of permission to uphold the privacy of my thoughts and feelings against premature exposure. We all need reassurance that we have control of the zipper that opens us up (Fossum & Mason, 1986; Mason & Fossum, 1987). There is no adequate substitute for knowing my own inner reality.

Another reason to Name It now and Talk About It later is to allow time and emotional space for an intervening stage, Feel It. Premature talking about shame may tend to codify or arrest the full development of feeling and its ramifications. "We will serve no wine before its time" is a good motto for both the shamenik and the vintner, especially because newfound shame is usually "green."

Because shame-bound families perpetuate shame from generation to generation (despite benefits that they may also perpetuate), it's usually helpful to name shameful events in family history. Considerable relief comes from acknowledging that my grandfather periodically deserted his family, leaving them impoverished and undoubtedly ashamed. Whether he did this because of alcoholism, mental illness, or wanderlust I can only guess; his reasons were never discussed. It isn't difficult to imagine how my father became my grandmother's "lover" in the emotional sense, and how confused and ashamed he must have felt.[1] I still feel a bit ashamed to admit that I was an unwanted child, a contraceptive failure, the only child of middle-aged parents during the Depression. I feel shame, but it clears out a lot of garbage, in that something inside gives me permission to be the way I am, to be carrying a load of emotional wounding that will take time to heal.

Please avoid using family history to support playing a manipulative Victim role (James & Jongeward, 1971; Everingham, 1995c). Grief is appropriate, but Victiming counterproductive. Grief subsides with time; Victiming often intensifies.

I consider it important to name shame wherever it's encountered, whether it be in personal interactions, advertising, television programs, comics, male and female socialization, or wherever.

Name It, along with Talk About It, form a one-two punch estimated to relieve a lot of shame in a relatively short time. In bringing shameful secrets to light, the fear of exposure is substantially relieved, and we give up trying to hide from ourselves. Thus, Name It breaks the rules of Denial and Disqualification in one instance, and Perfectionism, No Talk, and Incompleteness in another.

## FEEL IT

More than books, talk, thought, or the experience of others, our own body and emotions constitute our basic text. How shame feels was described previously and in chapter 1. The primary emotion is much more accessible to our bodies than internalized shame, but it too can be felt with practice and the use of keys previously mentioned.

It's valuable to stay with shameful feelings for as long as possible. This applies also to uncertain feelings which are only suspected to be shame. Recall that feeling ashamed is rarely destructive in itself. Don't make this your life work, of course, but try it when you sense these feelings deep and heavy inside, or if you're in a mood to learn something about yourself. Shame is such a silent emotion that it takes special effort to get friendly with it.

In a memorable therapy session, I sat frozen and ashamed, with my head down and eyes closed, for more than half an hour. My therapist briefly checked in with me occasionally, but mostly encouraged me to stay with the feeling for as long as I wanted to. I learned to be less afraid of shame, and certainly less ashamed of feeling it. And I learned something else, difficult to express in words; perhaps it's about really honoring my own personal experience. At other times when I've reminded myself about staying with the feeling, I've been able to do so for perhaps 10 minutes, or even just 1 minute. That's much better than jumping past it to fear, or the "medication" of an addictive practice, hardly noticing that I'm feeling ashamed.

Sometimes shame presents itself as confusion, or a feeling of not knowing what I want, or feeling bad without knowing why, or vagueness. It's wonderful to be able to sit with these vague feelings for a while, not in a crusade to "find the answer," but simply to honor myself. This kind of experience is often necessary after Hitting the Wall.

Feel It breaks the rules of Control, Blame, and Perfectionism; and internally, the rules of Disqualification, Denial, and Incompleteness.


## TALK ABOUT IT

Using this tool is the culmination of the previous four tools, and it's here that the big payoffs become apparent. When I'm able to talk about shame to at least one other person, my insides are saying, "I'm okay even though I . . ." and "I won't die even if they know that. . . ."

Talk About It can be as simple as saying, "I feel shame, I'm ashamed." Or perhaps a man will tell of situations in the past: "I was an unwanted child; my uncle sodomized me; my mother kept calling me her little man; the guys always teased me about my size." It's especially helpful to talk about feelings you're ashamed of, especially male-mode feelings (Bly & Meade, n.d.), or feelings you know may deeply offend others. Some examples: "I hate my father because he always put me down, but I was too ashamed to tell him. I feel like a traitor." "When the war ended, I felt let down. It was the most exciting time of my life, and sometimes I wish it wasn't over." "I wanted to rape her, then and there. To hell with rubbers and foreplay!"[2]

In addition to feeling ashamed of myself, sometimes I feel ashamed of a friend or family member. This shame is really being ashamed of myself for being associated, in someones mind, with the other person. I think it's important to tell the person involved, because it's likely to be picked up nonverbally and corrode the relationship.

A man can talk about his shame in confronting style: "When you don't call back, I feel ashamed; it feels like you're implying that your time is more valuable than mine." "That tone of voice pushes my shame button."

Many programs emphasize the value of telling one's story (see *Alcoholics Anonymous*, 1976, pp. 171–561). This practice establishes a ground of shared experience, and a vehicle for communicating hope to the listeners. It also uses the Talk About It tool for healing shame, for the "knower" most feared may be myself. At a

12-step meeting in Los Angeles, a wise old veteran of the program said, "We come here not so much to listen to each other's stories, but to be supported and encouraged in listening to our own."

Talk About It directly violates the No Talk Rule, and Perfectionism, Denial, and Blame as well.

## HIT THE WALL

There comes a time of blockade. I'm into heavy emotion, but have no idea where to go with it. I'm scared and confused. Usually one or more of the keys to internalized shame are present, often inarticulateness (Baumli, 1995).

Successful strategy is to back off, cease trying to drive through the fear. After a few hours or perhaps weeks, my internal process tells me what I'm ashamed of. Then I can cycle back and Name It, Feel It, Talk About It. We all have stout protective mechanisms against too rapid exposure, but acknowledging that I've Hit the Wall helps me to tolerate the impasse. As with Feel It, it's good to stay with the feeling of being blocked for as long as possible.

Hit the Wall breaks the rules of Perfectionism, Control, and Disqualification, and if the cycling back is successful, it also breaks one of the subtler shaming rules—Incompleteness.

## INTEGRATE HEALING INTO YOUR BODY

I don't know any way to plan the use of this tool, but when the opportunity comes, seize it. For weeks my 20-year-old son had been furious at me. Released by the New Warrior training from his usual inhibition about confronting the old man, he was letting it all hang out. He raged at me for committing slow suicide by overeating; he was contemptuous of my dispassionate treatment of his brother; he grieved for the years when he lacked an effective male parent; and he was disgusted when I'd had enough, and withdrew from him and others. I imagine that he was frightened by some of his feelings toward me. Most of all, I think he was frustrated that his rage seemed to have no positive effect.

Some little thing sparked his fury again, and his anger kindled mine. We didn't just pass it off, but went to a park nearby and faced each other man to man. As my anger cooled, shame came up. When I haltingly told him that I was afraid to have him see me as a phony, he looked at me with love in his eyes and said, "Dad, I've known for years what a phony you are, and its okay."

It was as if a heavy suit of armor melted and fell off my body. The secret I had been striving so mightily to preserve all these years was revealed as common knowledge. And he loved me anyway! My elaborate defenses against shame were completely ineffective, and moreover unnecessary. So I let them fall off me, to my great relief.

Over the years, I've had recurrent dreams about being inside a large metal boiler or tank, as large as a house. I've banged and banged on the walls of this metal prison; always it has been unyielding. The boiler hasn't visited me since this experience with my son. It was as if my body released the grief and rigidity of so many years of self-alienation, and began to reestablish a sense of belonging.

It's unclear what rule Integrate Healing breaks. Probably Control, and possibly Incompleteness. Words seem inadequate to describe fully the experience, and I hope we'll learn more about it in the future.

## ESTABLISH AND MAINTAIN BOUNDARIES

Shame-bound men usually feel that the handle of the zipper to our insides is located on the outside, so that anybody can invade us at will (Fossum & Mason, 1986; Dougherty, 1988b). We often take on others' problems and feelings as if they were our own, and are especially vulnerable to carrying shame, pain, and fear that rightfully belong to somebody else. Facing and healing our own pain and shame may make us less likely to offer ourselves as emotional beasts of burden. In my experience, boundary problems change slowly, but they do change. Cognitively, it may help to honor the concept that "I am I, and you are you" (Perls, 1969; Peck, 1978), or ask, "Whose problem is it?" (Gordon, 1974). A consideration of the Rescue Triangle (James & Jongeward, 1971; Everingham, 1995c) may be helpful.

## CONFRONT SHAMING BEHAVIOR

Examples of using this tool are: "When you . . . , I feel ashamed." "That's one of the rules we've been using to maintain shame in our family or organization." "I'm really offended by the way you use 'patriarchy.'" Analyze family structures for inappropriate vertical relationships (Mason & Fossum, 1987), role reversals, boundary violations, codependency (Fossum & Mason, 1986). Break the conspiracy of silence.

In recent years, we've tended to rely on others to do our confronting for us—lawyers, police, government officials, and a variety of activists and advocates. I'm recommending personal confrontation. Stand up, look 'em in the eye, say your say. You don't need to explain or justify. If the behavior triggers shame in you, tell them about it.

As I see it, Confront Shaming Behavior can break any of the 10 shaming rules. Jackpot! But I'd be cautious about using this tool too early and often; some prior experience with Recognize Shame, Name It, Feel It, Talk About It, and Boundaries is recommended. Confrontation is discussed further in chapter 15, under the Incompleteness rule.

## BUILD AND REPAIR INTERPERSONAL BRIDGES

Let's acknowledge our need for love, validation, attention, touch, respect, sex, blessing, and the experience of seeing another's face light up in response to our presence. Let's reduce our shame about feeling needy, and learn to distinguish genuine needs from playing a manipulative Victim role.

We can reach out to others, genuinely offering the same things. Let's be patient, for the self-surveillance and self-absorption characteristic of internalized shame may be slow to heal, and self-absorbed people start to wear on others' nerves after a while. This is the voice of experience, from both sides. But genuine love and caring will begin to flow as shame lifts.

But let's not be naive. As good engineering often requires the tearing down of old rickety structures, so ways of relating to people can also be tested for soundness and proper function. I'm learning to ask myself honestly about what I really want from being with this man or this woman. And if I'm not getting it, ask for what I want, be willing to negotiate, or perhaps bid them good-bye. If being with someone feels uneasy, we've got to find alternatives based on emotional honesty. And I sometimes find that I've fallen into a pattern of hanging out with certain guys just because they're more available, or I think are less likely to reject me. It's important for me to ask myself who I'd really like to be with, availability aside, and then make some effort to that end. I find that these things somehow clear out emotional junk and make "space" for more satisfying, more nurturing relations.

If a breach has occurred, make an amend, get back into integrity with the other person. If it's true, say, "Your friendship, warm and unencumbered, is important to me. I want to find a way to be friends without violating the integrity of either of us" (Paul & Paul, 1983). If your friend says "No," grieve; and then move on.

Interpersonal Bridges is one of the most important tools for maintaining ourselves free of the most toxic effects of shame after significant healing has occurred, as well as in the initial healing. Good interpersonal relations break the rules of Unreliability, Incompleteness, Disqualification, and Denial. And beyond tools and rules, they are channels for the healing flow of love.


## EAT THE SHADOW


The Shadow represents parts of myself that I deny or try to hide, and usually project onto other people (see chapter 1). Mostly, these parts are in the Shadow because I'm ashamed of them. But these disowned entities have a way of coming out sideways, and they're likely to be nastier after escaping from burial alive.

Projection onto others is one way the Shadow comes out. When I'm denying my own inner violence, I find some violent guy to feel both afraid and contemptuous of. If I'm hiding my self-righteousness, there's always some self-righteous phony to get angry at. When I'm ashamed of my desire to be persuasive or popular, I find some lawyer or actor to feel jealous of, as well as contemptuous. Although it spoils the joys of self-righteous anger, when I pause to ask, "What disowned part of me does this bastard represent?" I usually find an answer. Bly (1988, p. 56–59) discusses other worthwhile ways of using anger to honor the Shadow.

"Eating the Shadow" is a metaphor for retrieving, claiming, owning, integrating, embracing, and assimilating all those exiled shadow parts. This process not only reduces the power of the Shadow to make mischief, but it becomes an occasion of joy to welcome home aspects of my personality long banished from their rightful place of honor. Every homecoming strengthens the true self. The genuineness of the welcome may be judged by attending to my physical response, which is usually warm vibrations, and often tears of joy. Ritual homecoming celebrations, with a few good friends present to witness and bless, are recommended.

Robert Bly (1988, pp. 29–43) presents "Five Stages in Exiling, Hunting and Retrieving the Shadow." The first stage is projection, already described. In his second stage, "Something doesn't fit anymore, and we hear a rattle." The rattle can be very disturbing, and we may angrily blame and shame others, particularly our children. The third stage intensifies this effort as we promote our violence to the status of a moral crusade. The fourth stage happens when a man finally sees himself as diminished, because in giving away (projecting) his negative Shadow, he gives away the positive side too. The fifth stage is retrieval, and here the "eating" begins. It's usually a slow process, involving grief and a heightened sense of being limited in a fundamental way, and it requires active effort. I cannot do justice to Bly's excellent treatment in a summary paragraph and urge you to read the original.

Some men's groups practice "shadow naming" from time to time, in either a ritual or an informal way. As ritual, men may stand in a circle, arms on shoulders, breathing slowly and deeply, in an attitude of honesty and introspection. Each man has an opportunity to name the part of his Shadow that he's most aware of now, and his friends answer with a non-judgmental "Thank you." Any man may choose to pass. "My Shadow is the shame I feel, and try to hide." "Thank you." "My Shadow is that I'm afraid to be really intimate with a woman." "Thank you." "All my life I've been devising strategies to resist authority." "Thank you." "I truly hunger and thirst for revenge on (name of man)." "Thank you." "My Shadow is that right now I want to just pack it in, and die." "Thank you."

Sometimes a man will recognize that he shares with the speaker the shadow element just named, and raise a hand in acknowledgment. We take time between speakers to let things sink in. There may be grunts of recognition, "mmmm's" of approval, or sighs of relief. Men look into each other's eyes and perhaps nod in recognition, but we abstain from questions and comments, or defer them. These are sacred moments—when we trust our brothers with our innermost shame, with matters that we have hidden from *ourselves* until very recently. The relief of internalized shame is palpable, as is the bonding and mutual respect.

After some practice at eating the Shadow, I can feel in my body both a sadist and a masochist, as well as a man capable of fidelity and focused action for the benefit of self and others. These figures coexist and usually balance each other, but each will get the upper hand at times and be acted out, in the same way that each of various characters in a play has its turn at center stage. Shadow figures become dangerous when one of them is so magnified that it completely outweighs the others. Then we may speak of possession, by the tyrant Shadow of the King archetype, for example. This illustrates the important concept that conscious balance is a key characteristic of emotional health.

Eating the Shadow breaks the rules of Perfectionism, Blame, Denial, No Talk, and Disqualification, and offers substantial support for resisting Moral Intimidation.

## EXPERIENCE THE ORPHAN

Stories of orphans abound in ancient myth and fairy tale, as well as modern comics. The Orphan doesn't belong, through no fault of his or her own, and feels inferior and ashamed. Carol Pearson (1986, 1991) and Lucille Klein (1990) describe the characteristics of this Orphan figure; most of them look and feel like shame to me. It's helpful to consult these works and read the original stories, or perhaps do a bit of "Orphan theater." Then I begin to identify, in my bones, with a significant piece of my life history, and really experience, in a somehow protected way, feelings that I've been trying so hard to avoid. It can be the homecoming of a long-banished portion of the true self, profoundly moving and satisfying.

Experience the Orphan breaks the Denial and Disqualification rules, and may help with Control and Perfectionism.

## ACKNOWLEDGE YOUR WOUNDS

Listen to Robert Bly (1985) and Patrick Dougherty (1988a, 1988b) on audiotape. Their voices speak to this subject with a resonance which that cannot be matched on paper. Dougherty's first tape

provides vivid examples of both intrusive and neglectful (depriva-
tion) abuse, and shows how it's often difficult to get a handle on
neglectful abuse, such as never being held. I offer a short poem on
this subject:

Little Boy Hiding
Wounds  by their forgetting turn  to shame
Ashamed, I fear the gaze of a child
    and learn to hate the little boy within.
Acknowledgment begins the healing.

the Wild Man  shows his wounds
    machismo savage *tries* to hide them.
We see you in there, little boy
You don't have to come out
                until you're ready.

Wounds  in their forgetting  turn to shame
Remembering  begins the healing.

Acknowledging my wounds is a necessary precedent to taking
full personal responsibility for healing them—another necessity.
There is some danger that we'll get stuck in Victim mentality, and
use it to avoid taking our lives in our own hands. But I think most
men shift too soon, before the wounds phase has become fully
operational, so that the responsibility part has a fatalistic and un-
productive air. We need to acknowledge our emotional and spiritual wounds in the full depth of their pain and disability, avoiding
both undershooting and overshooting. In chapter 14, John Giles
(1995) presents some of his experience, which illustrates these
points well and extends the process to forgiveness.

Acknowledge Wounds breaks the rules of Denial, Disqualification, and No Talk. It helps with Incompleteness as well, by facilitating closure with people now dead or unwilling to participate.

## LET GO OF VICTIM

Interactions of the *manipulative* positions of Victim, Persecutor,
and Rescuer are described in chapter 13. We've considered elsewhere today's double standards favoring Victims who dish out

public verbal abuse. "MEN R SCUM" is an approved auto license plate in Illinois.

Several consequences occur. The politically "incorrect" may stand silent (and ashamed) or slink off, but their internalized shame and anger builds and gets more vicious. I view this as a natural consequence of shaming, not an indication of some kind of moral depravity.

It's doubtful that overt shaming or shaming threats help the social situation in the long run; they're effective mostly for short-term social control and carry a hidden time bomb. Along with reinforcing the prejudice, shaming drives it underground where it's more difficult to see by either party, but likely to erupt without warning. On the social and political level, the Victim turned verbal Persecutor often ends up shooting himself in the foot.

On the personal, emotional, and spiritual levels, hanging out in the manipulative Victim position is equally damaging. Barely audible voices inside say, "I can't . . . ," "if only they (she, I ) hadn't . . . ," or "I never had the opportunity to . . . ." These voices maintain the core belief of incurable unworthiness. To heal the buried shame, I need to turn up the volume so that I can hear these voices clearly, feel the force of their emotional impact, and claim them as my own. The "I can't" becomes "I won't."

Shifting from Victim to Rescuer or Persecutor derails the healing process by hiding the internalized shame behind "righteous" anger or "caring" service. This kind of anger rarely clears the air or accomplishes anything interpersonally. The "service" doesn't feel clean or do much to diminish anxious self-surveillance, and all too often it's not really appreciated by the recipient. Back to Victim again.

Groups or individuals often compete to establish themselves as the more worthy or bigger Victim, thereby to gain the upper hand in the moral pecking order. In such competition, there's a heavy price to be paid for winning. A serious question needs to be faced and, after a time of reflection, answered honestly: To what extent am I hanging on to the manipulative Victim position in preference to actions that can really change things? Despite the irrationality, I have several times found myself clearly preferring the "misery" of Victimhood. Awareness is a welcome jolt.

In addition to being a giant stride out of the Rescue triangle, Let Go Of Victim breaks the rules of Blame, Denial, and Disqualification.

## FORGIVE

Forgiveness heals the wounds of shame by reconnecting the broken interpersonal bond. If done well, the bond is usually stronger than before. True forgiveness breaks the Blame and Perfectionism rules, and probably Control as well. My favorite essay on this subject is our chapter 14, "Forgiving the Unforgivable," by John Giles.

Several additional points deserve consideration. There seems to be an optimal time to forgive; if it's done too early or late, there are likely to be problems. Dougherty (1988b) tells of his experiences with premature forgiveness—similar to Mark Twain's comment about how easy it was for him to give up cigars; he'd done it a hundred times! Forward (1989) warns that too early or easy forgiveness may lead us to discount the seriousness of our wounding, and Dougherty (1988b) explains how this may inhibit necessary grief.

Conversely, Giles (1995) describes some dangers of delaying forgiveness too long. Holding a grudge is likely to harm me much more than the other party. In addition to those presented by Giles, *Alcoholics Anonymous* (1976, pp. 551–553) describes a forgiveness technique that many have found surprisingly effective—repeated specific prayer for the other person, persistently done even if insincerely at first.

It's almost impossible truly to forgive another person if we can't forgive ourselves at the same time, or to the same extent. Giles's account illustrates this point; it seems to me that the specific naming of his mother's offenses provided him with the self-forgiveness necessary to truly forgive her.

Often an amend or makeup is preferable to a naked statement of forgiveness. The makeup acknowledges that the interpersonal bond needs repair, but maintains equality between the parties. Sometimes the "injured" party refuses, offering forgiveness for "free." Maybe it works, but sometimes the "forgiver" maintains a subtle air of moral superiority, while the man "forgiven" wonders why he still feels shitty and ashamed.

When a breach between adults is serious or long-standing, we usually find that both parties have contributed to the rupture of the interpersonal bond. Mutual forgiveness may be desirable. Paradoxically, each party must be *willing* to forgive unilaterally.

## EMBRACE PARADOX

Here's a stanza from my poem, "Rowing the Rio," in which white-water rafting provides physical metaphors for life's emotional and spiritual journey.

> He takes me to a rock by canyon cliffs
> and bids me see faces
> of paradox—seeming opposites,
> like heads and tails of a nickel
> joined:
> battle/surrender
> Warrior/Lover
> Magician/King
> letting it happen/making it happen
> *Seeming* opposites, each profoundly necessary.

Cyprian Smith (1987, p. 44) speaks of paradox thus: "Two apparently opposed realities will be brought . . . into clashing confrontation, until the dualism separating them is transcended and their underlying unity emerges like sunlight after rain." Making something happen (like publishing this book) and letting it happen (going with the flow of inspiration) are two such apparent opposites; I believe them to be merely different aspects of the same whole, like opposite faces of a coin. We need both, for we get unbalanced if we refuse to hold the tension of paradox, and being enthralled by a half-paradox can be dangerous.

Perhaps you felt some of this tension as you read the previous four sections. The order was designed to set the reader up for the paradoxes of experiencing the Orphan and letting go of Victim, of acknowledging wounds and forgiving. One dangerous half-paradox is to focus on forgiveness without giving the wound its full due. Men who do this tend to get wounded over and over, in the same ways. They're likely to be found hanging out in the Rescuer position. The man who focuses on his wounds but rarely forgives is poised in Victim, ready to turn Persecutor and pounce. He may still complain of affronts ten years old, and most people learn to avoid him. Perhaps he couldn't forgive himself for giving up such a lovely grievance.

Alcoholics Anonymous contains a famous paradox in its first step. "We admitted we were powerless over alcohol" becomes, paradoxically, the foundation of power to recover from addiction (*Twelve Steps and Twelve Traditions*, 1950, pp. 21–24). I am truly powerless over my addiction, *and* there is power in myself, in a group, in a program, and in a Higher Power sufficient for recovery. Then there's the grace of God paradox. When I don't have it, and know I need it desperately, then I have it; when I figure I've got it, I just lost it. The truth lies, not in some middle ground, but in embracing the whole thing—loss and gain, need and confidence are all parts of a unitary whole.

Perhaps you have a sense of what this holding of paradox feels like. (I obviously have a strong preference for the tactile/kinesthetic mode of expression. Eye and ear men may wish to translate into their preferred modality.) Sometimes it's like restraining two angry tomcats, and we may speak of holding "the tension of paradox." Other times, it feels easy and comforting, as if a paradox were embracing *me*. No matter how it feels, I cannot overestimate the importance of seeing that there's more than one side worth cheering for.

Embracing paradox implies a certain open-mindedness, an unwillingness to go off the deep end. For example, revealing our secrets has considerable value for healing shame, and so does maintaining our personal boundaries. Some therapists and group leaders use the first half of this paradox to justify breaking expected confidences. It takes hardening of our boundaries to convince ourselves that we can exercise this option when necessary; only then is it safe to soften them. Men and women have to see each other as different, almost foreign, to gain the respect that allows us to be truly intimate. That's paradox.

Our attitude toward internalized shame or addiction can be paradoxical. It's destructive and I want to lessen it, but it may serve to drive me to explore spiritual values, which are wonderful. As Barasch (1993, p. 310) says, "healing is not just a method of fixing-up, but a way to express the multiplicity of the soul."

Embrace Paradox works powerfully against Disqualification and Moral Intimidation, and is helpful with Perfectionism, Blame, and Unreliability.

## DANCE THE FOUR QUARTERS

Moore and Gillette (1990) have been engaged for some years in "decoding the deep structures of the masculine psyche," and their work is magnificent. The basic idea is that men (and women) have emotional / behavioral / spiritual patterns that—like our bodies— are shaped by biological evolution. To be healthy, we must live in harmony with our emotional deep structures—our biopsychologi- cal "hard-wiring"—in the same way that we accept both the strength and the limitations of our physical bodies. We honor our maleness, emotional as well as physical.

From extensive cross-cultural study, Moore and Gillette distill these inbred patterns into four basic areas—four realms. Each realm is represented by a mythic figure, an archetype (Jung 1964, 1983; Stevens 1983): the King, the Warrior, the Magician (Magus), and the Lover.[3] These four archetypes symbolize patterns that are encoded within us all, and in this view, remind us of our deepest longing and our highest purpose.

Balance and development toward maturity are key concepts here. Archetypes can be numinous, powerfully attractive, and dan- gerous as hell. One way to avoid being "possessed" by *one* of these dynamos is to carry all four actively and consciously, so that they balance and support each other. This active balance is what is meant by "dancing the four quarters."

Another way is to contact archetypes in ritual. Here's a meta- phoric illustration:[4] The archetype is a 100,000 volt generator at Grand Coulee dam; if a man plugs his toaster into it directly, the toast will be seriously burnt. Ritual is like a step-down transformer or impedance device; it allows a man to tap into archetypal energy without frying his ass.

Every archetype has its healthy and unhealthy parts. The King in His Fullness is generative; he's responsible for creativity, for blessing, for right order, and he's willing to sacrifice himself for the good of the realm. The unhealthy, dark, dangerous parts are called the Shadow; Moore and Gillette (1990) consider each Shadow to be bipolar. For example, the shadow King may mani- fest as a tyrant or a weakling abdicator. As tyrant, he may demand adoration of himself instead of being truly pleased at the success and prosperity of his people; as weakling, he may shirk the re- sponsibilities listed previously, perhaps even claiming that they aren't important or that he "can't handle it." We all act out both mature and shadow aspects of any archetype—we can't escape it. But we can shift the equation toward maturity.

To avoid becoming "possessed," it is required to disidentify with an archetype. I may carry or act out the King from time to time (poorly, or well, or "good enough"), but I *am not* the King.

Recent events in Waco, TX, show the destructive potential of forgetting this essential point. Rotating leadership is one way to remind ourselves, and to provide each man the experience of carrying the King archetype.

Dancing the Four Quarters heals internalized shame by promoting self-acceptance of ourselves as men, and as men fulfilling a mission in the world (Greenwald, 1995; Miller, 1995). We learn to recognize and *somatize* carrying the Archetypes in Their Fullness (Moore & Gillette, 1990) and are quicker to notice when we're acting out the Shadow. As we contact and derive energy from King, Warrior,[5] Lover, and Magician, we learn to understand and be proud of our male bodies, our male feelings, our masculine mission, and our male divinity.

## GO BEYOND SHAME

Important though it may be, let's not make a career out of healing shame. It's a means, not an end. In classical regression *à la* Erikson (1963), I find myself moving into trust issues. This received impetus as I wrote the section on the Unreliability rule in chapter 15, and discovered that I had never trusted myself to be reliable as my *own* best friend. Aha! However, I consider healing of shame issues to be prerequisite to effective work on trust. I can recall being so ashamed of my mistrust that I wanted to hide it.

Lindall (1995) stresses the value of letting go of fixation on recovery to focus on living. At some point, we have to say, "Forget self-improvement. I'm going to enjoy myself *as I am.*" Let the celebration begin.

These 18 tools may be used independently, or they may form a rough sequence, with plenty of cycling back. By analogy, I see them as operations, or subprocesses within a larger process. What follows are additional suggestions which I view as programs—structured approaches that incorporate some or many of these tools, and are likely to be quite helpful for healing internalized shame.

### New Warrior Training Adventure (weekend and weekly integration groups)

I carry in my body—indelibly imprinted—the sense of male bonding acquired on my weekend. I found in my bones the male mode of feeling (Bly & Meade, n.d.), and learned to speak in male voice, trust male intuition, and love men nonsexually. Surely this provides healing for the shame of being male (Schenk, 1995a). Greenwald (1995) expands this theme considerably, placing the New Warrior programs in the context of men's initiation, historic and modern.

The New Warrior weekend is designed to reinstitute that initiation into manhood which male elders in our culture have long neglected (Bly, 1985, 1987; Bridges, 1980). Although the process obviously cannot be accomplished in a 2 days, it can be well launched. Traditional rituals from several cultures are combined creatively with the modern. As in traditional initiation, men are tested: physically, emotionally, and spiritually. Most find within themselves deep reserves that they hardly knew existed.

To avoid misunderstanding, let it be clear that we honor and draw energy from the Lover, King, and Magician, as well as the Warrior. Our effort is to balance these archetypes consciously, and so avoid becoming possessed by any one of them (Moore & Gillette, 1990).

Presently, New Warrior training is offered by men centered in 12 cities: Chicago, Houston, Indianapolis, Louisville, Memphis, Milwaukee, Minneapolis/St. Paul, Philadelphia, Rochester, San Diego, Tucson, and Washington, DC. Additional training sites are being developed, as well as weekends for special groups (e.g., clergy, veterans, and high-profile men; call 508–544–0001). Integration groups meet weekly in these cities and others (Madison, WI; Windsor, ON, etc.), and are available to men who have completed the initiatory weekend. Analogous experience for women is available in southern Wisconsin and Minneapolis/St. Paul.

## 12-Step Programs (AA and Dozens of "Anonymous" Organizations that Follow the AA 12-Steps)

Step 1 ("We admitted that we were powerless over alcohol, . . .") is a powerful Name It and breaks the rules of Control. Denial, Perfectionism, No Talk, and Disqualification. Steps 4–9 look like they were designed for healing shame, as they involve honest personal inventory, the sharing of deepest secrets with someone, readiness to change, humility, and the process of making amends (which tends to repair broken bridges, both with others and with oneself). Beyond this analysis, I regard the AA program, for the last 50 years, as the world's most successful approach to healing a serious emotional/behavioral problem; it behooves us to learn from the best (see Bradshaw, 1988; Everingham, 1995e; Fossum & Mason, 1986; *The Twelve Steps: A Healing Journey*, 1986).

There is one drawback in 12-step groups: Confrontation between members is rare. It's as if there are No Talk and Incompleteness rules being enforced concerning our negative feelings toward each other. This is not to gainsay the outstanding effectiveness of 12-step programs for many people, but only that you'll probably have to go elsewhere for confrontation. Nobody's perfect.

## A Spiritual Solution

AA describes itself as fundamentally a spiritual program. Ley and Corless (1988, p. 102) point out that spirituality is difficult to define, but I find their description illuminating: ". . . a state of 'connectedness' to God, to one's neighbor, to one's inner self. It has variously been described as man's relation to the infinite, as the capacity to be energized from beyond ourselves, and as the basic quality of a person's nature—what the person is and what the person does. Inherent in all these definitions is a sense of dynamism, of movement, of reaching out. . . . religion may or may not be part of an individual's spirituality. For example, atheists also face the challenge of coming to terms with their own spirituality. The capacity to forgive, to create, to love and be loved is not necessarily dependent on one's belief in God."

Mickel (1988) calls attention to the fact that serious problems often require a spiritual solution. Although there are many forms of spiritual practice, it seems to me that they all involve contact with some deeply felt force, or entity, or "Presence" (*The Twelve Steps: A Healing Journey*, 1986). Often this force is experienced as *both* within and beyond oneself. I feel such contact as a sense of grounding and inner calm, often available from deep breathing, meditation, prayer, reading, music, poetry, or the experience of lying in a woman's arms after sex—and always requiring the will or willingness to ask or reach out for it.

Beyond theological argument, and regardless of appellation— God, Higher Power, Collective Unconscious, the Transcendent, spirit of the Universe, healing power within—I regard conscious companionship with this power and daily spiritual practice as significant for healing shame. Three reasons come to mind. A deep sense of being "in the flow" or "in the place we ought to be" transcends shame and makes ordinary anxieties seem petty. Conscious companionship overcomes that sense of not belonging which is so integral to internalized shame. Finally, we develop a sense of reliance on a healing spirit: loving, wise, and potent. All these help to combat the anxious self-surveillance and grandiosity/dejection extremes so characteristic of deep internalized shame (Miller, 1981).

Conscious companionship with God, as I understand Him, is becoming the major focus of my life, and internalized shame is a major roadblock. "Where shame is, God is not" (Dougherty, 1988b). And what is desired begins to provide the means to achieve it. Conscious companionship and reliance on God becomes both goal and process, process and goal.

## Psychotherapy

Therapy can be of great help if you have a therapist who understands the modern view of shame and is healing his own. For men with big shame issues, I recommend against therapy with someone not clued in; for me, it led to more shame, confusion, alienation, and rage—mostly at myself. If the prospective therapist says that shame isn't important, or implies that it's mostly about bathroom functions, I'd head for the exit.

A variety of methods for healing shame in therapy is to be found in our chapters 5 to 12, and 19, as well as in the writing of Kaufman (1989), Fossum and Mason (1986), Schneider (1987), Nathanson (1987), Bradshaw (1988), and others.

In the presence of a therapist who has descended into his own shame issues and returned, the client feels permission to go as deeply as he wants. The therapist is unlikely to become frightened or disgusted, because he's been there himself. This is the "vessel" or "container" that is built by a good therapeutic relationship, and it's much more important to the client's healing than the therapist's cognitive armamentarium.

## Support Groups (Men's Group, 12-Step Groups, Study Groups, Therapy Group)

We make use of "the magic of shared experience," which first shows us that we're not alone in our shame, and then gives us a safe place to experiment with breaking the rules—a place to come out from behind our facade, try out the liberation of being our real selves, and act out our shadow parts.

Throughout the book we describe methods for dealing with shame, and many of these can be adapted to support groups. Undoubtedly more will be developed soon. One potential problem is that support groups sometimes unconsciously adopt some of the rules for maintaining shame, especially Control, Denial and Disqualification. There's more about this point in chapter 15.

## Bless and Be Blessed

Blessing is part of our biological hard wiring (Moore & Gillette, 1992a). We all need the experience of seeing someone's face light up when we enter a room—it's one way that social mammals signal welcome and belonging (like tail wagging by a dog). In humans, this 'biological' blessing is communicated fundamentally by touch, eyes, face, and tone of voice (perhaps by scent). Cursing messages—"You don't belong here. Get out! If you stay, adopt a permanent posture of inferiority and shame."—are delivered using the same modalities. We humans were bred to respond to nonverbal blessings and curses long before we learned to use words, and our personal and planetary health demands that we honor these instinctive responses.

Just as I need to be blessed, I need also to bless others, and bless myself. And I may require a "refresher course" in the arts of giving and receiving blessing, and avoiding cursing.

Blessing heals shame. Potent blessing is a mighty healer of toxic internalized shame. Shame says, "There's something wrong with me. I'm so defective that I don't belong here. If I can hide my defectiveness, maybe they won't notice and let me stay. So far I've managed to fool them, but I live in constant fear of being exposed as a fraud and sent away—to die."

Blessing says in a loving voice, "I see you. I see you as you are, with all your defects—real and imagined; and I see your Shadow larger even than you see it." The sacred King in me sees you and says, "You belong here, just as you are. You're one of my men, one of the first-class citizens of my realm. You're a valuable man. You don't need more self-improvement to belong here. I want you with me—now. Welcome. Welcome home." He puts his hand on my shoulder and gazes at me with smiling eyes.

Then the King invites me to a leisurely walk in the woods. Just the two of us. We talk of my mission, and he blesses it. We discuss honestly my feelings and the events of the past, without needing to judge anything. He tells me that I have a wonderful future to enjoy, and that he's committed to love and support me always (Smalley & Trent, 1986). He says he expects me to fuck up once in a while, but it's unlikely that I'll do it so badly as to lose his blessing. And I feel wonderfully warm and fulfilled, trusting and unashamed.

Blessing makes us feel at home in our communities and decreases friction in our work together. Sometimes we engage in some bad habits of inadvertent shaming (Everingham, 1995d) and other types of cursing—intimidation, posturing, or too many White Knight assumptions (Moore & Gillette, 1992b). This is not to deny the many powerful benefits of our Brotherhood, but only to say that we can do better. My vision is that we develop a new Culture of Initiated Masculinity (Greenwald, 1995) and learn the art of honest blessing, with masculine potency.

Embrace Shadow . . . Return with Blessing!

Fearful Shame

The Invisible Dragon still fixes us with his evil eye
        and seeks to shrivel our souls
                                with his fetid breath.
But he's worried.
    He has been so dependent on his invisibility
            that he quails at the prospect
    of strong men wielding swords
sharpened by awareness.
He fears that we may soon drink blood
        from his severed neck
and in our joyous celebration
forget
            that tradition of bringing him back
                to life again, and requiring a gift.
His fears may be justified.
So BROTHERS   let's quit farting around
                                        and start kicking ass!

## NOTES

1. See Fossum and Mason (1986) on vertical and horizontal relations, the discussion of "structural abuse" by Dougherty (1988a, 1988b), and Baber's (1989) moving personal memoir.

2. It's my firm belief that the best way to stop rape and murder is to give full

acknowledgment to the killer and the rapist *in me*. A nod of recognition is just the beginning, but may lead to full-bodied integration and transcendence. Denial, soft-pedaling, or failure to express these violent internal structures makes them more likely to erupt in destructive acts. See discussion of the Shadow in chapter 1, topic 19, and later in this chapter.

3. An archetype is conveniently seen as an anthropomorphic figure represented repeatedly in myth or drama, as well as in modern life and literature. To set the record straight, this usage is derivative to Jung's basic concept. "The term 'archetype' is often misunderstood as meaning certain definite mythological images or motifs. But these are nothing more than conscious representations; it would be absurd to assume that such variable representations could be inherited. The archetype is a *tendency to form such representations of a motif*—representations which can vary a great deal in detail without losing their basic pattern" (Jung, 1964, p. 67, emphasis added).

4. This illustration probably originated with Robert Moore. I first heard it in a workshop led by Bill Kauth and David Kaar.

5. Some men feel such revulsion at the sadomasochistic bipolar Shadow of the Warrior archetype (Yes, Virginia, modern warfare is masochistic as well as sadistic) that they cast the entire archetype into their personal Shadow. Not only are they projecting their own sadism onto others, but they're inhibiting the development of their Warrior virtues (Moore & Gillette, 1992b; Greenwald, 1995). The basic mistake is to confuse the archetypal Shadow with the entire archetype.

# 7

## Involving Men in Healing Their Wounds of Socialization

*Compiled by Roy U. Schenk*

Efforts to help men deal with the intense shame messages they receive almost from birth will prove fruitless unless men can respond positively to these efforts. It is a long known and often discussed reality that most men do not seek counseling, or other help on emotional and feelings issues. This chapter is devoted to exploring why that is so and what we can do about it.

The writings in this chapter are a response to an inquiry we addressed to a couple dozen men who are involved with assisting and counseling men in some way. The questions we asked are: (a) Why is it that relatively few men turn for help to counselors or therapists, or to men's self-help groups? and (b) What does it take to get men involved? The answers we received ranged from a short paragraph to near-chapter-length articles. We have printed them here and then completed the chapter with a summary and reflections on what these men have written.

### RESPONSES BY TWENTY-THREE MEN

*Gershen Kaufman:* Men are ashamed of expressing feelings like fear, sadness, and shame itself. Men are particularly ashamed of needing any-

**120**

thing. That's why they have so much difficulty asking for help or appearing vulnerable. Men need to learn that needing is a source of strength, not a sign of inadequacy.

*Robert Bly:* Young men need to hear old men tell of their failures, so that they won't feel so ashamed of their own failures.

*John Everingham:* Most therapy is conducted (even by men) in the female mode of feeling, or in some demasculinized, hybrid, or neutral mode of feeling. Do it in male mode and *bingo*!

*Roy Schenk:* Men's sense of shame for being male makes them feel they deserve the bad things that happen to them. It's hard to change what you feel you deserve. We need consciousness raising to change this.

*John Higgins:* One-to-one extension of male caring, particularly with the AIDS-related intensification of homophobia, has become only more constricted. My personal experience with New Warrior weekend, which has a real chance of succeeding in the face of these odds, says that there is not only safety but comfort in numbers.

The irony is that it does require true strength of character and one-to-one extension of masculine caring to extend this experience to each other. Leading by example is necessary—someone has to be willing to take the risk. The group provides an umbrella from which the individual can extend a hand up to his brother.

*Al Ring:* Since early experiences of shame and attendant fear of recurrent shame are among the most intense feelings a person can encounter—perhaps more so for boys who are expected to be macho, to hide feelings, etc.—an entire facade, mask, or way of "looking good" to others is developed.

To get to the root of the shame and fear, which are deeply buried in the psyche, would require stripping away layer after layer of protective covering—something most men are loath to even attempt. For many men, the only hope is through the trust and love engendered by groups such as the New Warriors.

*Asa Baber:* Frankly, any seminar or meeting that allows men a safe space in which to talk about their lives and problems is a worthy exercise. I do think men need time and safety before they are ready to reveal their deeper thoughts. A good model might be the New Warrior Training Adventure. I'm not saying it's the only model, but it does seem to work, and it does allow men to explore their lives.

*Rich Tosi:* I participate and grow in situations when it is "safe" for me. Safe means:

- I will be protected from hurting myself and others both emotionally and physically.
- The trainers/counselors are initiated men.
- That I will be led into my deepest shadows protected from shame and self-hatred.

*Dieter Ammann:* How can I write about why men don't seek help when I have avoided seeking help for years? I really don't even know why I don't ask. So, rather than speculating, let me just tell you what got me to the Warrior Training and beyond.

First of all, I recognized at the time that I was in some pain around my personal relationships, particularly with women. I also just about hated my job and found it exceedingly difficult to focus on my work tasks. Even though I was encouraged to go to the weekend by a close female friend, in the end, it was the persuasive talks of some men friends at my church that induced me to go.

Going to the weekend was, however, no great trick since I am an experienced workshop goer and presenter. What was different was that it was an all-male event. My male parenting had left much to be desired, and I was not comfortable in all-male settings. So maybe the first clue for not asking for help derives from this. If my father was not there for me physically and emotionally and he continually disappointed me, what could I possibly get from a male stranger-therapist? I wouldn't risk it. Besides, what would this person possibly know about my problem that I hadn't explored already? So, I felt superior and used that to avoid asking.

Now what gave me the motivation to keep on with my men's group after the weekend and later to join Accelerated Behavior Change Training (ABC)? I think I needed a powerful experience, powerful enough to get and keep my attention. I learned to trust and love men, something I had never done before. Also, for the first time, I was able to drop my masks of competence and sophistication before men. So, I think that men need such an experience before they allow themselves to become vulnerable and needy enough to ask for help. Something powerful is necessary to overcome the cultural conditioning. And it has to be something that shakes a man to the core. Otherwise, he will "sort of" ask for help but never get down to business. At least that is how it worked for me.

At this point, I still have not gone to a therapist. However, my ongoing integration group as well as my year in ABC has more than adequately served my therapeutic needs. I don't know if there is a common denominator. I do think that men are ashamed to ask for help. I also think that most men don't know what therapy is and how it works. There are too many therapist jokes and the movies often portray the therapist as a funny/weird/strange person. So how can one go for help to someone who one's peer group makes fun of?

I do agree with Bly that the absence of the older men has caused substantial damage to the younger generation. Since the family no longer incorporates the old family members in a useful way, some forum is necessary to bring old and young together. I would like to see a special event devoted to this topic where some brainstorming can be done.

*Lawrence Diggs:* The reason that few men turn to counselors is that counselors have passive therapy. That is a nice way to say that all they do is talk. Men learn by doing. The psychoindustry is oriented to women, just as the schools are oriented to women. If a man cannot express what is bothering him verbally the psychofolks are usually useless.

Too many of the people who are in the mind-bending business have decidedly female perspectives. Their solutions work as long as you are on the couch, but do not apply in real life.

Men do not feel comfortable letting people mess with their minds. To allow this requires the utmost of trust, the utmost of desperation, or the utmost of stupidity. We have to ask ourselves what events in a man's life lead him to feel that he can take off his armor. Women are taught that it is their right to be protected, and the expectation of this right is reinforced all of their lives.

They know and men know that men will be punished severely not only for causing them harm but for failing to protect them. Men have not been socialized that they can expect the same kind of protection. So as men we wear armor full-time, and the helmet is the last piece of armor we are going to take off.

If we cannot trust the woman of our life enough to take off our armor, if we cannot trust the men in our lives enough to take off the armor, then we are certainly not going to take off this armor to someone who usually talks a bunch of "bull.". . .

Take a look at the solutions most of the men's conferences offer men. They are knee deep in bull shit. The words and ideas are molded to be politically correct. Everyone is so concerned that they don't hurt women's feelings that they forget that they are talking to and about men. They give men solutions based on a composite woman that for most men does not exist. They ask men to change before there is a society which will allow this change.

In short, these psychos are asking men to take off their armor while they are under the most vicious attack in recorded history. For a man to do this would be idiotic. Enough of complaints—Solutions:

I think we need to be teaching men to use light armor. The warfare has changed. Men need new weapons, new armor, and new tactics. I don't think the pop-psyches can do this.

Men need to get a hold of their spirituality and their sexuality. They need to be encouraged to value and look after their own needs. They need to be shown that if they fail to look after their spiritual needs, most of what we seek will seem meaningless even if we accomplish it.

I like what I know of Robert Bly's work for it's contribution in this direction. I think we need to build on the idea of bringing men and boys together not only in groups but, more importantly, to one level.

Activities bring men out. They don't want to hear a lot of 411 by a bunch of airheads who must live on some other planet. They need views they can use rather than complicated social theories and mysterious poems. Women have time to figure that out, men do not. We are busy protecting and providing.

Let's concentrate on creating space for men to think rather than trying to tell them what to think. Events create the opportunity to meet men and form relationships. Small groups work better than large ones because there is less politics and more issues. Small groups also allow for more two-way exchanges.

Men are repelled by the hard sell. We need to create a reason for men to be together and stimulate conversation. Note that I did not say guide the discussion. We don't need them to talk about the issues right away. Just put out some contradictions and when they have time they will talk about it.

Creating events for working-class men means lowering the rip off prices for some of these conferences. Okay, everybody has got to eat, but some of these prices seem to be set in order to discourage middle- and lower-income people from attending. Though I can sympathize with such a sentiment, really I can, it will be counterproductive in the long run.

The medium is the message. Let's start putting men's issues on cassette tape and video tape. When we do write, make sure there are plenty of photos and graphics. Why? Because men receive information better when they hear, see, and do. In short, reading is for women. The magazine industry knows this, it is about time the men's movement came to this realization.

I know I will hear a lot of esoteric bull about this statement, but the bottom line is that men don't read. As a dyslexic, I take particular offense that the only way or the best way to get information is through print. It is one way. The world did not begin or stop with Gutenberg's press. Let's use every kind of media possible to get our message to men, including print.

To summarize, men don't go to therapy because they feel it will fuck them up even more than they are. If therapists want work they must develop relevant modalities.

*John Gagnon:* I and a buddy have run a program at our local church called "Men Freeing Men," based upon the book by the same name. It is turning out to be a very successful program. The men who have come to it are liking the structure of the book, and unlike the less structured group we had run in the past, we are finding that the wide variety of articles written by so many different kinds of men offer an opportunity for the participants to feel freer to be themselves and to say who they really are (rather than what they think the men's movement or Robert Bly suggests they ought to be as men). Some common grounds *are* emerging, of course, but the most important starting point has been the acceptance of each of these very different men *as they are,* with their own particular mix of androgyny, masculine stereotypes, beliefs, identities, and personality traits. In short, I believe that it is important for each man to find his own energy, his own sense of maleness. The book, *Men Freeing Men,* allowed us to do this to a great degree.

The sense of basic male worth has an essential place in the men's movement. I think that the underlying message that men are not all that important needs to be addressed head on in the men's movement if we are to continue to grow in a lively and significant manner. It is not enough for a man to join the movement when he feels "bummed out" and then to quit when he lands that job he always wanted or finally straightens out things with his wife and kids. He has got to see that his very presence in the life of other men is essential. Each man can begin this process, I believe, by accepting himself as he is first. Part of that self-acceptance will be the "sense of maleness" which he perceives as right for himself. I then believe that he can go on to accepting "maleness" in a more general way in other men.

*Buddy Portugal:* I have been working with men for many years and have found that their hesitation to seek out "help" generally centers around the deep inner feeling/thought that getting help means *dependency* on others, and that should be avoided as much as possible. For many men being dependent on others relates to inadequacy and self-depreciation. Men need and strive for independency and self-sufficiency as a basic requirement for success and recognition. This craziness has its beginnings in our childhoods, where boys are encouraged to be, and recognized for their independency, which is equal to power and strength. Much of this learning takes place, and has taken place in the son's identification with father, who was generally perceived as independent and usually was recognized for this characteristic.

As long as men perceive that they need to do everything on their own, as a symbol of power and strength, they will stay away from "help." I lead a weekend experience with an associate called the "Men's Room,' which centers on these issues regarding how men struggle with their longing for contact with others, and the blocks that interfere with men having real intimacy in their lives.

*Bob Porter:* My introduction to counseling took place in high school. I attended an all-boys Catholic school run by Jesuits. For the most part, I hated school, having been a classic "underachiever." However, the school did provide a valuable counseling opportunity. Each student was allowed to choose a teacher or staff member as his counselor. We were allowed to leave any class, with the teacher's permission, to talk with our counselor.

At first, my primary motivation for talking to a counselor was to get out of class as much as possible. But I soon discovered, much to my surprise, the tremendous relief of having someone to whom I could safely tell my troubles. Here was a man, a grown-up, who would actually listen to me, take me seriously, and *care*! I was used to thinking of most grown-ups as people who could never understand my adolescent angst, and whose mission was to spoil my fun, limit my freedom, and criticize my viewpoints. I remember crying a little at one point, expecting to be mocked. Instead, he simply handed me a box of tissues, and let me know he understood. Incredible!

Since then, I've been in various forms of therapy several times. I've experienced individual, marital, and group therapy, attended experiential personal growth workshops, read plenty of self-help books, been massaged, and Rolfed. I've participated in several men's and mixed-gender support groups, both as member and facilitator. My interest in personal growth and healing led to my present career as a professional psychotherapist. My interest in men's issues led to my teaching a three-credit course on Male Identity Development at the University of Wisconsin–Milwaukee, which I taught annually for several years.

As a male psychotherapist with an acute awareness of gender-related issues, I have often wondered how therapy can better serve men. As it is with most therapists, my caseload has always consisted of many more women than men. Since I know how much I've benefited from my experiences in therapy, and I've seen many men in my caseload benefit as well (often to their surprise), I can't help but wish more men would take advantage of the support and challenge that a good therapist or group can offer.

Usually, the men I see in therapy are there in response to a woman. A wife or lover threatens to leave or leaves. She complains about his lack of communication with her (i.e., verbal, feeling-articulate communication). She complains about his excessive devotion to work, his alcohol or other drug abuse, or his temper. Sometimes, she knows her behavior is part of the problem, but more often she believes that if he'll change, all will be well.

Another common avenue by which men come to my office is a problem with one of their children. Nearly always, his wife phones to get help for the child or adolescent. Since I am trained as a family therapist, I always ask that the entire family be present for the initial consultation. Often, the wife and mother will insist that her husband won't come in, but I've rarely found a man who refused to participate in family therapy once *respectfully* asked.

Occasionally, a physician sends a man to me because of stress-related medical problems. Employee Assistance Programs sometimes send me a man whose work performance is suffering due to depression, anxiety, or family problems. I had two male clients, both in their late 30s to early 40s, who were sent to me for therapy by their mothers! And yes, some men do call for an appointment on their own initiative, and the number seems to have been increasing over the years.

It's no secret that most men feel threatened by psychotherapy of any kind. We are taught to be self-reliant. If we can't solve our own problems, we often feel like failures. We may withdraw into denial, alcohol, television, or silence, or deny any responsibility for change. I believe that many therapeutic modalities make it much harder for men to participate than women. Therapists who insist on clients quickly getting in touch with feelings, or who automatically emphasize verbiage over action, bias the therapy in favor of women's traditional strengths, not men's.

I like and generally agree with the first seven answers to the question of why more men don't get involved in therapy, which you outlined in your query. The exception is that I don't know what John Everingham means by "some demasculinized, bastard or neutral mode of feeling." For that matter, I'm still not sure what Robert Bly means by "male mode of feeling," other than that most men access feelings more slowly and articulate them more hesitantly (if at all) than most women. Also, unlike Roy Schenk, I have found just as much shame, and the concomitant sense of "deserving" bad things, in women as in men. I don't see shame as a men's or women's issue, but as a human issue, although I do know that there are some differences in the specific content of the shaming messages received by each gender. A book I've found useful in this area is *Men in Therapy: The Challenge of Change*, edited by Richard L. Meth and Robert Pasick (New York: Guilford, 1990).

*Michael "Bull Moose":* Tough questions, but I will tell you about my history and motivation. Since my New Warrior weekend (December 1989), the pieces are beginning to fit. Shame and Flying Boy have become more than words. They explain much of my life and behavior.

I am 45 years old and have been interested in behavior since I was 19. I first sought help when I was 23 and realized how self-destructive I was. I was afraid I was going to kill myself and felt that I had almost done it, and if God would give me one more chance I would do it right.

I did Freudian analysis for 2 years and didn't think I was getting much out of it and quit. From my perspective now it was the right thing to do. I got involved in Bioenergetics Therapy in 1980. Getting grounded in feelings helped me get out of my head and into my body. I did that for 5 years and for 2 was a part of a training group.

I got into that because I felt my marriage was over, and I was losing my mind. The therapist was a woman, and there were many women in the training group. I got a lot of experience with women and their issues. I dropped out because I found the angry woman energy toxic and I had gotten everything I could out of that group.

I studied Neurolinguistic Programming for several years and that led to the Warrior group. In July 1989, I found the book *The Flying Boy*, and felt that I had read much of my personal history. I have often wondered the same questions we were asked to respond to.

In the bioenergetics therapy I ran into a lot of John Wayne programs, for example, Men don't cry. (I learned to cry.) I also learned a lot about codependency, alcoholism, and adult children. The honesty, the brutal honesty it takes to do this work on the self is not of the slightest interest to most men. Ego, power, clever manipulation is what is worshipped in our society. Brutal fathers, narcissistic fathers, kiss my ego is a commodity, and anybody who tells the truth is regarded as simple, not smart enough to lie to get what he wants, a sucker, gullible, an easy mark, somebody easy to rip off. You can get points for deceiving somebody and putting one over on him. Or just overpower him; football, hockey, etc., sanctioned violence and power, soccer, all games of power and deceit.

I am a tool and die maker and work with my hands, much of it in factories. All the men of this caliber do not even have mental models of what this work is about, which makes it next to impossible to describe. Many of the better-educated, salaried types are on a power drive and not interested in the feeling mode and feel threatened by it. The only means they have to interpret openness is as a trick—that the open guy has lost his mind and wants to get fucked over.

I think it takes a major crisis to get a man's defenses open enough to begin to wonder if there is another way. Men have always needed to control and deny pain in order to survive, the strongest has always won, the one with the greatest stamina will prevail, in a battle for women, food, or land it has always and will always be.

Women by role have always needed to be open to pain, to feel the pain of the young to see that they survived. People, like plants, will grow to fit the shame of the container they find themselves in. But like living things put back to grow to their own nature, they will become unstunted in their growth and more natural in their manner.

*Robert M. Adler:* As I understand it, your main question is, "Why is it that relatively few men turn to counselors or therapists for help, or to men's self-help groups?" I contend the answer to this question lies hidden in your later question, "We suffer as much as women; why don't we go for help as often as they?" I also want to address your question, "What does it take to get men involved?"

Your statement that "we suffer as much as women" sounds true to me, and everything I've observed points to this being accurate. However, this statement equates male suffering with female suffering—and I know very few males who would acknowledge their equality with women in *any* areas. In my view, here are the reasons why far fewer men go for help:

- Men are *afraid* to show their suffering.
- Men are *afraid* to express their feelings.
- Men are *afraid* to ask for help.
- Men are *afraid* that there may not be a bottom line or cost/benefit ratio.
- Men are *afraid* of "growth journeys".
- Men are *afraid* of hearing about older men's failures.

And in my observations men are afraid of the reactions of both women and other men. The "path of least resistance" is for men to stuff their feelings, not communicate, not ask for help, and just put on the best face they can—and as Robert Fritz makes very clear, every living thing in nature follows *The Path of Least Resistance*.

Of course, this "path" only works for men in the short run . . . For in the long run, it is well known by wiser folk that whatever one resists, persists—whatever we fear we attract to us. So having grown up in a society that places stress on men as the performers, breadwinners, and macho machines, the "outer man" may *act* in a strong manner, but the "inner man" is constantly reacting. And, of course, the inner man usually will not effectively communicate, or even be in touch with this inner reacting. Strong women may want strong men, but all women want a man who is in touch with and communicates his feelings. Perhaps the real question we should be asking ourselves is, what's so great about being strong men? Or, what does it really mean (and to whom?) to be a "strong man"? What are the benefits, and what are the costs?

As a consequence of this confusion and societal pressure, people make statements such as "Most therapy is conducted (even by men) in the female mode of feeling . . ." and think it's a perfectly valid statement. The problem lies in that it is so deeply imbedded in man's psyche that he is superior to women that there is very little chance of a man acknowledging his female energies. For by doing this, the man would acknowledge that he *is* a softer, more sensitive being, and would surely be judged as being "weaker." Of course women don't have this problem, because for them to acknowledge their male energies can only bring them *strength* (they have some deeply imbedded ideas in their psyches as well!). So especially in this day and age, women have a lot less to lose and a lot more to gain by becoming more aware of their feelings, expressing them, and acknowledging their male energies.

Finally, what is the answer to getting men involved? In my experience, the answers to getting men involved are *perseverance*, *toughness*, and *timing*. But especially timing. For I have observed that when men finally say yes to the kind of help we're talking about, they feel they are surrendering to their weakness—"throwing in the towel"—swallowing their pride . . . until they find out about the wholeness available to them in some of these experiences. But men will only say yes when they are sick and tired of being sick and tired—when they can no longer bear their pain and shame.

I did the New Warrior Training in June 1989. I am not a man who's ever had trouble expressing his feelings—I've been in therapy and have done EST and everything they've ever offered, the Life Training, LRT, and lots of other searching—and got value out of all of it. But in my opinion, the New Warrior experience beat the hell out of all of them put together. I came back to Houston with the idea of possibly trying to get it here—to enroll 15 to 20 men to go to Chicago for the training so that we'd eventually have the staff to conduct a training here. I thought about it all summer—in the meantime, I realized that the experience of the training was *growing* on me.

I shared my experience with 42 men in Houston, and in February 1990, one friend who was "sick and tired of being sick and tired" with his issues traveled to Chicago for the Warrior Training. Since that time the number of men involved has increased rapidly. The Houston New Warrior community at this time numbers more than 400 men, and we are doing eight trainings a year.

I have another dear friend whose life will dramatically change when he does the New Warrior Weekend. He is stuck in an unhappy marriage situation, an immature attitude about his wife and his marriage, and a generally weak and wimpy attitude about himself. The fact that he also lives with his daughter and his wife's daughter doesn't help—it only magnifies his apparent wimpishness. And from time to time—when he gets sick and tired of it all—he calls me for help and nurturing in his life. And I tell him that I cannot support him anymore than I have attempted to already—that when he gets sick and tired *enough*, he will do what I have told him, because I said so—and experience the Warrior Weekend. I cannot offer him the soft nurturing he seeks—because that is what he's getting almost everywhere else—and that's what's keeping him in his rut. It's his own inner strength that is eluding him. There is no doubt in my mind that he is going to do it; the only question is, when? You can lead a horse to water. . . .

I've been accused of being an extremely direct, bottom-line person—sometimes to the point of being obnoxious. But I prefer to think that I call a spade a spade. Some men would read this letter and wonder if it was written by another man. I am only being true to my own experiences. I do not dislike men—on the contrary, I have grown to love other men in a profound way. I can't stand the fact that most men are unwilling to get off their egos and go for help. For many years I hid behind my shame—unaware of it—and acted out the victim role of my life not working out. Now that I realize some of the reasons it didn't, I am very involved indeed in "forwarding the brotherhood."

*Irwin Aloff:* As boys we were taught what a man is: A man is responsible and strong. He works to support himself and his family. Later we saw that we could get our women with work and strength (which equals power).

Going to therapy implies weakness and vulnerability—an admission that we don't have our lives under control. We can't work, support, be strong and responsible if we aren't in control. Thus, therapy looks like a threat to our security, even to our basic sense of self. Men won't readily seek and accept therapy until we change two strong beliefs: vulnerable = weakness, and weakness leads to our ultimate demise.

To get men into group work, we need to offer *empowerment* as the bottom line (ultimate enticement). We need to confront powerfully and accept lovingly, thereby modeling the behavior that many men feel they lack. They may even think that we can give them what they lack, but, of course, that's not true. We can't *give* them anything, but we can offer the opportunity to learn to be powerful in a new way, with a new definition of power.

Descartes said, "I think, therefore, I am." Therapy says, "We think, we feel, we believe; therefore, we are." Men have the opportunity to be whole.

*Frank Dilallo:* Being in the counseling field for the last 15 years has been and continues to be a wonderful opportunity to serve others and a challenging quest into my own psychology. The first 5 years of counseling I worked in chemical dependency treatment, and approximately 95% of my caseload were men. Approximately 99% of these men were mandated by the court. Any man who entered counseling in this milieu voluntarily was a rare exception. The last 10 years in private practice, approximately 75% to 85% of my clientele have been women. When men come in for private counseling it is usually with a spouse and if alone it is often at another person's request (i.e., spouse, mother, friend, or adult child). It has been my experience when given a choice most men do not seek counseling as an option for help, at least not voluntarily. The small percentage of men who do seek out counseling with me have been a joy to work with. It is a powerful experience for both of us.

One of the perks of being in this field is to have had opportunities to participate in dozens and dozens of trainings, workshops, and experiential weekends. Most of my experiences have been positive. However, following several of the experiential weekends, I recall feeling angry about being the only male or one of the few. I was not angry at women. On the contrary, I honored and envied their ability to gather collectively and create such a depth of experience. I would ask myself, "Where are all the men?" I felt so alone, like I was the only man doing this work. This changed for me 5 years ago, however, when I had an opportunity to attend a very intense weekend training designed for men only. The New Warrior Training Adventure gave me hope and validation as a man and for men. This spirit continues as I have been involved in an ongoing weekly group for men, born out of this training.

Below, I would like to offer some of my experience and perceptions of why more men have difficulty seeking and engaging in counseling.

In order for anyone to come into counseling, they need to admit first of all there is a problem or problems, and second of all they do not have the resources to handle this problem on their own. In essence they are powerless or inadequate to some degree. In seeking counseling services I am acknowledging a certain level of defeat. Messages or words that are consciously or unconsciously synonymous with defeat include impotence, castration, loser, failure, unsuccessful, powerlessness, and death. There is a great deal of shame wrapped up in all of this for men.

As a man one can understand why we do not like to admit defeat. Competition can be a healthy motivator. However, our culture promotes a "win at all cost" or "winning is everything" mentality. This "win–lose" orientation forces men to adapt an "I'm okay, you're not okay" position psychologically to defend against loss or defeat. This inflated position is exemplified in self righteous, "holier than thou," or blaming stances, which prevent us from accepting responsibility for our wounds. If I am in this inflated position I cannot engage with others, and, therefore, keep distant from love and intimacy.

Counseling is an engaging and empowering (both of us win) process. Seeking counseling could be perceived by men as a "one-down" experience, because I am searching for an expert to assist me in coping with something bigger than myself. Competition as it is promoted in our culture is the antithesis of empowerment. If I feel a lot of shame already about admitting defeat, what a shaming experience it would be to see a counselor (especially another man) who has more education, possibly more status or position, and may make more money. Statements such as, "Why didn't I see that? . . . How do you know all this?" continually are raised in my counseling sessions with men. These kinds of statements, although subtle, speak of the competition between male counselor and male client. It also speaks of the hidden shame present for men around having "blind spots" or not having all the answers. In my own counseling I find myself feeling shame about not knowing as much as my analyst does. This experience, although humbling, helps me to be more conscious of what other men are experiencing.

Messages or words synonymous with counseling, consciously or unconsciously, are "sick," "crazy," "helpless," or "dependent." Also, the word *shrink*, although used in jest, has a negative connotation and gives counseling a bad rap. Also, if inflation is what I am into as a man, a "shrink" is the last thing I would be looking for.

Our culture is set up for quick fixes, solutions, and instant relief from pain. Pain, discomfort, and suffering are inevitable realities and yet we are inundated with media messages inviting us to deny, cover up, or escape our wounds. It is no wonder we have an epidemic of addictive behaviors.

The hero speaks to this business about men and counseling. All men identify with a hero. A hero often stands alone and does not usually need help. He always seems to be confident and self-composed; rarely if ever revealing human frailties. I have never seen a movie or TV program where a hero has gone in for therapy. In this context, men believe they should be able to do anything alone and without help.

When I was a kid I used to fantasize in church that armed robbers came in to steal the offering, and I single-handedly "saved the day." I can recall feeling very high or inflated from this fantasy. This hero stuff is even played out in our own field by male therapists who rescue clients. I have done this as well and have paid the price. It would be revealing to do a survey of those in the counseling field to determine how many of us are counselees.

I think one of the pitfalls to being in this field is that it is easy to move away from our own wounds by being a "hero" for others (clients, patients). One of the wounds common in all of us as men is a lack of appropriate fathering and an overabundance of mothering. Accessing the hero seems to be a way men overcompensate for this father lack. By remaining in this hero or inflated position, I separate myself from my wounds. Also, Father may not be physically or psychologically available to help me separate from Mother. Father's absence creates a psychologically incestual relationship with Mother to fill the void. Mothers have a tendency to unconsciously keep their sons little boys. This, in turn, creates a tremendous fear of engulfment and castration fear for men. My guess is the latter also impedes, inhibits, or prevents men from engaging in counseling. Counseling connotes dependency for many men and is not perceived as a self-reliant or resourceful step.

If we look generationally at where we have come from, all of us have either depression era parents or grandparents. When it comes to economics, many of us are conditioned to be in a "survival mode" financially, and counseling could be perceived as an unnecessary expense or luxury. Also, many of us consciously or unconsciously use money and what it can buy to inflate from our wounds. As a result, the counseling expense could be viewed as prohibitive of buying other "things."

I know that my own work, journeying inward and deepening as a man is extremely important to me. I hope I set some sort of precedent for men. As a man, I cannot do this alone; I need men to mentor me as well. We must support and empower each other in order for healing to occur.

*Bill Kauth:* Since 1973 I've been organizing men's groups. From then until now the common denominator has been one man reaching out, and the other man being able to trust enough to take the invitation extended. It was true for my small-sized men's support groups in the early 1970s and it continues to be so for the more than 4,000 New Warrior Brothers over the last 10 years.

*Jack Kammer:* On November 22, 1963, I was in seventh grade. My teacher, on learning that the injured President Kennedy had died, stood up behind her desk, and with fire and—dare I call it hatred?—in her eyes, leaned forward and said, "Do you see what you boys grow up to be? Murderers!" I consider myself fortunate that I had the presence of mind to realize that the person whose death so enraged her had been a boy who did not, indeed, grow up to be a murderer.

Why do so few men go for counseling? My guess is that men perceive counselors as subscribing to what Dr. Schenk calls "morality as the codification of female self-interest." I don't buy the idea that men refuse to ask for help. Men ask for help all the time, as in "Hey, Jim, can you give me a hand here with this forklift?"

What works to get men involved? I can't say I've had monumental success in getting men involved, but I think the success I've had can be attributed to validating men's anger. As you know well, men are afraid of their anger (especially toward women because it violates the code), but every man, I think, feels a lot—even if he has become numb to his feelings. Making no bones about my own anger, but expressing it in calm, confident tones, is the best way I know to help other men feel free to express theirs. Once the anger has been identified and coaxed into the open, humor seems to be a good way to make it touchable so that we can make it less frightening and turn it into constructive energy.

*Ian M. Harris:* Being a man implies being a stoic, denying pain. Stoics don't show hurt. Courageous fighters, they bravely face adversity. Because crying is feminine and boys are not supposed to be like girls, they shouldn't show emotions. Throughout their lives men are conditioned to hide their feelings.

Life deals everybody bad breaks. A stoic does not admit having a hard time when shit hits the fan, but rather grits his teeth and toughs it out. Because a man who shows fear can be taken advantage of in fierce male environments, stoicism can be necessary for survival.

Men neither admit pain nor show emotions other than anger because years of gender role conditioning tell them that real men do not express tender feelings. Wanting to create a male identity that will earn the respect of other men, males construct walls around vulnerabilities that don't let others close enough to see their wounds. Males who fear not living up to the rigorous demands of masculinity go through life tangled up in knots, never unlocking their emotions.

Men start to tear down these walls when they are encouraged to be sensitive. A woman's support for a man can only take him so far because women ultimately fear men's pain. Men have to help each other take a hero's journey inside to confront inner dragons.

Men sometimes get encouragement from other males for confronting their dark sides in a bar or though drugs, where an altered state will lower the moat and let the dragons out. Men need more articulate, caring male models than that of a man in a drunken stupor crying in his beer.

Although men's support groups can help men open up to other men, explore their gender conditioning, and share their wounds, most men's groups are too polite. Governed by the same norms that demand male rigidity outside the group, few men's groups deeply challenge men to explore their darkest secrets. Men who fear letting down their defenses stay locked in chains.

Men's weekends like the New Warrior experience, developed in Milwaukee, WI, are the best way for men to confront their destructive behavior patterns. At these intense experiences, men are required to take a hero's journey inside. The encouragement they receive for so doing teaches men they can trust their brothers. Receiving such tenderness from other men opens men's hearts to the possibilities of nurturing father love, perhaps for the first time in their lives. The staff at these weekends model caring male behavior. Sensitive males are the best midwives to conquer male fear of shame and give birth to masculine emotional sensitivities.

*Jim Lovestar:* Some years back, as I was hitchhiking to Denver, I was picked up by a truck driver headed west. As we rolled through Iowa and Nebraska, I asked him about his life. He told me he was married and had two kids. I put this together with something he had said earlier about being on the road 5 out of every 6 weeks, and remarked how hard that must be on his marriage and family life.

His reply startled me. "We fuck the first night I'm home and get along okay until the second day. Then we just fight. I usually can't wait to get back out on the road."

I asked this man if he preferred driving a truck to being at home with his family. "Shit, yeah." He replied. "I know how to do this just fine. There's no place for me at home. The wife, she does fine without me."

I realized that anyone would choose to do what he is good at. For this man, driving a semi was a lot easier than relating to a woman and children. He chose it with the attendant boredom, loneliness, health risks, and physical danger because he could *do* it.

Would this man go to see a therapist to talk about his issues of alienation from the family and the risks of his job? What do you think? What if this man thinks he's too busy driving a rig from city to city to take the time to go sit down in a therapist's office to talk? Where does that leave the therapist who expects people to come into an office, fill out forms, and talk about their feelings? Probably giving counseling to the wife.

What can be done? How can we address this man's needs? Perhaps the first step is to acknowledge our ignorance of his needs. If we presume to know what he needs and try to give it to him, we might end up in the position of the man who wondered why his tomcat never ate the oatmeal that was set out for him.

What if someone asked the truck driver what his life was like, what his needs are? What if that someone did this over lunch at a truck stop rather than expecting the driver to come into a clinic? What if that someone was just someone who was concerned rather than a pad full of theories of human behavior? *And* what if when those needs were expressed they were seen as a part of the human condition rather than a problem?

Maybe this truck driving man would be interested in talking. Maybe in talking, he would discover ways to meet his needs. Maybe he would begin to enjoy life and want to give something of himself to others. If this happened, would we call it therapy? What if all this happened by talking with another truck driver rather than a trained and certified therapist? What would we call it then?

More questions: What if this man were told what feelings are and had them demonstrated for him in a simple, direct way? What if he were told he was capable of having and expressing his feelings? What if he were consistently supported in the expression of those feelings, even the ugly ones? What if he were told he is the expert about his life rather than some well-dressed professional sitting behind a desk taking notes? What then? Can we trust this man to know his own inner life? What if he feels a sense of his own personal power? What then?

What if this man meets other men who are angry at and afraid of women? What if these men, with compassionate guidance, can express all this and discover ways to deal with it? Ways that feel good and bring them closer to women? And if their confusion about relationships with women is honored rather than attacked?

What if these men who are accustomed to criticism of their behavior were blessed for who they are rather than what they do? Who would do this? Who do we look to for blessing? Who do *you* look to for blessing? Perhaps that one in the mirror is a place to start.

I'll speak for myself. I've tried to do life right for a long time. I've often failed. One way of compensating for my failure was to show others how to do their lives right. I had a lot of answers that I readily volunteered without being asked. I saw men in pain and wanted to fix them. For some reason, I often encountered resistance, or compliance that led to only temporary change.

I was told many times to let the man state his questions and find his own answers; then support him in those answers. This is a simple definition of blessing. As time went on, I became more able to do that as I experienced it myself. I realized I needed blessing more than I knew and I learned I could ask for it. Traditional therapy expects us to just go and ask for it without having received it. Have you ever tried to drive a semi-truck backward?

*Francis Baumli:* "No, there's no leaving shame after all—not down here—it has to be swallowed sharp-edged and ugly, and lived with in pain, every day" (Thomas Pynchon, 1973, p. 637).

Men go to therapy less often than women because men are being justifiably self-protective. They sense that therapy is a relatively inaccessible, even hostile, environment for men. I believe there are nine reasons why men perceive therapy and counseling this way.

1. In our society men are viewed by others, and by themselves, as workers and providers. A counseling session can easily consume 2 or 3 hours of one's time (if one considers not only the session but also the travel time to and from a session). And a group therapy process might involve using up the better part of an entire evening every week. Men, whose work is their primary role, rarely have the leisure to participate in such a time-consuming process.

2. There is a social stigma that prevents men from seeking out therapy; a man in therapy is often considered laughably weak or suspiciously pathological. Few men care to subject themselves to these prejudices.

3. Therapy is expensive. Men who are constrained by the habits of machismo are not accustomed to giving their emotions much in the way of healing care. They are likely to claim that the counseling process is frivolously self-indulgent and a poor financial investment.

4. Men are aware that therapists are no more neutral on issues that pertain to men, especially concerns about women's supposed moral superiority, than is the average person in our society. With few exceptions, therapists have never really thought about men's liberation issues and have never examined their pro-woman stance, much less begun to purge themselves of their own anti-male prejudices. Men suspect that therapists know little more about the deeper pathologies of the male psyche than do their male patients. Indeed they are correct in this suspicion. A male therapist is himself likely to be afflicted by unconscious male shame, and a female therapist is likely to inflict upon her male patients further shame.

5. Men also avoid therapy because of the very ways they are crippled by shame. Male shame is one of the most toxic and painful neuroses pervading our society. Yet few men can articulate this feeling, or even give it a name. Shame, for them, is merely the feeling that "something is terribly wrong with me." This shame, vaguely felt, scarcely identified at the cognitive level, is a painful mystery which most men would rather avoid than deal with.

6. Not only therapists' personal views, but also the general ideology behind therapy, is anti-male. To give some examples: The average therapist, despite all the research and sound evidence on the issue, still believes that a battered spouse is always a woman. Also, the average therapist continues to refer to "impotent" men while eschewing the term "frigidity" in describing women's sexual problems. Helen Singer Kaplan's view that a man is afflicted with premature ejaculation if he can not give his female partner an orgasm, with only intercourse, at least 50% of the time, is accepted as standard doctrine by many sex therapists. Therapists routinely counsel divorced men who are being denied their children to be patient and wait until their children are grown adults before seeking to have contact with them.

The average man who reads newspapers, watches televi-

sion, and goes to movies, receives occasional, if limited, exposure to this general ideology. He may never put it into precise
words, but he is self-protective enough to realize that the tacit
ideology of therapy does not speak truthfully to men about men.
Moreover, if this average man does muster the courage to visit a
therapist, upon entering the session room, he very likely will encounter bookshelves sagging beneath the weight of titles like
*Against Our Will, The Women's Room, Beyond God the Father.*
He will see the names of authors such as Betty Friedan, Gloria
Steinem, Andrea Dworkin. If he thereupon believes that this is a
pro-male environment, then he needs to have his head examined—not by a psychologist, but by a brain surgeon.

7. Another reason men avoid therapy—even have a revulsion for
   therapy—is because they are aware that in our culture the self-
   help books pander to women primarily, the advice columns in
   newspapers have an audience that is 90% female, and no small
   number of women look upon therapy as an indispensable
   weekly visit to their emotional cosmetologist. Such behavior is
   viewed by men as immature and counterproductive; they believe
   that these female toys are not likely to be useful tools for achieving male health.

8. The women's liberation movement of the 1960s soon trans-
   muted into feminism. Since then, feminism has, for the most
   part, been little more than an anti-male ideology which has in-
   sinuated itself into most of our cultural institutions, including
   psychotherapy. This is apparent in the scholarly journals of psy-
   chotherapeutics. For example, during the late 1970s, the notion
   was generally held that, in this country, the vast majority of alcoholics were men. Any suggestions to the contrary, based upon
   preliminary empirical evidence, were immediately silenced by
   feminist "theorists" who claimed that these suggestions were
   chauvinistic, anti-female, and intended to show that women are
   as prone to social deviancy as men. But then, in late 1980, indis-
   putable evidence surfaced proving that there indeed are as many,
   or almost as many, female alcoholics as there are male alcoholics.
   The main difference being that female alcoholics, whose domestic status allows them to do their drinking at home, are more
   adept at concealing their problem than are men. Within 6
   months of receiving this evidence, the very same feminist theorists who previously had denounced the evidence pointing to female alcoholism, did an about-face and immediately began publishing articles claiming that all along there had been a male

conspiracy to conceal the problem of female alcoholism and thus divert funding away from helping female victims (sic) of alcoholism.

This is but one example which illustrates the extent to which feminist ideology has taken over (and distorted the methodology of) the profession of psychotherapy. How is the average man, who might otherwise be drawn to therapy, aware of this feminist distortion and consequently deterred from seeking therapy? This "average man" learns from the female-oriented popular television talk shows that it is female therapists, with a harshly feminist viewpoint, i.e., harshly anti-male prejudice, who are today being accepted as the experts on emotions in our society. He also is aware that the therapeutic superstructure, ranging from the plethora of pop-psych books to the smorgasbord of group-therapy encounter groups, have all encouraged women with liberationist leanings to take the feminist attitude that men are the cause of every woman's every problem, whether it involve sexual dissatisfaction, domestic discontent, or lack of success in the workplace. But most of all, men are aware that the therapeutic process, which touts "professional value neutrality" has actually taken a strong anti-family view. The traditional family, and the tradition of marriage, are now viewed by most therapists as archaic, outmoded, and dispensable. Intimate relationships are expected to be ephemeral, and divorce is considered a healthy option—often the preferred cure—for a troubled marriage.

Even though men are socially conditioned to be sexually active and relatively uncommitted to only one loving partner during their early, sexually active years, when they do choose to "settle down" they desire stability, that is, continuity, in their intimate or sexual relationships. But men know that the Big Sister of Feminism is looking down upon them, and they know full well that hers is a malicious gaze. Have it her way, and all women would cast men aside. Unmarried women would spurn men, married women would abandon their husbands, and fathers would be stripped of their parental rights. No wonder, then, that men avoid therapy. It has become one of the most effective bastions of feminist subversion, constantly undermining most men's hopes for one day having a lifelong, happy relationship with a mate.

9. A final reason men avoid therapy is because they see what its consequences have been for its primary clientele—women. Over

the last few decades, therapy has perhaps helped women feel better about themselves, but it has not made them better human beings. Instead, it has provided them with but temporary diversion from their emotional pain, it has given them a scapegoat (men) to blame their pain on, and thus by leading women toward blaming behavior, it has blocked healthy change. Men observe women who, upon exiting therapy, pronounce themselves cured and henceforth blameless in any emotional conflict with another human being. Men observe other women who are forever addicted to therapy, and pronounce themselves incurable because our supposedly patriarchal society oppresses them. Observing these two types of women, men justifiably say to themselves: If this is what therapy has done for women, I want nothing to do with it.

––––––

A further question remains: Why is it men do not go to self-help groups as a way of dealing with their problems? I think the answer is clear. Men are not at ease in the emotional sphere, and the idea of going to a group of other men to deal with one's emotions is quite terrifying. Some men, of course, overcome this fear, and do go. I have perceived, however, that many of these men, after having attended but a few meetings, never go back. Why? Because, for the following reasons, such groups fail to satisfy their wants:

1. Men in our culture are very dependent on women for fulfilling their emotional needs. Instead of providing men with an alternative way of dealing with emotional needs, such groups often serve as little more than a forum wherein men complain about how they are not being successful in their relationships with women. Grievances against women are aired, advice is given, and then the men go home, maybe feeling better for the moment, but not having done anything to make themselves less emotionally dependent upon women.

2. The reaction men have to their own emotional vulnerability in such groups often prevents such groups from ever attaining an emotional atmosphere. Some men are so afraid of being macho or competitive that they scarcely participate, doing little more than murmuring sympathetic responses to each other's self-disclosing statements. Other men react to their own emotional fears by reverting to stereotypical macho behavior, talking loudly,

dominating the group, seldom listening to those who are not so forward.

3. Generalizing somewhat, we can say that in our culture women are socialized to *be*, and men are socialized to *do*. When men approach a new experience, their reflex is to deal with tension, excitement, or enthusiasm by doing something physical. Self-help groups tend to be sedentary; they involve people sitting around and talking. Hence, they neither utilize nor channel male energy—the kinetic response men have to an emotionally charged situation. Like schoolboys held in during recess, the men grow restless. When they leave, they feel unserved and drained.

4. Some groups, for example, the wildman warrior groups, do inject a certain level of physical activity into their gatherings. Unfortunately, such activity is so channeled via ritual, so given to fictional mythology and play-acting, that little of what is explored under the auspices of "male identity" can ever translate to the real world where play-acting and fairy tales get a man nowhere. Men often feel an initial enthusiasm in these groups, but soon realize that all those rituals, instead of channeling male energy, are self-indulgent emotional thrashings. A keen disappointment sets in as that "primordial male" they have supposedly rediscovered loses his way in the civilized world. Nevertheless, the wildman warrior groups have a strong appeal and attract many disciples. The problem is that they leave in their wake men who are weaker, and more bewildered, than they were when they joined these groups.

*Tom Williamson:* Why don't men seek help from therapy as often as women, and what does it take to get men involved are two questions that were put to me recently by the editors There are many forms of "therapy." Among these are psychotherapy, counseling, support groups and outreach programs. All have elements in common: They work with the mind, and, in so doing, each form addresses mental conflict, a "void" in one's life and/or changes in attitude. I will address all of these forms in striving to answer why men don't seek help as often as women and what it takes to get men involved.

We must consider at least three things in order to answer the questions posed: 1) The level of public acceptance for men to seek help from others or to seek self help forums, 2) The setting or surroundings in which activity takes place, and 3) The content of therapy itself (e.g. is it sex biased?).

1. There is little or no public acceptance for men to seek help or to accept it when offered. To a significant degree men have internalized the expectation that it is unmanly to seek or accept help. However, for some men, this expectation can be overcome if there is a public policy to encourage them. For example, I conducted a private study on the battered husband in 1978. I examined the policies of two public services. I looked at their willingness to offer services to men, and I looked at their means of promoting their services to men.

   [The year] 1978 saw the beginning publication of a growing body of research showing that battering of men by women is a significant problem. Two organizations decided to keep an open mind and make their professional services available to men if men wanted them. They were the New York City Mayor's Task Force on Rape and the Victim's Information Bureau of Suffolk County, NY.

   The NYC Mayor's Task Force on Rape located their crisis centers in hospital emergency rooms, where there were trained personnel to spot suspected spousal abuse. In addition, the task force embarked on an ambitious public relations campaign that targeted male victims and that specifically encouraged husbands to seek professional help. The results were reported only in a qualitative fashion. No quantitative statistics were kept, because the task force had only been mandated to study and help women, not men. For example, the number of men calling for telephone counseling was verbally reported by counselors as a "flurry of calls" or "many calls" after each public service announcement, talk show interview, or news broadcast announcement. The task force also picked up male clients in another way: They identified battered men who had come to the emergency room for medical treatment (sometimes being brought in by ambulance).

   By contrast, the Victim's Information Bureau of Suffolk County (VIBS) reported not getting so much as one inquiry. VIBS is located along a major highway. The staff was mainly experienced with women as clients. The public service campaign sponsored by VIBS attempted to be gender neutral. They used the word "spouse" in place of "husband" or "wife"; as in "spouse abuse." The gender-neutral phrase did not communicate well to males. In this case, "spouse" implied "wife," because abuse has been so widely defined and accepted as a female problem. Not one male contacted VIBS as a result of [its] public service campaign. Yet, that same year, VIBS conducted a county-wide study of the incidence of "spouse" abuse and obtained results that showed that 52% of battered spouses were men. Thus, while there are battered men in Suffolk County in need of help, the VIBS approach was unable to reach them.

*Conclusion.* If there is widespread paid advertising or widespread use of public service announcements that encourage men to seek counseling, therapy, or support groups, men will come forward. However, the advertising must be specifically targeted at men, their interests, and their needs. There must not be any hint of shame or any suggestion that men seeking help are at fault or are weak.

Beyond this we must be sensitive to political forces that see it in their best interests that men not seek help. For example, most organizations that are formed to help battered women do not want to see the subject of battered men legitimized. We will see in a moment that the so-called helping professions are greatly influenced by a politically motivated ideology that is part of a newly emerging power structure with an ever-increasing ability to exercise social control.

2. The setting or surroundings in which therapy takes place is very important. Tom Clark (1975) describes the reluctance of males to seek counseling in family planning clinics where the decor is feminine and the intake workers communicate negative attitudes, both verbally and nonverbally, toward maleness. At this same conference, papers were delivered that showed that family planning outreach programs aimed at inner-city males could be very successful if the program and surroundings were geared toward the male. What was described were programs designed to change macho male attitudes about pregnancy (i.e., where a man feels that getting a girl pregnant proves his manhood) and fatherhood (getting men to take more responsibility in child care).

*Conclusion.* The physical facilities must be attractive to men and the personnel on hand must act in a positive manner.

3. The content of therapy itself can be discouraging to men. There are many different approaches to therapy and counseling. However, what has some observers alarmed is the degree to which feminist doctrine has seeped into social and psychological theory. The extent to which this has happened depends on the subject matter. For example, the topic of the battered husband is often ignored. There is resistance to funding abortion counseling for men. The subject of male victimization, especially when at

the hands of a female, often is not dealt with. One example of this is sexual abuse of males by females.

LeRoy Schultz, MSW, professor of docial work at the West Virginia University, Morgantown (private interview, March 25, 1991), says a great deal of social work and counseling is dominated by the narrow view of feminists toward power. Generally, this view holds that physical power resides with males who can then abuse it. More specifically, this school of thought holds that the abuse of women by men is mainly an issue of the need for men to dominate women. For example, the Ellen Pence method (The Duluth Domestic Abuse Intervention Project) for counseling men who batter their wives is based on a model in which men use power to control women. The therapy, itself, assumes the worst about men and imposes shame. Recently, the state of Wisconsin began considering funding counseling for men who batter. Their guidelines for qualifying mandated that male bonding be prevented in therapy and that a course on sexism be provided. All existing courses on sexism, to date, use the feminist model and avoid concepts of interaction.

By contrast, Tony Kubicki of Batterers Anonymous in Milwaukee, WI, has developed an alternative method for counseling men who batter. Kubicki specializes in counseling men who have battered women and also women who have battered men. His method assumes that couples want good relationships and that "people" who batter have not learned certain social skills, are under stress, and have observed or been victims of battering as children. He does not see spousal abuse as a gender issue (i.e., where it is men versus women) (private interview, March 23, 1991).

Two therapists, John Macchietto, PhD, (Counseling Center, Tarlton State University, College Station, TX) and Eric Mendelson (State University of New York, Binghamton, NY) have gone further in independent articles. They conclude that therapists often completely ignore both the male perceptions of problems and male victimization, especially that perpetrated by a female. Macchietto (1992) demonstrates resistance within the therapeutic community to consider male victimization even when they are made directly aware of this situation. He proposes that these forces of resistance should become a topic of self analysis for the therapeutic community. In his article Mendelson (1990) describes a resistance that resembles attitudes of a "political" nature.

One of Professor Schultz's strongest criticisms of the therapeutic and counseling disciplines is that all forms of power are not considered. Currently the move in therapy is to explain everything as "male versus female." Schultz specifically cites for criticism such mainstream publications as *Journal of Interpersonal Violence*; *Affilia: Journal of Women and Social Work*; *Working on Wife Abuse* by Betsy Warrior; *Women and Violence* by Susan Schechter; *Wife Battering: A Systems Theory Approach* by Jean Giles-Sims; *Ending Men's Violence Against Their Partners* by Richard A Stordeur and Richard Stille; *Participants Manual: Court Mandated Counseling for Men Who Batter, A Three Day Workshop for Mental Health Professionals*. These are sources which are used by both professionals in practice and professors who teach young students.

John Robertson and Louise Fitzgerald (1990) conclude that therapists are apt to take a negative attitude toward nontraditional role behavior in men. Insofar as the application of therapy enforces "the mold" (politically correct thinking, as it has come to be known), therapists can also be expected to take a negative attitude toward men who have not adopted a feminist ethic. This last point is demonstrated in Mendelson's article cited earlier. Much of the therapeutic community cannot see beyond the feminist theory. Robertson and Fitzgerald concluded in their article that therapy can function as a means of social control. Therapy as "social control" was earlier discovered to apply to women. Now, it seems, it also applies to men.

In fact, one of the things that we must watch for is the content of forced therapy, which is very widespread and is used as a means of social control. Examples of this are court-mandated therapy and required corporate outreach programs on such themes as sexual harassment. Sexual harassment courses never deal with false accusation, never deal with females who use sex to climb the corporate ladder, and never deal with women sending mixed signals to men. Attendance at these courses is mandatory in some corporations and schools, which have an extreme definition of sexual harassment that the general public might find unacceptable. For example, some institutions define sexual harassment as unwanted looks even if they are unintentional. It is in the area of forced therapy that we find large numbers of men. What we are witnessing is the blurring of politics, gender scapegoating, and mental health into a unified theme.

Both Macchietto (1992) and Mendelson (1990) are mainly

concerned with the relevance of therapy and counseling for men. Both make suggestions for how to make therapy more relevant to male clients, and, ultimately, how to attract and then maintain a male client base. Macchietto (private interview, March 23, 1991) and Schultz (private interview, March 25, 1991) feel strongly that most male clients would not continue with voluntary therapy if guilt and shame promoted by the feminist approach is the attitude presented by the therapist.

*Conclusion.* LeRoy Schultz, MSW, said, "The majority of men are prone to drop out of therapy where the feminist power approach is invoked. Where the therapist identifies with the problems men have, they are more apt to stay with it." In citing the problems men have, Schultz points to: stress, lack of having been taught certain social skills and stereotyped cultural expectations, such as those placed on men to be the defender and provider. John Macchietto commented, "Most men will not go into therapy if they view the therapy as feminist in orientation."

Certainly, it has been my experience in the National Coalition of Free Men (NCFM) that any shaming or condemning of men has acted as a deterrent to membership and to continued counseling. In NCFM's experience, any feminist aggression, gender polemics, or antimale sentiment adds to the male's already reluctant mood to be involved in such issues as changing roles and behavior. Many men are just plain fed up by always being attacked in the media. Feminist therapy, with its attitudes toward power and sex, adds insult to injury where a man has become vulnerable enough to try and open up to therapy.

## SUMMARY AND ANALYSIS

*Dmitri Bilgere:* First, let's look at these authors' answers to the question: Why do so few men turn to counselors, therapists, or men's groups for help? The men who responded to this question had a wide variety of wonderful answers, but they returned again and again to three key ideas.

First, almost every author mentions *shame* at least once. Men, they note, have been socialized to feel ashamed of themselves if they aren't absolutely self-sufficient and if they don't fulfill their responsibilities perfectly. Our society has imposed the ideal of the rugged individual, these authors notice, much more on men than on women. Women are socialized to need help and to ask for it; men are socialized to laugh at pain and ignore difficulty. Other writers noted men's *denial*—our culture rewards men for producing and shames men for "complaining." In light of this, it's no wonder men aren't interested in even acknowledging, much less exploring, their feelings.

Second, these authors cite the *irrelevance* of therapy, counselors, and men's groups to men living the traditional male role. Roy Schenk and Francis Baumli point out that while society values what men do and empowers men in activities, society also values what women feel, and empowers women in relationships. Men are programmed to succeed materially, and women are programmed to succeed in family and relationships. Therefore, these authors say, it is cost-effective for a woman to get in better touch with her feelings so that she can have better relationships and a healthier family.

For the traditional man, being in his feelings simply does not make good business sense. Men are trained to compete, and being in his feelings during competitive situations, like in business, can be economically fatal for a man. While there is a payoff for the traditional woman to get therapy and to get to know her feelings, that payoff really does not exist for the traditional man. While feelings help women in their expected role, feelings hinder men in theirs.

Third, there is a very real and legitimate concern among these authors that many therapeutic modalities are not relevant to, or are even destructive for, men. Several authors discuss how talk therapy is better suited for women than for men because women are more discussion oriented, whereas men are more action oriented. There is evidence for this. Studies by psychologist Martin Seligman found that women are much more likely to ruminate about their problems than are men. Men are more apt to take action when troubled even if only to have a drink or to kick the dog. Because of this difference in style, talk therapy demands that men change their style just to begin. Therapy doesn't do much to meet men on their own emotional ground, or even to meet men halfway.

These authors also note that men are suspicious. They are tired of being blamed, and are uninterested in getting in any situation where they are blamed more for the problems of others, especially for the problems of women. Men see, they say, the feminist books on the therapist's shelf, and feel the feminine environment of the therapist's office. Like an auto shop for women, the therapy office is not a naturally welcoming environment for men. The result of all this is that men stay out of therapy and don't look for help.

So, according to these authors, the shame men feel about needing help, the irrelevance of therapy to traditional male goals, and the poor quality of most therapy available to men keeps men isolated, out of the men's movement, and not seeking help.

To this list I would add several items of personal opinion; there are things the men's movement itself does that turn men off, and keeps them away.

Men have plenty of problems and responsibilities in their lives already, and are not at all interested in taking on more unless they absolutely have to. Yet often the men's movement, especially the political men's movement, tries to sell problems to men rather than solutions. The men's movement often seems to want men to see just how bad they really have things. This is very unattractive to most men, who have enough problems already.

Men in the men's movement, like anyone else, can become pessimistic and hopeless in the face of the magnitude of their problems. Recently I read an article in a political men's journal about the journal's letter-writing campaign to companies that did antimale things. This article reported victories as if they were failures; it reported a victory in which a greeting card company withdrew a male-bashing card with such an air of doom that the success seemed like only a tiny drop in a huge ocean. Instead of glorifying and celebrating this success, their pessimism made this victory appear tiny and insignificant. This turned me off, and I imagine it would turn off many other men, too.

Further, men don't want to be associated with a movement that might seem extreme, different, or antiwoman. The extreme views of some of the men in the men's movement, the seemingly odd rituals, like drumming, men's spirituality, or "wild man" weekends scare men off, just as the extreme aspects of feminism scare off women. This is not to say that we should get rid of our radical opinions or stop drumming with our brothers; but we do need to know that we scare off some men.

Most men aren't interested in a movement that sells hopelessness, distance from women, a feeling of victimization, and a sense of women being the enemy. To the extent that the men's movement does this, it keeps men out. Selling awareness of men's problems is in itself a problem. Until joining the men's movement and getting help looks like a *solution*, rather than a problem, men will continue to stay outside of it.

It would appear, from the answers of these authors, that *solutions* are, indeed, a main reason men get involved in therapy and in the men's movement. There were two answers to the question: What does it take to get men involved? Men seek help and get involved in the men's movement, these writers say, when they are in a time of crisis, or when they learn to really trust another man who then suggests their involvement.

Both in crisis and in trust, the man who joins a man's group or who seeks therapy has decided that those actions can improve his life. A man in a real crisis, such as a divorce, may suddenly see the men's movement or therapy as real and viable solutions to problems that are so severe they must be addressed. His crisis gives him a new perspective on personal growth.

Bill Kauth and other proponents of the *New Warrior Adventure Training Weekend* discuss *trust*. Most men, they say, who choose to go on this often-transformative weekend, go because they trust a man who recommends it to them. A man they trust, then, can get men involved in activities that will help them heal. Outside of cases of crisis and trust, however, none of these authors holds out much hope that the men's movement and therapy can draw men on their own.

With this in mind, these authors suggest that men befriend men and begin to build trust. We can be there for our brothers, build the trust and friendship, and when the time is right, we can share what we have learned about ourselves, and our feelings, with them. When the time is right we can introduce them to personal growth for men. And if they have a crisis, they need not be alone; we can help them into a supportive brotherhood of men.

Men in the men's movement can also, I think, look to selling solutions instead of problems. We can sell the movement by talking up how it makes men's lives even better rather than by talking only about the oppression men experience that they must, for some reason, come to understand. Men's oppression is just too bitter a pill, at the beginning, for most men to take. We can create a movement that supports and empowers men optimistically, and we can avoid the temptation to see ourselves as helpless victims of women and society.

These authors understand that man by man, we build trust and brotherhood. With each man we share trust, and prepare for growth and the men's movement, we change the world.

*Roy U. Schenk:* When we initiated this inquiry, we had some sense that shame contributes to men's reluctance to seek counseling help. What came through loud and clear in the responses to our query is that men avoid seeking help *primarily* because they have been shamed so intensely for seeking help or even for expressing feelings in the past. What men have learned is that they must "do it alone" and that it is unmanly to seek help. Tom Williamson stated: "There is little or no public acceptance for men to seek help or to accept it when offered." As a result, men are very reluctant to subject themselves to further shaming that they believe they will experience if they seek help.

For a man to seek for help he must be experiencing a crisis so severe that the pain is worse than that expected from the added shaming he anticipates experiencing. It also means that men often drop out again when the pain level has diminished. *What this means is that the disease itself creates the conditions which make it extremely difficult to seek a cure!*

As Francis Baumli remarked: Men "avoid therapy because of the very ways they are crippled by shame. Male shame is one of the most toxic and painful neuroses pervading our society. Yet few men can articulate this feeling, or even give it a name. Shame, for them, is merely the feeling that something is 'terribly wrong with me.' This shame, vaguely felt, scarcely identified at the cognitive level, is a painful mystery which most men would rather avoid than deal with."

The respondents regularly note that current methods of counseling and therapy are not designed to assist men. This is attributed to either the passivity of the process or to its hostility to men. As Lawrence Diggs expressed it: "The psychoindustry is oriented to women." Several writers referred to their own experiences that revealed a serious bias against men. This seems to have been amplified in recent years by a "feminist" orientation.

Because feminism is presumably about equality and justice, this might seem unexpected. However, in practice, a great many, if not most, feminists have regularly continued to accept the societal myth or traditional belief in women's moral superiority/men's moral "depravity," which is the source of men's shame feelings. These feminists have continued to blame and shame men as the evident method of choice for attaining their goals of women-favoring legislation and for silencing criticism.

This blaming and shaming attitude has flowed over into the counseling and therapy areas. Yet one can wonder: Why would male therapists accept and enforce such antimale biases? The answer is simple. As feminists state it: "Oppressed groups regularly buy into the value system of their oppressors." Oppression is a direct result of being seen as inferior. So men buy into or accept the blame and shame associated with the belief in men's moral inferiority.

Another way of saying this is that men just as much as women believe the societal myth of female moral superiority, which translates to perceiving women as victims and creates in men a sense of shame for being "inferior" males. Unfortunately, myths are so "true" that it is difficult for people to recognize them. As a result our society's treatment of women as victims is not generally recognized even though it is so prevalent.

The result of this is that traditional counseling and therapy have tended to enhance men's shame feelings. This is certainly adequate reason for men to avoid and distance themselves from "help." Even today, most mandatory counseling for men, for example counseling for men who physically batter their wives, evidently continues to use shame as a primary technique for altering and controlling these men's behavior. Because shame is the source and trigger for the violence, such programs try to make things better by making things worse. Actually, the concern tends to be with the women involved; and little compassion tends to be evident for the men.

How can we enlist men to transform their lives to be more fully human? The answer provided by many of the respondents is that men need to have a safe place to work on their issues—especially a place free from the perpetual shaming they fear. What are the characteristics of a safe space? To Rich Tosi, safe means: "I will be protected from hurting myself and others both emotionally and physically; the trainers/counselors are initiated men; and I will be led into my deepest shadows protected from shame and self-hatred."

In addition, Tom Williamson proposes that a "public policy to encourage men to seek help" will encourage many men to overcome their reluctance and fear. However, the efforts must be specifically targeted at men and must avoid any hint of shaming or blaming."

Another point is raised by the recognition that men need a safe space in order to work on emotional issues. That point is that men live mostly in an unsafe environment. What are the characteristics of this unsafe environment, beyond physical risk conditions? The respondents regularly describe it as an environment filled with shame and blaming. In other words, our society is programmed to shame and blame men.

Where does this shame and blaming come from? It is my belief that this shaming is based on the fundamental belief of our culture, perhaps even worldwide, that we must divide and judge people on the basis of superiority and inferiority. This judging begins in a newborn child's life at the moment we learn its sex and immediately project differing expectations on it depending on its sex. We also instantly begin treating babies differently based on these differing expectations. We immediately begin judging a child's behavior based on these expectations; and shame the child when it does not conform to society's expectations.

In addition, women are in contact with babies far more than men are. As a result, they do most of the transmittal of societal messages. Naturally, women transmit to infants the message that women's behavior is good behavior. Male babies then get the message that in any way their behavior differs from women's behavior, their behavior is bad. This occurs even while male babies are being taught the expectation that their behavior *will be different* because they are male. This message is well learned by male infants before age 3 because males are already into over-achievement, a shame response, by that age. Since girl's feelings of achievement inferiority become dramatically evident around puberty, boys' inferiority feelings may be learned much earlier in life than are girls' inferiority feelings.

In summary, few men will willingly expose themselves for any extended period to a counseling environment where they are shamed or where their legitimate concerns and needs are ignored or even discredited. Therefore the most important way to get men involved and to keep them involved in seeking help for their emotional problems is for the process to become conscious of, to be sensitive to, and to address men's concerns honestly and without shaming.

# 8

## On Men, Guilt, and Shame*

*Francis Baumli*

It was when working as a therapist that I first became aware of the necessity of distinguishing guilt from shame. This awareness came about during a time I was working with a fairly large number of male clients who came in unaccompanied by wives or female lovers.

Seeing a man in therapy when he is accompanied by a woman who is significant in his life is usually a very difficult experience. She quite often presents herself as the "emotional expert" in the relationship; she knows what is "wrong" with the man, and wants to solicit the therapist as her ally in getting the man to do as she wants. Dealing with a male client in this situation presents a host of problems, which I will not here go in to. But I mention this type of man because he contrasts so much with the man who comes in by himself. The unaccompanied man presents problems for the therapist too, but they are problems of a very different sort. For example, he is often very difficult to get moving. He says he wants help, but he does not talk very much. When asked what his problem is, he presents it as a general malaise: he is depressed, although he isn't sure why; he says he isn't feeling good, but he can't really say what feeling good would mean for him; he may try

*Modified from the original article published in *Transitions*, 7(6), 5–15 (1987), entitled: "On Men, Guilt, and Shame: An Open Letter to Roy Schenk."

to summarily define his problem by saying, "I just don't communicate well with others," but as a therapist I can not get very far with this revelation because he is not communicating very well with me.

Seeing all those unaccompanied male clients was quite a burden for me during this time. I was nearly at my wits' end, trying to pry some of these men loose, when I began noticing that over and over the men were using the word "guilt." The term came up in contexts so various I certainly could not draw parallels between the men, but I was curious about the frequent mention of this emotional state. I began pushing at this guilt. "What do you feel guilty about?" I would ask. The men couldn't really say. "When do you feel it? Are there specific times it comes in?" They would answer that it might come in at any time, or that, in one way or another, it is always present. "Do you remember ever feeling this in earlier years? Perhaps during your childhood?" Yes; they remembered feeling this way in earlier years. In fact, they had always felt this way. But now they were tired of it, and wanted to do something about it. "Well, what *is* this guilt?" I persisted. They could not talk about it. It was there, it was painful, they wanted to do something about it, but they felt helpless.

I was more than challenged by all this; I was mystified. Here were several men, all referring to a similar feeling, but none of them able to articulate it.

It might have been easy to have dismissed this impasse with the general judgment that men have trouble discussing their feelings, and have left it at that. But such a judgment would have been inappropriate. Some of these men were very articulate about feelings, and however sparse they might be with words, they were not at all afraid to open up—at least in therapy. I knew that something besides inhibitions, or masculine armor, was blocking these men.

A breakthrough came. I do not now remember what brought about the realization, but one day I saw something. These men were using the word, "guilt," but maybe they were actually talking about something else. If so, what was this "something else"?

I was taking a stab in the dark the day I interrupted a client, who was talking lamely about feeling guilty, and asked him, "What are you *ashamed* of?" My question stopped him cold. He wasn't sure, but it was obvious that we had found an important key. Later, that same day, I asked another male client about shame. Again it was obvious that something important was being probed. Neither of these men could answer my question. They gave halting answers like, "Just ashamed of my*self*," or, "I don't like my-self," or, "I feel bad because I *exist*."

Curiously, these men could not talk about *what* they were ashamed of. Nor could two other men I saw later that week.

The following week I was chaffing at this mystery. At one point, I angrily interrupted both myself and a client by saying, "I don't *want* to know *what* you're ashamed of! I want to know *why* you're ashamed!" The man looked at me in surprise, started to say something, and suddenly began sobbing.

For some reason, changing that "what?" to a "why?" opened the lock, not only for this man, but for every one of the other three men I was seeing that week! These previously inarticulate men could now speak! They talked about their mothers, their wives, their former wives, early dating experiences, female co-workers, early elementary school teachers, and on and on! And *always* these men talked about shame in relation to *women*.

It was from working with these men in therapy that I first was struck by, and gained some insight into, the need to distinguish shame from guilt. But insight does not make for understanding, much less for theory. I knew that if I were going to be a responsible theoretician and figure this thing out, then I would have to probe it as a social psychologist, and not as a therapist only. Furthermore, I would have to do some reading about this matter, dialogue with other psychologists, and also do some careful, personal reflecting about it.[1]

I first began looking within myself. Yes; I had some guilt in me, but I had already pretty much dealt with that. But shame—it was everywhere! In fact, the very memory of certain select experiences caused a lancing shame to pierce through my entire body.

Allow me to recount just one such experience:

I was 18 years old and it was my first semester in college. I was dating a girl who was slightly younger than me. Our habit for the last several weeks was to go to a movie, or some such thing, and then drive about 10 miles out to an old rock quarry and park. We did a lot of kissing, necking, and such, but she put up a strong resistance to my doing anything else—like touching her breasts, or going for the "down-there zone." But then the night came when something was different. This girl was squirming and moaning beneath me and I was tired of holding back. She let me open her blouse, she let me fondle her breasts, she had a hand pushed under my jeans and was gripping my ass, she let me kiss her breasts, so I raised up and reached a hand down to her inner thigh, and . . . quite suddenly she tensed, her body went rigid, and as she pushed my hand away she said in the most accusing voice, "Don't you have any *respect* for me?"

A burning, nauseating shame filled my groin. My whole body went numb, and quite unexpectedly—I say "unexpectedly," given that, at this point, even though my penis was erect, I felt no sense of sexual arousal at all—I ejaculated. It was a long ejaculation, with many a throb, and at the end I was totally drained of both semen and desire. Even amidst the shame, I felt amazed at that ejaculation—a hard erection, a very *protracted* ejaculation, but with no pleasure at all, no orgasm, just a mechanical, far-away pumping. (Yes; this experience should surely lend credence to Herb Goldberg's assertion that a "premature ejaculation" is simply a man's way of saying, "I don't want to have anything to do with this sexual experience." But this is another topic, and I will not belabor it here.)

I felt horrible. I still feel horrible, right now, 20 years later, writing about it. What do I mean when I say that I feel horrible? I do not feel guilt. How could I feel guilt, when there was nothing specifiable to feel guilty about? If I had felt guilty, then I could have gotten angry, or I could have apologized, or I could have asked for clarification; but as it was, I wasn't even sure as to what I had done that was wrong. She had put her hand under my jeans, and she was, if anything, being more aggressive than I was, and . . . but you see? The very attempt to explain it only mirrors the confusion. No; it was not guilt I was feeling. When it's guilt, you know *what* you are guilty of. This was shame. I wasn't sure *what* I was ashamed of, because I wasn't really ashamed of any*thing* I had done. But I did know *why* I felt ashamed. I felt ashamed because right when I was feeling accepted, welcomed and desired, a woman had rejected *me*. And she had done it by putting herself above me: i.e., while nothing was said about her respecting me, *I* was supposed to respect *her*; which meant that she was somehow superior to me. Moreover, since I *should* respect her, but was not even moral enough to *show* this respect, she was even *more* superior to me! How very, very shameful of me! I felt awful. I still feel awful. Yes—awful, horrible, ashamed. Not a very articulate way of putting it, is it? But then, that's the way shame is: inarticulate, inchoate, bewildering, seemingly irresolvable.

Allow me to give a few more examples:

1. How many times have you heard a woman say of a man, "He's a total *jerk*!"

    "Why?" someone asks.

    "He just *is*! He's a *jerk*!"

    Okay; he's a jerk. So what has he been accused of? Nothing in particular, of course; just everything in general. And how is a man going to defend himself against an accusation like that?

2. "He's a *loser*." (Same consequences as above.)
3. "He's a wimp with women!" (Same as above.)
4. "I hope you feel *embarrassed* when you realize what you did!" (Same as above.)
5. "That just *isn't done*!" (Same as above.)
6. "He's starting to make some changes. Maybe he's finally starting to grow up." "*Finally*," she says. In other words, he has a long history of something to be ashamed of. *Maybe* he will change from that detestable state he was in before. He is indeed making progress, but since he is just *starting*, he can continue to feel ashamed until he does finally succeed in *growing up*, whatever this means. It apparently means something a man never quite attains, as long as a woman can continue to shame him by telling him he hasn't attained it. But as for *what* it means, he will probably never figure this out.
7. (This is the big one!!): "You should be *ashamed* of yourself." Yes; she comes right out and says it. She may be his mother, his high school date, his lover, his wife, his female coworker—all of them women, feeling a little uncomfortable with something he is doing, or just wanting to exercise a little more power over him. So they tell him he should feel ashamed, and he is so accustomed to this judgement that, however much he may bluster and try to appear otherwise, he reflexively grovels inside.

I clearly remember an instance when four men (myself among them) and a woman, all senior members of a large counseling center, realized that if we were going to get our project done for the next day, we all would have to stay late after work. Once everyone accepted this, the mood became light, people were talking of ordering food, and the charts were being brought out. "Too bad the secretaries [not all female] have gone home," one of the men said, "they could have helped."

The woman, her briefcase still closed, turned to the man who had spoken and said sharply, "You *men* should be *ashamed* of yourselves!" and with her nose in the air she left the room and went home.

The men's egos toppled like bowling pins. They were all too embarrassed to even say anything to each other about what had just transpired. Instead, with all levity gone, they proceeded to the task at hand, each aware that what had been said could indeed have been construed as something lewd, even though it wasn't, but if a woman could take it that way, then maybe it should never have been said in the first place, which makes it difficult to know what you can say without getting into trouble and feeling this way—vaguely guilty, very vaguely guilty, so vaguely guilty that it really isn't guilt, but rather, is this shame that paralyzes a man into inarticulate acceptance of a woman's judgement about how he is somehow morally inferior to her. When really, if these men could just *say* what they feel, or, more accurately, quit feeling what they feel so they could speak the truth, (you see how quickly shame fosters confusion—verbal and otherwise!) then they might point out that it was not "men" who made the remark, but one man, so if anyone is to be ashamed, it is that one man only, and moreover, that one man meant exactly what he said, nothing underhanded implied, since he was fully aware that without the secretaries this job was going to take about twice as long as it would otherwise, but then . . . yes, the female co-worker goes home while the men stay late to do the work.

The next day, none of the men bring up the issue with the woman. Each of them feels like he should apologize, but no one is sure what to apologize for. Each of them would like to protest her leaving; if she was that upset, then she should have confronted the man and dealt with it instead of leaving; besides, when she left she took some of the files with her, which made the men's work that much harder. But the men are too ashamed to protest. It is not until a couple of years later that these men finally discuss the matter. They all agree that she acted inappropriately. But it is also obvious that they still feel somewhat ashamed . . . of something . . . they are not quite sure what.

Enough with examples. It should be obvious by now that shame, although an elusive concept, is a very present and danger-ous feeling. Can this feeling be better understood? Let me try to better expose the feeling for what it is by here entering upon a brief analysis.

I am convinced that guilt and shame are two terms which, from a phenomenological point of view, are decidedly different feeling states. Is it possible, then, that shame can better be understood by looking at it alongside guilt, while being very careful to not confuse it with guilt? Let us see what a comparison reveals. I here list six observations—or speculations—about certain aspects that I believe are salient, even defining, qualities of the two terms:

1. *Guilt* is often referred to as a burden. A guilty person complains of feeling oppressed, weighed down, crushed, smothered. Guilt is often accompanied by a bodily sensation of something weighty which is spoken of as a burden on one's back, or a lead weight in one's belly. Note that the Zen Buddhists speak of guilt as, "a corpse you carry on your back."

    *Shame* is often referred to as a void. A person who is ashamed feels empty inside, without ballast, lacking a sense of self-centeredness or emotional certainty. Shame is often accompanied by a bodily sensation of tactile fear, i.e., a fear that seems to be actually crawling over one's skin, or writhing in one's belly. It often results in an actual physical nausea.

2. *Guilt* is something quite determinate, i.e., specifiable. One has a pretty clear idea of *what* one is guilty of.

    *Shame* is something quite indeterminate and unspecifiable. The feeling is so ubiquitous that one can only begin to grasp it, i.e., give it a determinate boundary, by attaching the shame to something quite all encompassing—usually one's entire self.

3. *Guilt* is felt in terms of something one has *done*, e.g., one will say, "I feel guilty because I spoke sharply to my son this morning."

    *Shame* is felt in terms of something one *is*, e.g., one might say, "I feel ashamed when I [sic] spend time with my mother."

4. It seems that *guilt* is largely learned early in life from one's father, whose masculinity is oriented toward the performance of, or failure to perform, specifiable tasks; it also seems that guilt is learned from other men whose masculine conditioning orients them toward competition, fear of failure, and success-oriented values wherein one never quite succeeds.

    It seems that *shame* is more often learned from the mother early in life, whose approval of us causes us to feel pride in our entire being, or whose disapproval causes us to feel ashamed of ourselves. Shame is also learned from other women whose values, (a) instill in us a sense that morality is something feminine, (b) teach us to fear women's disapproving of us, and, (c) give us the sense that we never quite measure up to their expectations of good, moral behavior.

5. I suspect that in our culture a women feels more *guilt* than shame. Conversely, I rather suspect that in our culture a man feels more *shame* than guilt.

6. *Guilt* is a difficult emotion to grapple with, but once one has the courage to face it, it can either be quite spontaneously discharged via an angry assertion that one is reformed with regard to what one was previously guilty of, or it can slowly be cast off as one takes on a new state of awareness—exercises different choices or actions—thus rendering the old guilt irrelevant to one's current intent and values and perhaps also remedying any harm to others that one has previously done.

   *Shame* is equally difficult, but it can never quite be grappled with because it has no specific form. Attempts at dealing with it tend to leave one feeling helpless. Attempts at being angry have no clear avenues of expression. And shame therefore is much more likely than guilt to persist as a toxic, crippling feeling which engenders an anger that, turned inwardly, becomes self-destructive.

Such is my analysis, which, if true, leaves men—the primary victims of shame—in a rather sorry state. Women's justifiable anger over the burden of guilt our culture has heaped upon them has, for the last 30 years, been finding expression. I do not at all believe that such expression has always been healthy; too often, women's anger, via a feminist ideology, has taken the easier route of hatred and blaming toward men. Hence, their ways of ridding themselves of guilt have scarcely been kind; still, I believe they have quite effectively cast off most of the burden of guilt they have carried for too long.

But men? Well; we have scarcely begun. A few of us are beginning to articulate the problem, but perhaps our most valuable insight thus far has been to observe that the very nature of shame is such that it can scarcely be articulated. A sorry beginning, no?

In dealing with shame, we are not entirely without resources. We do have anger. The problem here is, of course, that our anger too quickly feels ineffectual, impotent, and . . . already ashamed of ourselves, we are also ashamed that we can do nothing about our shame.

Anger, however, is a bipolar process. It sets up boundaries which say no to the encroachment of others. It also—and this aspect of anger is too often minimized—is a fierce affirmation of the self. As such, it can strengthen oneself to the point that a new independence—a newly created self—begins to emerge. In this emerging process, shame can not be cast off in the same way guilt can. But it can be dealt with in a different way—it can be eclipsed by the newly emerging self, and thus become irrelevant to one's being and actions. When we men experience this new self, we can feel pride and excitement at who we are, and experience a sense of indefatigable joy as we discover new dimensions within ourselves—exhilaration at our new-found emotional power. It must be noted here that this new-found power is pride based, not upon our *approval* of ourselves, but upon our ability to fully *be* ourselves. Moreover, this pride hurls anger at anyone who reproves us, or expresses displeasure with us, by condemning our entire personhood.

But I deal with this process of self-creation so abstractly. How does it become concrete?

Well; this is what we are doing. Contrary to what I above implied, we actually have begun the process. This self-creativity is, to a great extent, what The Coalition of Free Men is all about. It happens every time we join a consciousness-raising group and, rather than spending all our time complaining about the women in our lives, talk about who we have been, who we are, what we want to *be*, and how we are moving toward becoming happy, i.e., accepting ourselves. *We discover that we men can only leave our shame behind when we break our addiction to women*!! Only when we are free of this addiction can we learn to enjoy ourselves, and subsequently (perhaps not so paradoxically) learn to truly enjoy women too.

But to enjoy women is to run a risk. In this culture, women are the primary promulgators of male shame. They often feel very threatened by any man who is clearly enjoying himself, celebrating himself. They will try to smother his joy. At the very moment he is laughing, relaxing, they will say something like, "Are you *drunk* or something?" "Can't you *behave* yourself?" "When are you going to *grow up*?" "*Now* look at what you're doing!"

How can a man defeat these attempts at shaming him into self-abnegation? The fact is, he can *not* defeat them! It is impossible, because the moment he consents to do battle—to argue or get angry or fight it out—he has given a woman's feminized scheme of values too much validity. He has acknowledged the threat, which means he has acknowledged her power and his own tendency to diminish himself.

No; a man can not defeat a woman's attempts at shaming him, but he can transcend them. He can transcend them by refusing to give up his self-enjoyment. By refusing to forsake joy for battle.

Does this mean he ignores a woman's attempts to shame him? Perhaps. But if he wishes, he can still interact with her, not by battling with her moralistic judgement, but by setting himself over against it in a way that diminishes her judgement. How? Simply by projecting his self-enjoyment through humor. A humor that is directed, not *against the woman*, but *from himself* and *for the sake of his own self-enjoyment*!

To give but one example—a true one:

A woman said to me, "You know, last night at the party, you really weren't acting like your usual self."

"Oh really?" I replied.

"Yes. You should be *ashamed* of yourself!"

"*Shame* on you," I said, angry and yet laughing, that is, enjoying myself, "for trying to make me feel ashamed of myself. Shamey, shame, *shame* on *you!*"

It worked. Not, I believe, because I clearly reflected to this woman what she was doing, but because I demonstrated quite clearly that, at least for that moment, *I was not at all ashamed!*

Which for her was quite disconcerting, given that much of her self-image, her sense of power, was based on a sense of moral superiority—the same sense of superiority which is used by many women and which nourishes itself by occasionally heaping shame, that is, a sense of inferiority, on men.

Perhaps—and this is very important—when confronted by the kind of response I gave, a women may feel so disconcerted that she will get angry. And out of such anger, she then may begin making accusations—letting a man know what she is upset about. This is all well and fine. We men can then deal with *what* she is upset about. This "what" is then a conflict that can likely be resolved. And as long as it is dealt with in this way, i.e., as long as we can deal with a *what*, we do not have to feel ashamed of our*selves*.

Of course, I have given here but a brief account, along with a few examples, of my initial conceptual reckoning with the shame I myself have experienced most of my life. And I have proffered a rather brief, even cursory, analysis of shame and guilt. And my prescription—my view as to what men can do to overcome their shame—is obviously rather abstract; i.e., I must confess that my attempts to incorporate this prescription into my own personality are only sporadically successful.

*But we must not be timid about paltry beginnings!*

As we begin to escape shame, each escape will nourish what well may become a continuum, not only of *escape* from shame, but also of *freedom* from shame. I above listed but one example of how I have dealt with a woman's attempt to make me feel ashamed. In this example, humor is the key. Realizing this, I have several times used humor in other ways when dealing with women who have tried to shame me. For example, one comeback I have used several times (it has become part of my instant repertoire) is, "Maybe you're right. Excuse me for a couple of minutes while I try to grovel." Of course, I am smiling while I say this, and along with the smile there is a bit of a smirk. The women then know—they know fully well—that they did not succeed in their attempt. And I have learned to vary this response somewhat. "Pardon me while I grovel," works well, and so does, "Oh God! Now I feel so ashamed of myself I'll probably sob into my pillow all night long!" Or, just as effective, "I guess I'll have to spend all day tomorrow whimpering in a corner somewhere." Always, of course, there is laughter with the comeback. And sometimes, this laughter by itself is enough.

Humor, then, is my way of escaping shame—at least at the particular moment the shame is inflicted. I am sure other men have their own, individually tailored ways of escaping it. As for ridding myself of old shame—shame that is several decades old—that is a different process, and I have not been very successful at it.

But, as I said, we should not be timid about paltry beginnings. Humor is a beginning, and I am slowly learning other approaches. Meanwhile, there are other men escaping the yoke of shame. We must seek their advice on this matter too.

## NOTE

1. I did not discover that shame was the crucial problem of all my male clients, nor, for that matter, the crucial problem plaguing *any* of my male clients at that particular time. However, my experience as a therapist had for many years shown me that, when counseling a male client, certain important variables, i.e.,

aspects of the man's personality, must *always* be taken into consideration, regardless of what the basic problem is. These aspects are: the man's relationship with his parents, his sexuality—both identity and satisfaction, his relationship with his current family—if he has one, and how his job affects him. I realized, since Dr. Schenk's visit and discussion in September, 1986, that an equally important variable to be explored—which must always be explored when counseling any man—is the extent to which he has experienced, or experiences, shame as a male.

# 9

## Basic Male Shame

*John Gagnon*

Listen   Brothers   Listen
The alarms are too late
This is the hour for
amorous revolt
Dare to take hold
Dare to take over
Be heroes of harmony
in bedfellow bliss
Man must love man
or war is forever
Outnumber the hawks
Outdistance the angels
Love one another
or die

—James Broughton, 1990

In the two decades I have worked as a psychotherapist, I have met men and women with many different psychological diagnoses, and I have traced their disorders to a variety of sources.

**167**

While many of my clients suffered from low self-esteem, I wouldn't have called their conditions "shame-based." It wasn't until I gave a great deal of thought to the concept of shame that I began to see its hand in so many psychological maladies.

I came to understand that shame was a component in many personality disorders. In the sanctuary of my consultation room, many clients struggled through the indignity and devastation of shame on their way to healthier living. As I watched them work through their shame, I developed an interest in treating people who suffered from shame-based maladies. I started to keep track of the many subtle, emotional variants that this self-consciousness or self-loathing takes. Out of my observations emerged a system for classifying different kinds of shame.

One classification that emerged from my experiences—not only as a clinician, but as a friend and fellow male—was what I call *"basic male shame"*: a feeling of shame and self-loathing for the existential fact of *being a man*.

As the concept became apparent to me, I was amazed at how widespread this fundamental disorder was in the male gender. Deep male shame appeared not only in men who came to see me for psychotherapy, but in men who were my friends, in members of the men's movement gatherings I attended, and in participants of workshops for men. I even encountered it within the day-to-day behaviors, thoughts, and feelings of my own being.

Understanding this basic male shame is important because it often keeps men who could benefit from therapy, peer counseling, or the consciousness raising of the men's movement from seeking the help they need. In men who do find their way to therapy, male shame seems to lie beneath other forms of low self-worth that are more readily apparent. When I developed a clearer picture of this gender-specific disease, I became more successful in treating the men I met in my practice.

Therefore, I want to address the insidious disease of basic male shame. I also wish to suggest a therapeutic approach for treating this disorder of Self. As you will see, my exploration of basic male shame has been a long one. This exploration unfolded over a period of 20 years and touched every important aspect of my life: my work as a psychotherapist, my relationships with other men and, most important, my relationship to the core of my own thinking and feelings as a male child, and ultimately as a man.

## BEGINNINGS OF SHAME

Basic male shame results when a boy sees the intrinsically male part of himself humiliated or denigrated within the familial or social context. For example, it can result when a boy is unloved or even rejected and abandoned by the most significant man in his life: his father. If a boy never receives love, protection and nurturing from the man who raises him, the boy never develops a sense that he is worthy of care and nurturing by other males. What results is male abandonment, a feeling that to be a man is to be—and consequently feel—fundamentally unimportant and of little or no worth to other men. This is one starting point for basic male shame. There can be others.

From birth, male children experience different developmental influences from those that female children experience. Boy children are held less, breast-fed less, spanked more, and desired less by mothers (as demonstrated by "reaching out" and "cuddling" behaviors). Boys receive numerous messages that males are worth less during their early life development (Jesser, 1987). This pattern of gender-distinctive treatment occurs all through the male child's development, and culture and society strongly support it.

The pink and blue we use to differentiate our babies have less impact on the male psyche than the nonverbal communications—the looks and tones of voice—that little boys receive. These messages are often tougher, louder, more demanding, and harsher than those given to girls. Even the violent, work-oriented toys we give to boys reinforce the early messages that men must learn to be rough and tumble, fight, and even destroy one another. Men are supposed to eschew more tender and nurturing feelings. The preceding verbal and nonverbal directives that shape one's view of oneself as a particular gender or role are known as *stereotyping events.*

Stereotyping events include, therefore, persistent and long-term cultural attitudes that give to males less physical and emotional worth than females. These messages are repeated so many times in childhood that a man's negative self-view is well established long before he attempts to engage in adult relationships.

## WHAT SHAME DOES TO MEN

Long before I learned about the causes of male shame and arrived at my theory, I encountered, first hand, the results of the destructive way we raise male children. In the mid-1970s, I joined a local chapter of a famous male liberation group. The group began with approximately 30 men, ranging in age from the late teens to the early 70's. For the first time, I heard men talking openly about male anger at women, the devastating effects of the macho stereotype, the inequality men experience in divorce court, and other topics. Many of the men shared their personal pain and some even cried openly, expressing how important it was to "have the support of other men."

But, when these same men began to feel better, they started to skip meetings and eventually dropped out. This kept occurring until the group dwindled to three members, one of whom was the president and one of whom was myself. Throughout this decaying process I searched for what had gone wrong. Weren't these men getting what they had come for? Didn't the group satisfy them? I asked these questions of several ex-members and most of them merely replied, "I got what I needed from the group, so I just decided to leave."

At this same time I was also examining my relationship with my own father. During my childhood, my father, a hard-working man who had been orphaned at the age of 8, had done everything he could to keep me at an emotional distance. He did it by simply ignoring me, or by telling me aimless stories, playing solitaire whenever he was in the house, or with partial deafness caused by his job and his refusal to use a hearing aid.

Mostly, my father used pet projects in his workshop to keep me away. For a while, I tried to be his apprentice, but he found ways to reject me there. I was forever holding the light *wrong*, or handing him the *wrong* screwdriver, or holding a piece of wood for him the *wrong* way. He also rejected me outside of the workshop during his favorite pastime, fishing.

The single time he took me fishing, I managed to hook something, but it pulled me off the slippery rocks and into the river. I didn't know how to swim and began to drown. I can vividly remember seeing my father, calmly unaware of me, facing in another direction while I choked on the muddy water. After I slid to the bottom of the river bed and managed to crawl up on shore, my father came running up to me and said, "How dare you fall in and lose my favorite pole, you stumblebum. I will never take you fishing again." He never did. Although it took more than this single event to make me feel worthless in the eyes of my father, the story is a powerful metaphor for his persistent rejection of me.

Over the years I ached for my father's love and acceptance. I yearned for, but never saw, a change in his feelings. So I chose to reject manual labor—I would be bookish, an intellectual, a *wunderkind*. My father and I grew steadily apart. In the mid-1970s, when my father was 83 years old, he was diagnosed with stomach cancer. During those last 2 ½ years of his life, I visited him more than I had in any previous period of our lives. I talked with him, and I tried to share feelings with him in ways we never had when I was growing up. I made every effort to have him understand that I loved him and that I needed to hear affection from him. Finally one day, when he sat wrapped in a blanket like an old Indian, he looked up at me with his sunken eyes and said, "You know, Johnny-boy, I love you and your brother Ernie, and I've always been so proud of you." Despite my 30 years, I ran from the room and screamed in pain. We opened the door to a hole in my core that existed since my childhood, but that hole could not be filled by a single statement.

I don't know how many times I tried to capture that lasting sense of love and acceptance with my bosses. I put on all kinds of shows for them: I achieved great things, won awards and even lied about the things I had accomplished to get their loving approval. But I never got satisfaction, and that is how it should have been. These bosses were not my father, nor were they the right men to help me find self-love (Osherson, 1986). I slowly began to realize my need for connection with other men, males who could and would love me as a man.

## A SEARCH FOR THE RIGHT OUTLET

I decided to gather my closest male friends and develop some kind of men's group through my local church. My hope was that we would talk over liberation topics, and become close and loving with one another. The first meeting would be a potluck dinner at my house. The men arrived one at a time. Almost every one of them looked genuinely uncomfortable at having to make a dish of food and bring it to a meeting of only men. One man joked, "So when do the dancing girls arrive?" Another asked, "We gonna see some porno flicks later?"

When I responded that we would have neither dancing girls nor porno flicks, the tension grew palpably. As the evening wore

on, these men, who were my dearest friends, felt increasingly uneasy without an agenda to relieve their anxiety at being in one another's company. At first, I chalked this up to homophobia, and
shared this concern with them openly. They denied that they
were homophobic. Most of these guys could hug one another and
myself freely, and they didn't feel uncomfortable with men on a
one-to-one basis. But somehow, this men-only meeting disturbed
them. There was no fishing, no baseball, no television, no porno
flicks, no poker hands to play. What the hell was a group of men
supposed to do? Talk? About *feelings*?

Some admitted that they were unaccustomed to talk about
how they felt with other men and that to identify with their feelings seemed somehow . . . unmanly. In other words, male shame
kept them from admitting their vulnerability (Astrachan 1988).

After a fashion, we did talk, and what came out was a fundamental malaise that these men felt about being male: Men simply
could not offer each other safety, nurturing, acceptance and love;
they expected these things only from women. The idea that another male could be as important to them as the significant
women in their lives was totally foreign. When we talked about
going to singles bars with male friends, many men admitted
dumping their companions to go home with some "foxy chick."
Men who had been abandoned in these situations accepted this as
"natural," or "the way things are." Any suggestion that a bond between men might be more important than meeting a sexual partner was agreed with intellectually but shunned in practice. As a
matter of fact, not far into the evening several men left to go home
to their wives or lovers.

The men agreed, in principal, to meet like this on a regular
basis, but unless I consistently prodded them, the meetings never
happened. Finally, I gave up and decided to join a different group
of men. My church was holding a program for men on women's
*theology*,[1] the study of a female goddesses and how women think,
spiritually. Here was a men's group with an agenda. We had exercises and a format to follow. But what emerged from our weekly
meetings was a hunger for something more. Many of the men admitted that they had no personal relationship with a male God or
even to their own fathers. Others mentioned male friends but re-
gretted how seldom they got together since they were out of
school, where occasions for meeting had more easily presented
themselves. Several of us decided to start a men's group as soon as
the women's spirituality program was over.

This all-male group met once a week for 2 years. We talked over many issues in our meetings, but it was our discussion of male nurturing that revealed the most to me. Most men reported that they could, and did, nurture one another when the occasion presented itself, but none of them felt that nurturing was an important part of being male. Feelings of nurturing and loving applied to men simply weren't that appealing; their custom was to avoid these feelings toward other men, and consequently with themselves.

Even though we could explore this topic on an intellectual level, it didn't stop members from arriving late, skipping meetings without first notifying the group, or complaining that they "had better things to do with the family on a Sunday night." After 2 years and many changes in membership, the group dwindled to a few men and disbanded.

## A Theory Emerges

By the end of this latter group, I had developed a theory of basic male shame. I believed that men, raised by women and loved by women, had learned not to look to other men for love. I n other words, "If my father did not spend time with me, empathizing with me, holding and loving me, then why should any other man?" The corollary is, "If I am a man, then I am basically unimportant to other men" (Diamond, 1985). At its worst, it becomes, "If I am a man and men only love women, then I can mistreat another man any way I like."

I guessed that men dropped out of male support and consciousness-raising groups because of basic male shame: They believed that they simply were not that important to the other men in the group. They could experience the novelty of accepting love, empathy, and caring from other men, but they did not realize that other men needed them to return the gift. Once their own needs had been met, they were ready to move on.

This theory frightened me. If it was true, then the men's movement was doomed. No matter how many men sought out one another, they would not build lasting relationships because they hadn't learned to love maleness. In Jungian terms, it was as if men had no loving animus. The animus might be cruel or intellectual or a good rule maker, but it did not love other men. Worst of all, it did not love the male in the self. As a man, I myself found that several hours with an attractive and admiring woman fulfilled me more than a whole evening with a group of caring and nurturing men. Other men admitted feeling the same way. What was going on in us? Did it mean that every time we felt our own "male energy" that we had to deny it to keep from losing the love of women, the only gender we felt was a source of love? (Moyers & Bly, 1990)

I felt trapped. I wanted to make men more important to me. My friends felt the same way. But we lacked a deep feeling that men are important to other men as nurturing figures. We might work on feeling empathy and caring, but we couldn't love or desire another man, nor could we believe that he truly loved or desired us back. I'm not talking about homosexuality, but about heartfelt love. And I believe that gay men suffer from this lack of male love as much as straight men do.

Basic male shame prevents men both from loving other men and from ever really loving themselves. If I don't love myself then I will fall prey to a whole host of other problems: low self-esteem, self-degradation, stress, guilt for any imagined wrongs done to women (my only source of love), and a compulsive need to undo feelings of worthlessness when the woman I love leaves me. I may feel so mortified that I self-destruct when I cannot support myself after a woman rejects me. Like the men on television commercials who can't cook, clean, or find the medicine when their wives are sick in bed, I may play the role of the "male fool."

When I do encounter truly male thinking and feeling, I will probably reject them as antisocial, and feel misplaced guilt or shame for having them. For example, If I blow the whistle on a corrupt aspect of established order—a true act of male assertion—I may feel like I've done something wrong, that I've violated my mother's wish that I "shut up and keep the complaints to myself."

Basic male shame gives rise to a lack of commitment between men, male competition for virtually everything, and a desire to "dethrone" men who have already established themselves (Bly remembers "shooting arrows at the older poets" when he was young). Basic male shame leads us to the societal view of men as the disposable sex, expendable in times of war, or when the ship is sinking and men are told "women and children first," presumably because men cannot take care of children (Farrell, 1990). Basic male shame denies everything else that is male: noble behavior, love, beauty, feelings of tenderness, grace, integrity, morality, living healthfully, and identity with maleness.

## WITNESSING SHAME IN THERAPY

While I encountered the effects of male shame in my own life and in the men's groups I joined, I also witnessed how shame worked in the men I saw for therapy. Ted was a hard-working man, raised in an Irish-Catholic family in the Boston area. When Ted was growing up, his father and mother favored his three sisters and made it very clear that he was less in need of their attention because he was a boy. Ted was always blamed for any argument he had with his sisters, and he was even beaten by his father on several occasions. Ted took this treatment for granted; he thought it was normal.

Ted came to me with his wife, Jennifer, for therapy. Over the course of our 3 years together, I learned that Ted felt totally responsible for everything that made his wife unhappy. If she wasn't comfortable with something he said, it was his fault for not saying it in a way his wife desired on a particular night. She complained he was insensitive to her needs. He always felt like he was accountable for her feelings, especially if she felt anger, sadness, or displeasure.

In the sessions, Ted became increasingly aware of the shame he felt for being a man. He thought that he was morally inferior to his wife. After a few months of recognizing these feelings of worthlessness, Ted decided to change his behavior. He would treat his wife as he always did, but would no longer take responsibility for what she did not ask of him directly. He also decided he no longer wanted to give her everything she asked of him. Ted's wife did not like this decision.

At home, she became more manipulative. She concluded that Ted's interest in his own needs was due to selfishness alone. Ted eventually saw that he would no longer be happy in a relationship that contributed to his own sense of shame and worthlessness. He divorced Jennifer and continued to work out the sense of basic male shame that he had been taught as a child.

To help Ted resolve his feelings of shame, I employed several Gestalt experiments allowing him to express feelings toward his mother and father about the lack of support he felt for being a man. He became very angry in several sessions, and he cried a lot at the thought that neither of his parents wanted him for his maleness. In time, he resolved these unfinished experiences with his parents. Ted moved on to find more ways to love himself and care for other men. He eventually left his job in a large industrial corporation and became the director of a nature museum. Years later, he reports that these changes bring joy to his life.

Another client heard different messages from his parents but still grew up feeling male shame. Alex was a 38 year-old electrical engineer and very capable in his work. His intellectual parents always prized his ability to think well, but they gave him absolutely no support for playing sports, being with other males, feeling sexual, or loving his own father. In fact, his father was particularly cool toward him and, like many working fathers, spent a great deal of time away from home at the job.

Alex presented himself to others, as a very rigid, easily frightened man. He spoke with deliberate hesitation and often reworked his sentences until he had them "correct." He constantly monitored himself in front of me and others and felt basically ashamed of himself for being male. Alex had ulcers and other gastrointestinal problems, and was mildly anorectic.

Timid around both men and women, Alex told me that when he attempted to develop a relationship with a woman, he felt inferior to her and immediately tried to impress her with his intellectual prowess. This failed to engage most women either in or out of the work arena, and Alex had never been in a romantic relationship. Before therapy, he had no male friends, although he was highly regarded by several male colleagues. They might socialize with Alex around job-related projects, but they never discussed or showed their feelings to him. Alex reported feeling immensely isolated and in a "great deal of emotional pain."

When I began working with Alex, I had him make a list of "the messages you would have liked to have heard from your parents." He followed my instructions compulsively and listed, among other things: "that I can feel my feelings and show them to others," "that my body is O.K. and deserves exercise and sex," and "that I can have meaningful, contactful relationships with other men and nonintellectual relationships with women."

With time, Alex learned that he did, indeed, have a body. He became proud of his body and wanted to take better care of it through jogging and a healthier diet. He even started several friendships with other men and a relationship with a woman with whom he could relate in a more feeling way.

## OUTSIDE THE OFFICE

My clients aren't the only men who suffer from basic male shame. It also affects men I know and care about. My friend Jim is a police officer. His middle-class parents taught him to respect others and to have a high regard for ethical principles, but they also sent him another message. As he grew up, they made it clear to him that to earn their acceptance, he had to prove himself as a disposable man. To do this, Jim joined the Army during the Vietnam conflict and even renenlisted when his tour was over. He was often scared in combat, but true to his ideal of the macho man, he never showed his fear and always acted as if his life was totally unimportant. Jim never questioned the self-destructive messages his parents had instilled in him.

Jim has many macho buddies but no close male friends except me. He values our friendship and intimacy, and he often comes over to my house to talk about his feelings. Yet, while he shares his feelings with me, he admits shame over having fears and insecurities, doubts, and confusions. Jim still believes that he does not have a right to these feelings, and that he should avoid them to please his mom and dad. Jim's father died of a heart attack last year and Jim, himself, has suffered from angina for several years now. I am trying to help my friend take better care of himself, especially his "heart."

Three other friends have had heart attacks in the past 5 years. One of them needed a triple bypass operation. I worry about them and am often aware of the driven and stressful lives they all lead. Even my father was driven and self-destructive. He never complained of pain and eventually died of the cancer that developed from the stomach ulcers he never told his doctor about. Even though I wanted to be different from my father, I too felt embarrassed and sometimes ashamed of my physical pain, fears, and sickness.

## MY SEARCH CONTINUES

In the late 1980s I was still trying to unlearn the lessons my father had taught me. I wanted to take my life into my own hands, but it was seldom as easy as I had hoped. Once again, I went looking for a healthy group of men, a place where I could give and receive love, somewhere I could share the complete range of my feelings. But where—in this age of absent fathers and forgotten male initiation rites—would I find a group of healed, loving men? Where were the role models who would teach me to love and accept the man in myself?

I found some of what I was seeking in the work of Robert Bly. I attended several of his lectures but that wasn't enough. I wanted a complete, loving, and self-giving initiation experience, and I couldn't make it to one of Bly's weekend retreats. Instead, a friend and I organized a group of a dozen men to explore the possibility of initiating one another. We built our meetings around Francis Baumli's (1985) excellent book, *Men Freeing Men*. We gathered regularly to discuss and receive acceptance for the experience of our male sexuality, work, and daily stress, our male bodies and our male feelings.

At one session we conducted an initiation rite. The ceremony opened with a meditation on passage into manhood. Then we began drumming and chanting. We explored a complex ritual we had designed and one by one each male was initiated by the group. Each man had written his own "words of initiation" and had brought a personally meaningful item—a pocket knife, a fishing rod, a cooking pot—that for him symbolized passage into manhood. Another man chosen by him would say the words back to him and present him with the gift he had brought. We who attended got a lot and gave a lot during the ceremony. Several of us felt great sadness and wept openly in grief for the acceptance we had never felt before. Others laughed from the belly with great joy.

Several members of the group, however, missed this event and did not call ahead of time to say they would be unable to come. By now, I recognized this pattern from the other men's groups. I decided to raise my theory of basic male shame with the initiates. I found them generally accepting of the theory, but several men said they could not identify with it at all.

## PUTTING MY THEORY TO WORK

In my work as a psychotherapist, I found myself more aware of basic male shame and helping many men undo the shame that they had received in early development. The result? More of these men worked through numerous other issues more quickly and easily. I was amazed, and so were my clients and colleagues.

Here is an example: During a session with a group of musicians, Bill, a master cellist, told the group about an intermittent difficulty he was having with his performance. I asked Bill to play for us and he settled himself in front of the group, looked at us, then averted his eyes and began to play. His phrasing was precise and sensitive, his rapport with his instrument perfect, until the last few measures, when he looked up at someone in the group and faltered. I guessed that this eye contact was significant to Bill in some way, and I immediately stopped his playing.

I asked Bill what had happened at the time when he erred in his bowing, and he told me that he had looked directly at John, another musician in the group. At first he did not understand why this made him falter, so I asked him to try playing again while looking at John. He quickly realized that he felt "competitive and scared . . . of physically being hurt" by John—by any man.

Bill: "When I was a kid, my mother refused to let me play sports with the other boys. She frightened me . . . told me I would hurt my hands and then I would never be able to play cello again."

Therapist: "So now you frighten yourself with mama's warnings and when you feel like making playful contact with some man, you do become momentarily unable to play cello."

Bill: "Wow! I never thought of it that way, but it's absolutely true."

Bill's mother had shamed him out of aggressive male contact. I suggested a playful "wrestling match" between them on a soft rug. John agreed. Bill was reluctant but was willing to try as long as I acted as referee.

The two musicians grappled, first tentatively, then with more and more energy. Each tried to get the other onto his back. John seemed to have the advantage of youth and almost pinned Bill to the rug. Others in the group cheered for one of the wrestlers. Both Bill and John were grunting loudly as they tried to turn the other over. Finally, Bill's superior strength won out, and he held John's shoulders down as I counted John "out" and declared Bill the winner. The group cheered joyously. Bill was flushed and sweating but grinning broadly. Finally, he and John caught their breath, rose to their knees, and spontaneously hugged each other. The love hidden beneath Bill's fear of being hurt had emerged.

Bill readily admitted that he no longer feared assertiveness in himself or other men. When he was ready, he took up his cello again and rendered the sonata beautifully. Several times while he played, Bill looked up at one of the other men and smiled. And this time he didn't miss a note. Later, Bill wrote to me:

> It was a great relief . . . from those long standing and generally hidden fears. . . . You were most helpful in bringing these skeletons out of my closet. . . . We [John and Bill] found out we could wrestle and that we would not be hurt or hurt the other person . . .
>
> The musical accomplishment [during the session] was indeed profound for me. It was the musical expression of my state of ease: emotional connectedness to my male playfulness with John.

Bill was one of the many men in therapy who eventually benefited from a recognition of basic male shame as an underlying issue leading to other problems. Many of my clients realized that their poor health and reluctance to get a yearly physical examination was the result of their basic male shame.

## MALE SHAME IN THE MEDIA

The message that a man's well-being is not important, that being a man is a shameful exercise at best, comes to us from many quarters. Take the movie, *Glory*, for example. It was a deeply moving film about a Union Army regiment comprised of freed black slaves. During their long and rigorous training together, these men developed a profound amount of love and respect for one another. They didn't recognize this wealth of feelings until the night before they would lose their lives in a hopeless attack against a well-armed fort. In their prebattle celebration, one soldier says, "Tomorrow, we will be MEN!" There was a resounding shout of agreement, and much caring for one another. Watching that scene, I felt so sad for these men who could only revel in their maleness when they were about to give up their lives for some cause. This is not glory, but stupidity. Because we learn this stupidity first at the knees of our parents, we men desperately need to reparent ourselves, and especially to refather our inner child.

## BECOMING THE FATHER WE NEVER HAD

What can men do to reparent themselves in the face of so much negative familial and cultural programming? While I believe there are several ways men can undo the societal and parental inculcation of basic male shame, I will offer one that I have used with myself and others. It is called "creating a fantasy father," and it involves imagining a new father in one's mind. I learned it in 1979 from Stuart Alpert and George Rogers at Hartford Family Institute, but did not apply it for a few years.

When called on, this "father" always gives good advice and never asks the son to do anything self-destructive. He might say things like, "I love you, son, not for what you do or become in your life but just because you are you. I love you as you are, and if you never change anything, not even in your therapy, I shall always love you." A man can bring this fantasy father wherever he wants and can "talk" to him in his mind whenever he likes. He might not be able to picture his fantasy father's face, or visualize his physique or imagine his particular tone of voice, but that doesn't matter. The important part of the technique is that the man *feels the fantasy father's presence and loving support* when he needs it most.

If a man summons his fantasy father and hears a shaming voice, then he either has the wrong fantasy going, or he is listening to destructive voices from his childhood father or some other adult who injured him as a child. The goal is to dismiss these people as harmful and wait patiently until he can hear the fantasy father once again.

For men who have tried this, the results have been marvelous. They have experienced a new relatedness to the positive animus within themselves. They reparented themselves with the father they would have liked to have had when they were boys. At the same time, they experienced that to be male is to love the self as male and thus to love other men as well.

Like prayer and meditation in other systems, this therapeutic intervention must be practiced faithfully, for some time, before the effect is felt. But eventually a man learns to summon his fantasy father whenever he has a question that needs answering, and this is reinforced when the man learns that the "father" will give him a useful answer. The fantasy father never encourages selfishness, only self-love, so the man who calls on his fantasy father will also experience real humility in daily life and remorse whenever he hurts another.

After several months or years, the fantasy father becomes a very real substitute for what a man missed as a child. This "father" eventually recedes into the background, unless he is called forth for help with a particular question. In fact, the man who develops a fantasy father may not be sure his fantasy father ever really "existed." Nevertheless, the effect of this form of imaging seems to be quite powerful. One internalizes the ability to love oneself as a male. One learns to trust oneself and to develop lasting, committed bonds with other men.

There are other ways to internalize self-love. Robert Bly, Ed Tick, and Joseph Jastrab are but a few of the loving men who run frequent experiential workshops in which male bonding, affirmation, and love abound. In these workshops one gets the experience of being loved as a male from the other men in the group. One weekend, however, does not change the brain patterns of a lifetime. It takes many such exposures to loving men before this message can replace the basic male shame of childhood.

Whatever method you choose to follow to overcome male shame, remember to test the effectiveness of your personal change by getting together with men on a regular basis. Experience how important these men are to you and feel how important you are to them. This is not the clinging dependency of a child, but the ability of grown men to give and take adult love (Gottlieb, 1987). You should be willing to pursue this bonding; you must realize that despite their liberated attitudes, your closest friends may be struggling with their own basic male shame. You can't save them. But you can be an example. You *can* teach them with your own love that love between men is nothing to fear. On the contrary, love between men is deeply fulfilling and something every man needs to overcome the destructive effects of basic male shame, to stay nourished for a lifetime and to nurture others.

## NOTE

1. "The*a*logy" is a feminine form of theology.

# 10

## Male Initiation: Filling a Gap in Therapy*

### Christopher Miller

Men are less likely than women to enter psychotherapy. And when they do, it is often difficulty with women that, directly or indirectly, brings them to the consulting room. As a pastoral psychotherapist, I have noticed that my male clients are often poorly prepared to function in heterosexual dynamics.

Emotional awareness, expression of feelings, and the empathy often desired by females, are poorly developed skills in many men. Moreover, men seem to think they are more rational and objective than they really are, misunderstanding the emotional systems that influence their perceptions and behavior. This puts them at a disadvantage with women, who are likely to be emotionally aware and expressive in negotiating for their personal needs.

### TWO MALE STYLES

Generally, men in my practice seem to adopt one of two interpersonal styles. The more stereotypically "macho" men endure or

*Based on a presentation to the national conference on "The Men's Movement and the Churches," convened at Chicago Theological Seminary by Robert Moore, October 1991.

**184**

deny emotional pain, concealing their reactions behind a cool poker face or Marine toughness. Anger is usually the most acceptable form of emotional expression. Their aggressive energy is channeled into competition, dominance, and hierarchical structure. Although women may admire or respect these men for their power, they may also experience them as controlling, uncooperative, and demeaning.

In contrast, the stereotypically "soft" males will directly acknowledge pain in themselves and others but may have trouble expressing anger. Such men may channel their aggressive energy into niceness and cooperation, sometimes resulting in low self-esteem or a sense of inadequacy from compromising self. Women find them affectionate, understanding, and more compliant, but may also find them son-like and difficult to respect.

Neither type of man is adequately prepared to negotiate a satisfying relationship with a woman. Disregarding their spouses' positions or automatically adapting to them, both types miss the emotional cues in themselves and their partners, thereby failing to establish interpersonal boundaries through clear and direct communication. Unable to readily say, "I need," "I want," "I can't," or "I won't," they become overly dependent on women to interpret their feelings and positions for them, often inaccurately.

Culturally trained to disregard their own feelings, men may not know how to empathize with a woman's perspective and needs without losing themselves. They may experience women's expressed wants and needs as demands, criticisms, or orders requiring an immediate solution. The biological programming to protect the nest manifests in a "fix-it" syndrome—an automatic tendency to respond to female distress with problem solving. The male alarm system makes it difficult to tolerate conflict with their female partners long enough to generate win-win solutions. By abdication to what she wants or by dominating or oppressing women to control the situation, men may attempt to resolve conflict ineffectively. Women who would have preferred empathy to a solution will be frustrated and disappointed by a compliant or controlling response to their distress.

Neither the macho nor the soft style was enabling men to establish satisfying long-term relationships with women. Furthermore, the general tendency to focus their emotional needs only on their female partner and not into a variety of relationships as women tend to do was adding to the problem. These men were not only lacking skill in negotiating with women, but were also needing something that cannot be provided by a woman's love.

As a son must turn to his mother for all his emotional resources when the father is unavailable, so these male clients were looking to women. But the need for a father and the unexpressed grief about this father deficit cannot be met or resolved in the mother-son, heterosexual relationship. So my clients were vaguely discontent or openly hostile toward their female partners, experiencing them as somehow inadequate or withholding. The unfulfilled or underdeveloped father-son relationship was damaging marriages.

A boy needs to bond with a strong, nurturing male. The experience of closeness with his own kind positively mirrors his own maleness and alleviates overdependency on the female. For a boy to develop a shame-free sense of himself as male, he needs to experience *cellular contact* with the male, resulting from physical proximity to a strong male figure who models and teaches the boy life skills. From this he learns how to handle himself successfully with females. Ideally, the boy learns a way of relating that allows the exchange of physical and emotional nurturing without violating the integrity of either person.

The man who never experiences such male contact longs for a true soul protector with whom he can discover and fulfill his true self. The "hole" in the self he feels may drive him to compensate for the loss in any way he can. He may settle for substitutes, attaching dependently to a woman. Or he may be drawn to the exploitive boss, competitive coach, or drill sergeant. These people rarely function as adequate soul protectors.

## THE BENEFITS OF INITIATION

It has been difficult for men to find true soul protectors to satisfy their father hunger. Hope came when one of my clients attended the New Warrior Adventure Training. This male initiation weekend shows men how to meet their needs with other men and begins to fill the gaps our culture leaves in their own male development. My client and his wife were getting a divorce. He was angry and frustrated because he couldn't communicate with her. The New Warrior weekend helped him develop a remarkable new ability to be emotionally present and communicate with his wife, even though they continued to divorce. I made plans to attend New Warrior training for myself.

My experience at the weekend was profound personally and enlightening as a therapist. The leaders redefined the standards for what a man is. These standards were clearly mandated in stereotypical Western male style, which avoided the automatic resistance to female styles. We were directed to be present for each other and to give focus to each other. We were told that a man does the hard work of finding, naming, and owning his feelings. We were challenged to become men who act with integrity among other men, inner directed by our own sense of mission. We saw that a man needs men to love and needs to be loved by other men. We discovered new possibilities for being good sons and fathers.

This training allowed me to address my own personal issues in ways that would not have been possible in individual or family therapy. I participated in the emotional, physical and spiritual exercise of being present and intentional with other men, emerged deeply touched, excited and somehow changed.

As a psychotherapist, I can see that such an initiation experience facilitates discovery of the true self. It promotes awareness, objectivity and respect for the feeling system that directs our behavior more powerfully than the thinking system. Initiation grounds a man in honest acceptance and responsibility for himself. From this new viewpoint, he can pursue his goals by taking action that is response-able rather than reactive to others. He can acknowledge the unique experience of the other person. He becomes receptive, rather than reactive, to the stranger, especially the female stranger.

When men are good to each other, when they are soul protectors instead of adversaries, they create a positive approach to the world. When they say, "I need, I hurt, and I can't" to themselves and others instead of hiding behind a "macho" or a "nice-guy" stereotype, they can reach out to their environments rather than exploit them. Such men aren't codependent or adaptive to dysfunction, and they don't blame. They communicate clearly and directly about themselves and are good advocates for their own needs. They are neither the oppressor nor the oppressed.

## IMPLICATIONS FOR MEN IN THERAPY

Many men have sensed that something is wrong but haven't been able to name it. Many of us secretly concluded that something was wrong with *us*. We achieve goals that parents or culture establish for us, but then we hide in hierarchy to protect ourselves from the shame of being out of integrity with our true selves. If we are intelligent or otherwise talented, we usually master a false personality that is rewarded by our parents, wives, and children. Or we can defy society's conventions and other people, maintaining our selves by keeping others at a distance and avoiding commitment. Either way, we lose our souls in the long run.

Psychotherapy is difficult for many men because it contradicts a male code that includes denial of feelings and personal needs and a silent, do-it-on-your-own achievement orientation. Seen from a male perspective that rewards hierarchy and dominance, therapy resembles submission: A man turns control over to his therapist, who knows it all and will fix him. Thus therapy may feel humiliating, shaming, and wrong to many men. Beyond that, many therapeutic styles emphasize pathology and treat the client like someone who needs to be "fixed." Therapists who practice these methods devalue men and confirm the secret sense of inadequacy and shame that many men carry.

Therapy often subtly expects men to compromise themselves by adopting feminine modes of being and feeling. Male styles are often perceived as wrong by women and by men who have mastered feminine styles of communication. Men usually talk without facing each other or making much eye contact, and we generally don't match up feelings with language as easily as women do. Yet many therapeutic styles require us to face the therapist, sustain eye contact and name our emotions with precision.

Men have a unique mode of feeling and communication, achieving closeness in ways different from females (see chapter 17). Men in therapy have a fundamental need for their maleness and male styles to be understood, mirrored positively, and affirmed. Perhaps a woman therapist can do this, but the basic need for admiration by an older man suggests that many men need a male therapist. Father hunger in male clients must be addressed.

Because men are often at a disadvantage in female relational skills, therapists need to teach men how to negotiate for themselves in relationship with women. Men need to learn how to handle themselves when women are emotionally intense or expressive in ways that men can find overwhelming or threatening. Men need to learn aggressive empathy: Listening without reacting, then reflecting back what they hear, as an alternative to feeling hurt, manipulated, and enraged. Working with other men on identifying feelings is excellent preparation for male-female dynamics. We learn to understand the male mode of feeling and become advocates for our own emotions. When a man does not know what he feels, he probably doesn't know what he wants, so he can't tell his partner what he needs. This leaves him disabled in relationships. He then must choose to take whatever she gives him, or move on.

My experience with the men's movement confirms that men need to have a mission, and therapy should not overlook this. Personal change is much less difficult when it serves a personal mission. Therapy must consider the authenticity of a man's career choice in light of his larger sense of purpose or mission, and help him identify subtle and obvious ways he may be compromising himself and eroding his self-esteem. A man must learn to consider whether his life is consistent with his own ideals.

Therapy needs to challenge the usual style of male-male relationships and teach men how to connect securely with other men. Male clients should learn how much they need other men and be coached in developing relationships with them. And they also need to know what can and cannot be expected from relationships with women.

A man needs a therapist who is a soul protector. Such a therapist will help him rediscover his soul, and guide him in the art of being authentic, true to what he is meant to be, and graceful in his respect for himself and others. The therapeutic process should look beyond a client's defects and the issues he needs to resolve. A man deserves a therapeutic process that consistently serves to mirror his personal worth, blesses his manhood, reveals his mission in life, and teaches him to relate to others in ways that bring joy to his existence.

# 11

# A Shame-Based Model for Recovery from Addiction

## George Lindall

From my private practice of psychotherapy, I developed a therapeutic model that is effective for people addicted to a variety of self-destructive behaviors.

### THE ADDICTION MODEL

The model clarifies the forces involved in the perpetuation of addiction (see Figure 11.1). The addiction cycle begins when a child experiences victimization and learns to insulate himself from painful feelings and memories by developing layers of shame and later codependency. The child aspect of the model is called the *equipment* because it's a given (i.e., the person carries it with him from his family of origin). The *adult* aspect of the model includes acting out (compulsive behavior) and the shame the person associates with acting out.

Our traditional method for treating addiction places too much emphasis on the adult side of the model. I propose an "80/20 rule" for addiction: 80% of the feelings that drive addiction come from the childhood equipment, whereas only 20% of the feelings come from the adult shame an addict feels. The crucial issues are the childhood issues.

**190**

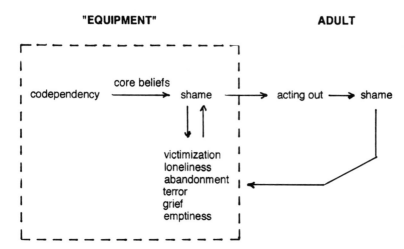

**FIGURE 11.1** Addiction model.

Concentrating on adult behavior and adult shame is likely to put a Band-Aid on the problem—and create a dry drunk or a straight junkie. Adult compulsive behavior (acting out) tends to obscure underlying issues, so it needs to be stabilized before the major childhood issues are treated. But this concern with obvious adult behavior is only a beginning; when it becomes the major focus of therapy, relapse is much more likely to occur.

## ASSUMPTIONS

This therapy for addiction starts with a set of assumptions about all people, whether or not they see themselves as addicts or are actively seeking treatment for addiction.

1. All human beings are addicts. All of us look for some form of distraction to protect ourselves from our existential predicament. We are each alone with God, as we understand him. Each of us entered this world alone and will leave alone. We are all fearful, to some degree, about this predicament. Recovery is about learning to face this fear.
2. All addicts are shame-based. Shame is the first distraction we turn to when faced with the pain in our lives.
3. All human beings are victims. When we were children, we all had

needs that were not met. In that sense, we were all abused in childhood. Whenever this happened, our emotional development was interrupted. So, every one of us has feelings of loneliness, abandonment, terror, grief, and emptiness. These painful feelings propel us to
seek distraction from our existential predicament.

4. All human beings are codependent. We all engage in caretaking,
   pleasing, and achieving behavior in the hope that it will make us
   feel better about ourselves. We look outside of ourselves, instead
   of inside, for our self-esteem.
5. Each of us has dysfunctional core beliefs that reinforce our addictive
   cycle. Subtly but powerfully, we tell ourselves things like, "It's not
   okay to be angry," or "Sex is my most important need."

## METHOD OF TREATING ADDICTION

A method for treating sexual addicts[1] arose from this addiction model
and these five assumptions. Although each addict has his own unique
reality and situation, the method covers issues each must face in order
to recover successfully. Are these issues best taken up in linear order,
one after the other, or interwoven like threads in a piece of fine fabric? I
see recovering people use both approaches. Although a client might be
involved with two or three stages simultaneously, there is usually an
identifiable progression from mostly stage 1 to mostly stage 2, and so
forth. What follows is a kind of check list of typical issues that addicts
encounter in their therapeutic journey.

1. Because acting out anesthetizes an addict's feelings, he must cut back
   his addictive behavior in order to start feeling again. Whether he's using alcohol, sex, food, or gambling to numb his emotions, he needs
   to reduce his coping behavior until it isn't as profound and powerful
   as it once was. Only then can he can get closer to his feelings and begin productive work on his childhood issues.
2. The addict must let himself feel shameful without medicating his
   shame with distractions. I believe that all compulsive behavior
   comes from trying to avoid shame. The cycle begins when we
   are children. We're victimized when our parents weren't there
   for us emotionally or when they abused us in some way. We felt
   shame as children, and we decided that shame hurts too much.
   We learned to avoid feeling it at all costs.

As adults, we still look outside ourselves to relationships, work, food, or sex to make us feel better. Sooner or later, we'll fail when we try to get our self-esteem from our environment. This triggers shame—that emotion we learned to avoid as children—and we try to escape it through compulsive behavior, which only leads to more shame.

We simply can't manage to avoid shame in our lives, nor do we want to. A turning point in treatment occurs when the client decides that his shame is to be honored, rather than avoided. Shamefulness is part of our personalities, and I want clients to learn that they can live through it without the anesthesia of compulsive behavior to distract them from feeling this emotion.

3. The addict must allow himself to make mistakes without condemning himself. During early recovery, I ask my clients to focus less on avoiding their compulsive behavior and codependency, and more on allowing themselves to engage in this behavior without beating themselves up. I'm certainly not encouraging people to get drunk, take drugs, overeat, or break the law. But I do encourage clients to be gentle with themselves and give themselves permission to be just the way they are. When addicts condemn their own compulsive behavior, all they do is reinforce their shame and the cycle of addiction.

4. The addict must hold his abusers accountable for his childhood victimization. He must learn that 80% of his feelings—80% of the power behind his compulsive behavior—arises from childhood issues.

We all suffered at the hands of our parents or the people who raised us. Each of us started life as a unique person with unique desires, beliefs, opinions—all of us had our own unique reality. And to some degree, each of us had parents who didn't allow us to be our own unique selves. They tried to force their own feelings, beliefs, and values on us. I call this abuse.

As recovering adults, we have to realize that although we are responsible for our adult behavior, we are not responsible for the "equipment" our parents provided us. This childhood equipment is part of us; it will always affect how we respond to life. But we did not create it ourselves. Recovering addicts must acknowledge the abuse they experienced as children and learn to hold their abusers accountable for it. It's really useful to stand up and say out loud, "It was not my fault. I didn't deserve this. I'm an adult now—no longer the child who didn't have enough power to stand up to you and your beliefs."

5. Once he learns to hold his abusers accountable, the addict must learn to express his anger about the abuse. Standard methods (yelling at surrogates, pounding pillows, etc.) are usually effective.

6. The addict must reach back to his unresolved victim feelings and be able to cry over them. This marks his safe arrival through an important series of emotional transitions. We have many layers of feeling, and shame is only the outermost layer, the one that lies closest to the addict's acting-out behavior. As his compulsive behavior wanes, the recovering addict comes to the realization that he has lived continually—24 hours a day, for years on end—in shame, depression, and repressed anger. Then he learns to feel his shame instead of medicating it. In time, the shame recedes, and he's left with his innermost feelings of abandonment, loneliness, grief, and terror. When a client cries, I know he has reached these victim feelings.

7. The addict must recognize his tendency to depend on others to make him feel good about himself, and begin to change. Now that he's in touch with his victim feelings, he starts to notice how his adult environment triggers these feelings, especially his fear of abandonment. He begins to see how he gives up his own power to others and that he can start taking his power back.

8. The addict must learn which of his core beliefs reinforce his addiction. For example, as a little boy he may have been taught that he wasn't okay unless he pleased everybody else. When he fails at this—and he's bound to fail—his shameful feelings will beckon him back into compulsive acting out. As he learns to counteract the belief, he gains strength to avoid active addiction.

9. The addict must make amends for past behavior that has harmed others. Making amends is step 9 in the AA program of recovery. Such action teaches the addict that he can survive feeling intensely guilty and ashamed, and that he can act responsibly while experiencing these emotions. Amends often restore broken interpersonal bonds, to the benefit of both parties, and reduce long-standing shame.


## FIVE STAGES OF RECOVERY


Elisabeth Kübler-Ross (1969) developed a model of five stages for working through grief. I've adapted and modified her model to describe the stages of recovery from addiction, because I think these are similar processes. Inside the adult addict is a child who

**Stage 1—Acting Out**

Caretaking, Overeating, Flirting, Fantasizing, Having lunch with a woman, Bragging about my sexual history, Going out with the old gang, Watching TV, Working out, Achieving, Performing, Telling sexual jokes.

**Stage 2—Denial**

Rationalizing, Controlling, Minimizing, Blaming, Depression, Using anger to control, Not listening.

**Stage 3—Anger**

Holding abusers accountable, Feeling shame, Doing anger work, Asserting myself, Standing up for myself, Naming the abuse.

**Stage 4—Grief**

Crying, Feeling empty, Feeling terrified, Feeling abandoned, Feeling a loss, Shaking.

**Stage 5—Acceptance**

Accepting responsibility, Making amends, Experiencing intimacy, Being good to myself, Getting excited about a sunrise, Feeling affirmed, Surrounding myself with recovering people, Exploring, Taking risks.

**FIGURE 11.2** Behavior during the five stages of recovery from addiction.

didn't get his needs met. He's grieving the loss of his childhood; grieving the loss of protection when he was vulnerable; grieving the absence of blessing from his parents; grieving especially that he was not allowed to develop in ways that are necessary for healthy adulthood.

These stages are slightly different from Kübler-Ross's, and are listed in Figure 11.2 with behavior typical of each stage.

To summarize the stages and the internal dynamic in each stage: In stage 1—*Acting Out*, the addict engages in various behaviors in order to escape painful realities in his life. In stage 2—*Denial*, he perceives that he must protect his addiction and the lifestyle he has created around it—in order to survive. In stage 3—*Anger*, the addict sees that he has been a victim and learns to express his anger toward those who victimized him. In stage 4—*Grief*, he grieves, and allows himself to feel his terror, abandonment, and emptiness. In stage 5—*Acceptance*, he accepts the equipment he carries from childhood and learns how to live with his childhood feelings without acting out his addictive behavior.

**From Acting Out to Denial**

Carnes, Patrick. (1992). *Out of the Shadows*. Minneapolis: CompCare Publications. *An overview of sexual addiction.*

Woititz, Janet G. (1990). *Adult Children of Alcoholics*. Deerfield Beach, FL: Health Communications. *Outlines the core beliefs and childhood origins of addiction.*

**From Denial to Anger**

Viscott, David. (1976). *The Language of Feelings*. New York: Arbor House. *Helps clients to recognize and label their emotions, and find permission to own their anger.*

Millman, Dan. (1984). *The Way of the Peaceful Warrior*. Tiburon, CA: H. J. Karmer, Inc. *A guide to being one's own person.*

Andrews, Lynn V. (1983). *Medicine Woman*. San Francisco: Harper. *Tips for being quiet and reclaiming one's identity.*

**From Anger to Grief**

Schaef, Anne W. (1985). *Codependency: Misunderstood and Mistreated*. San Francisco: Harper. *Understanding codependency.*

McNaron, Toni A. H., & Morgan Yarrow, eds. (1982). *Voices in the Night: Women Speaking About Incest*. Pittsburg, PA: Cleis Press. *Personal stories useful for sexual abuse victims, both male and female.*

**From Grief to Recovery**

Kübler-Ross, Elisabeth. (1969). *On Death and Dying*. New York: Macmillan. *An exploration of how people work through grief.*

**Recovery**

Woititz, Janet G. 91985). *The Struggle for Intimacy*. Deerfield Beach, FL: Health Communications. *The work of recovery can become an obsession. This book helps clients to help focusing on recovery and start focusing on living.*

**FIGURE 11.3**   Readings to facilitate a client's recovery.

Recovery from addiction involves moving through these stages. There are specific experiences, practices, and behavior that may help addicts make the transition from one stage to the next. Useful books for each transition are listed in Figure 11.3.

## From Acting Out to Denial

First the addict has to identify the things he does to escape from reality. When he engages in such behavior, he is abandoning himself. His task is to learn how to stay with himself. Part of being present for himself is setting goals for reducing his acting-out behavior and noticing how long it takes him to realize that he has entered an episode of acting out. But he doesn't need to do this alone. He can ask others to give him feedback when they see him acting out.

## From Denial to Anger

At this stage, he starts talking about his acting-out behavior. He goes back over his personal history and tells others how he acts out and how he abuses others. He starts to be honest with others and with himself. Group therapy provides a good opportunity to do this, and it also gives him a safe place to share his secrets. Keeping secrets reinforces the shame he feels and perpetuates the cycle of addiction. If he's going to work through his shame, he has to start sharing his secrets, even if this means compensating those he has harmed or serving time for illegal acts in his past. In this stage, staying with himself involves taking responsibility for his actions and for their effects on others.

He also needs to start identifying his own feelings. It's absolutely crucial that a recovering addict learn some basic labels for his feelings, learn to recognize his feelings and listen to them, and then learn to connect his feelings with the labels. I teach addicts eight basic feelings: mad, sad, joyful, scared, lonely, empty, abandoned, and shameful. I encourage them to use these labels because they're especially descriptive and specific. Words like "depressed," "addictive," or "confused" are dead ends—they tend to keep an addict stuck in the idea that he's diseased, and probably incurable.

My goal is to get clients closer to their own inner voices, to their own inner selves. Out of the true inner self, a real identity and personal integrity can emerge, along with behavior that's consistent with this real identity. This is a time to slow down and look inward. Sometimes it requires him to work less, give up television, or call a moratorium on family contact—whatever it takes to allow him the time and space to discover his own reality.

## From Anger to Grief

After the addict has learned what his shame feels like, and is able to stay with the shame without doing something to medicate it, he has to face his huge reservoir of shame from childhood. He needs to know deep down that it's not about his flaws but about what was done to him. When he was a child, he learned to abandon himself to please his parents. This was not something he chose freely, but was necessary for survival. It was perpetrated on him. Anger work—hitting pillows and yelling at his abusers—will help him experience his victim feelings of abandonment and emptiness and shame.

Presenting his victimization history is also helpful. He can talk about all the ways he was abused—most importantly how he was not allowed to be himself but forced to be what his parents wanted him to be. When he does this, he sets the record straight for himself: He makes a subtle shift from saying, "I was sexual with . . ." to "I was sexually abused by. . . ." Instead of telling himself that he was responsible for what happened to him, or that he participated in it willingly, he sees that it wasn't his fault. Sexual addicts begin naming the covert sexual abuse they suffered. Many of these men had fathers who were absent, and mothers who were invasive and intrusive. The mothers turned their sons into surrogate spouses, and the sons now learn that Mom's sharing and touching was inappropriate behavior and constituted covert sexual abuse.

## From Grief to Acceptance

The addict needs to learn how to cry and be able to get in touch with his victim feelings (e.g., emptiness, loss, abandonment) whenever he wants to. When an addict has a compulsive urge, he's less likely to act it out if he sees that it arises from childhood feelings, not from what's happening right now. In this stage, it helps to present his history of caretaking and codependency, both past and present. Going back to childhood, he talks about all the ways his parents forced him to be codependent with them. And as an adult, he needs to examine how he still gives his power away and allows himself to be a victim. He must see clearly how he continues to control, manipulate, and lie in order to please others. Although the pattern began in childhood, he needs to see himself perpetuating it in adult relationships with his mate, his kids, his boss, and others. When they decide to break up their lifelong patterns of codependency, I often ask clients to make the decision more concrete by writing good-bye letters and visiting graves.

## From Acceptance to Recovery

Eventually, the addict is ready to focus on the here and now, and prepare to move on with his life. He can look at the subtler ways he loses and abandons himself, and start to tighten up contracts he has made and boundaries he has set. His emphasis turns to the present moment, the present reality, his current relationships. He makes amends and leaves therapy.

Clients often stay in therapy too long. It's important to get out and take risks, one of which might be leaving therapy too soon. It's good to take that risk, and return to therapy if necessary.

## MOVING ON

What does a recovering person look like? How does he behave in order to keep on recovering? First of all, he sees himself engaged in a process (recover*ing*) which he can handle "good enough," rather than as one who has finished a task (recover*ed*).

My clients work hard to get in touch with their childhood victimization feelings. Instead of abandoning themselves, these recovering addicts stay with their feelings and follow them back as far as they go—whether that be the present moment or a painful childhood scene from long ago. That work doesn't end when their therapy ends. Staying healthy means using the 80/20 rule whenever the need arises, and that requires continuing access to childhood emotions.

But recovering addicts get beyond spending most of their energy doing this emotional processing. They learn to enjoy the sun's warmth and the light of love in another's eye. Perhaps they'll spend an hour a week remembering and taking an emotional inventory, but mostly they find excitement and joy in other aspects of their lives. Recovering addicts no longer see themselves as diseased, but feel some acceptance of themselves as they are, and tend to regard their histories of abuse, shame, and addiction as things that normal people may experience.

## NOTE

1. A sexual addict is defined here as a person who *compulsively* masturbates, has affairs, uses pornography, patronizes prostitutes, thinks and fantasizes about sex, exposes himself in public, etc. The repetitive and compulsive nature of these practices causes these people to feel intense shame and other emotional dis-

tress, and significantly harms their relationships, work, finances, and enjoyment of life. Most of these addicts are *not* sexual offenders or criminals, who rape, molest children, or commit similar offenses.

## ANNOTATED GENERAL BIBLIOGRAPHY

For therapists and other professionals. These books were the most influential in developing my therapeutic practice.

Bandler, Richard, and Grinder, John. (1979). *Frogs into princes*. Moab, UT: Real People Press.

Bandler, Richard, and Grinder, John. (1981). *Reframing: Neuro-Linguistic programming and the Transformation of Meaning*. Moab, UT: Real People Press. *Two books on effective and pragmatic technique, based upon trust of the body and its primary role in communication.*

Carnes, Patrick. (1988). *Contrary to love*. Minneapolis: CompCare Publications. *For professionals who treat sexual addiction.*

Ferguson, Marilyn. (1987). *The aquarian conspiracy*. Los Angeles: Tarcher. *A detailed discussion of the cultural transformation which we call recovery.*

Fossum, Merle A., and Mason, Marilyn J. (1986). *Facing shame: Families in recovery*. New York : Norton. *Understanding shame and its relationship to addiction.*

Grinder, John, and Bandler, Richard. (1981). *Trance formation: Neuro-linguistic programming and the structure of hypnosis*. Moab, UT: Real People Press. *The genius of Milton Erickson needs interpretation before ordinary folks can understand and use it.*

Hackbarth, Judy, and Lindall, George. (1989). *Against the tide: Why addicts aren't recovering in today's world. Unpublished manuscript, available from author.*

Haley, Jay. (1993). *Uncommon therapy*, 3rd ed. New York: Norton. *Introduction to the non-rational techniques of Milton Erickson.*

Schaef, Anne W. (1985). *Women's reality*. San Francisco: Harper. *Affirms clients' experience of never fitting in.*

Schaef, Anne W. (1988). *When society becomes an addict*. San Francisco: Harper. *Addiction is embedded in the culture, not just in the individual or the family.*

Yalom, Irvin. (1980). *Existential psychotherapy*. New York: Basic Books. *Everything you ever wanted to know about right-hemisphere psychotherapy.*

# 12

## Grandiosity: The Shadow of Shame

*David L. Lindgren*

> . . . if we now consider the fact that, as a result of psychic compensation, great humility stands very close to pride, and that "pride goeth before a fall," we can easily discover behind the haughtiness certain traits of an anxious sense of inferiority. In fact, we shall see clearly how his uncertainty forces the enthusiast to puff up his truths, of which he feels none too sure, and to win proselytes to his side in order that his followers may prove to himself the value and trustworthiness of his own convictions.
>
> —Jung, 1928, para. 225

## THE FALL

For the past 6 years, as director of a men's organization, I have facilitated hundreds of men who have attended our initiation trainings. The major focus of these trainings is to empower men to take responsibility for their lives. We emphasize in this work that a man examine the *shadow* side of his psyche. The challenge is in confronting the shadow and the natural resistance to revealing these deeper underlying feelings that men so frequently bury.

The strategy of our trainings is to confront the various de-

**201**

fenses men construct to avoid the shame of revealing to a group of men that they have indeed "fallen"—fallen into a pit of self-doubt and uncertainty. Becoming a man of real emotions and integrity tends to make superfluous the wrappings and armor[1] that we men have acquired. The urgency and necessity to expose our real selves is at once the most terrifying and the most exhilarating experience.

This circumstance appears universal, in that every man has taken a "fall." At some point in childhood, every little boy has a "fall from grace" and chooses to let go of his uniqueness—decides to become something other than who he is intended to be. A series of ego-splitting experiences occurs. The child "decides,"[2] at this point, that he cannot please his primary caretakers with a certain set of behaviors. He adapts by betraying his ego in order to receive the reinforcement he needs to proceed to the next step in his development.

There are necessary but painful losses at each step in the process. Manifestations of the "fall" may appear in different forms. Each child selects strategies to protect himself from further harm. Later in life, these strategies become armor that prevents him from developing in a healthy way. During an initiation training, the internal experiencing of this process is accelerated in time (Greenwald, 1995). Initiatory experiences heighten the drama of a man's life and expose it to intensive mirroring. Shame has little chance to escape exposure.


## CONFRONTING SHAME


Shame is a common feeling expressed by men who have reflected honestly on their lives. When men can acknowledge their shame, we repeatedly hear the phrase: "I am afraid of making a mistake . . . of not being good enough." An extreme but stereotypical pattern is that of a man who is frozen in a shame-bound state.

Many men are aware of the importance of shame (Bradshaw, 1988), and the desirability of examining the "little boy" inside. Some men appear to be the type of man who is "life-sustaining" and not "life-giving" (Bly, 1990). Instead of being generative and supporting of others, they themselves need nurturing. These men typically had mothers who were more dominant than their fathers, who are described as being weak or absent.

These men are waiting to project their father-need on the leaders, who are idealized for having personal qualities which they aspire to. Leaders are not always aware of this hunger and the propensity to project "father hunger" onto them. The holding of this idealizing projection by the leader is essential to the process in initiation. Leaders need to reflect this father hunger back to the man and then stimulate the idealization into healthy grandiosity.

While their life stories may range from the horrific to the pathetic, some of these men appear to have made a decision to stay in a position of shame. They reason that the world expects too much of them, and they are convinced that their resources are too limited. In effect, they seem to choose shame over examining the myriad other possibilities available to them.

The frequency of men holding their shame-bound position seems to be on the rise. By "holding," I mean that given a choice to express deeper emotions, a man will stay with shame as the emotion of choice. In his shame-bound state, he resists standing up as a man and "holds on" to a posture of being a scared little boy.

Most of these men did not take the rebellious route as children. They adopted strategies to please "dear old Mom."[3] These men have learned to sell out to the needs of women in a heartbeat (Bly, 1990). With the absence of masculine spiritual energy in their lives, they lose the will to resist. None of us is immune to this temptation. Given the possibility that Mom might leave us, most of us would do virtually anything to "hold on" to her love.

Such men hold their shame in their bodies. For example, we confront men with sloped shoulders and distended bellies with the necessity of standing up and grounding themselves. To enlist a man's pride or his inner beauty requires an assault on the enemy which is shame.

When these men drop their disguise of shame, they reveal the absence of father energy in their lives. They are ashamed that they were not "good enough" to be loved and respected by their father. Ultimately, what is revealed is hunger for the masculine spirit.

## MODEL OF GRANDIOSITY AND SHAME

Moore and Gillette (1990) describe the bipolar nature of the shadow of the major male archetypes. In their model, the particular energy of the archetype is split in the shadow realm. The more active, extroverted side of the split chooses a more exhibitionist, grandiose path. The more passive, introverted side involves more shame and fear of exposure. Together they form two poles—like two ends of a teeter-totter. If you push down one pole of the shadow, up pops the opposite energy. *Shame and grandiosity are opposite ends of the same continuum of self development,* much like introversion and extroversion.

Moore and Gillette (1990) present a developmental scheme wherein each archetype has opportunities for expression. If these energies are blocked, the child "decides"[2] on a basic strategy to disguise the "gold" of these archetypes. This strategy unfortunately creates a diminishment of the self with a splitting process that reveals the self as both underadequate and overadequate. Parents and adults appear disproportionately larger than reality.

We have observed in this process that "pride" and "fall" exist side by side. Pride and grandiosity are always a shadow dynamic with men who present themselves as shameful.

If we start with the passive side of the split in a man's self-presentation, we find that he may be stuck in his shame, exhibiting some hopeless/helpless anxiety. He claims that his issue is shame. However, on confronting the shame with a question such as, "What is keeping you from your goal?" the hidden grandiosity is revealed.

The man typically resorts to defending and protecting his tactic of withholding from view the opposite side of the split. And the challenge reveals the split in its paradoxical form. Yes, "pride goeth before a fall," and we also know that "pride" will resurface upon challenging a man's defenses. The direction of his process resembles more the "fall" preceding the "pride."

The active side is usually some manifestation of anger/rage or disappointment/grief. In either case, the basic energy of grandiosity is in play. When a man's shame is challenged, particularly the "holding" of the shame, he faces a choice (usually unconsciously). He can choose to recycle his shameful feelings, as he has for most of his life. Or if he accepts the challenge to be a warrior of his own heart, he can open himself to a profound transformation. He can stand tall, touch deep breathing and powerful sounds that resonate in his soul, defend his internal and external boundaries, and enjoy the forbidden fantasies he has previously suppressed with shame.

Having experienced his grandiosity in its fullness, a shame-bound man begins the transformative process to becoming an erect warrior. Men can then accept their ancestral heritage of waging battle against "evil," that is, against the admonitions that "I am bad/no good." This is the spiritual battle of authentic warriorship, which is "won" only by those willing to first risk feeling the grandiosity next to the shame. And those who "win" must first risk being seen as something other than how they presented themselves.

Self-psychology as presented by Kohut (1971, 1977) and more recently by Lee and Martins (1991) illustrates the developmental course of "infantile grandiosity" in children. By "grandiose self," Kohut (1971, p. 106) refers to "that aspect of a developmental phase in which the child attempts to save the originally all-embracing narcissism by concentrating perfection and power upon the self." Parents may react to this primitive bravery by shaming these initial excursions of the child away from the safety net of the family comfort zone.

Under favorable circumstances, the child is able to acquire, through various maturational stages, the capacity to recognize and accept his limitations in a realistic manner. The grandiose fantasies can be consolidated as ambitions through empathic mirroring principally from mother and father.

However, if the ego gets too attached to the deep self-structures within the unconscious (the archetypes), "inflation" of the ego occurs. Inflated, we have the potential to kiss the humility of the self good-bye. Manic-depressive psychosis awaits the "winner" of the "where did my humility go?" award.

Conversely, Kohut points out that the greatest achievements of our civilization did not come from men shrinking from ambition by de-flating/de-pressing themselves into curious, shame-bound onlookers. A poorly modulated grandiose self is the risk for men encountering this aspect of their shadow (Kohut, 1977).

To paraphrase Moore and Gillette (1990), grandiosity is a temporary but false energy state that can be self-stimulated to compensate for feelings of inadequacy and shame. It is a risk inherent in any challenge or ambition for the future. Continued exertion of the self in a grandiose state will deplete the self.

From my personal and "analyzed" experience, I can recognize the fusion of shame/grandiosity when someone asks me what I am feeling. My internal reflection is something like, "Dah, I feel nothing . . . (next) I feel empty . . . (next) what is wrong with me?" I know at that point that I have been hanging out over the cliff of self-denial by defending my shame with grandiosity. Rather than tell my feelings of shame to a friend or my significant other, I have chosen to deplete myself through ambitious efforts that create a false energy state. I stimulate my active side of grandiosity for fear that I will be seen as inadequate.

## Passive Side

Gary W., who attended one of our trainings, was 36 years old and had decided to marry for the first time. He felt ashamed of the fact that he had never married. He presented himself as emotionally shut down with feelings of inadequacy and a sense of hopelessness. Making the decision to marry had caused him to be uncertain and paralyzed in making future decisions. His fiancée, Julie, had provoked his uncertainty by hedging on her commitments— saying "maybe" or "I will have to wait" or "just let me think about it." Gary was overwhelmed with anxiety that Julie would not marry him, fearing that he would be deeply ashamed for again not succeeding in a relationship.

Gary's parents had frequently kept him waiting and parceled out their love in a "maybe" manner. As he became aware of this pattern, Gary released great physical spasms of hopelessness. Falling into grief, he cried out questioning how he could ever get married to a woman who would "maybe" love him. Severe shaming from his "aristocratic" family seemed right around the proverbial corner. Then he discovered the desperate requirements he had for a "perfect" girl/woman as his bride. Julie would spoil his plans for a perfect marriage by not fitting in with his "aristocratic" family. He became infuriated with Julie. "How dare she spoil my perfect plan." As he held on to his rage, he sounded like a spoiled little boy.

The fusion of shame and grandiosity is apparent in Gary's case. The rambunctious little boy appeared occasionally, but mostly he had taken the passive, shameful route. His world was a "maybe," tempering and controlling his every move.

If his parents had given in and pandered to Gary's demands, his infantile grandiosity might have been stimulated. Then he would probably have moved to the active side of the split—demanding special recognition rather than repressing his needs.

Gary was able to break through and work out his relationship with Julie when he understood how his repressed sense of grandiosity could be activated in a healthy manner. He learned to take responsibility for fulfilling his needs rather than projecting them onto Julie. He began organizing his goals and ambitions around more realistic expectations without resorting to false modesty or being overwhelmed with temporary disappointment.

## Active Side

Bruce M. was a flamboyant entrepreneur who perpetually was either on the verge of making millions or filing for bankruptcy. I asked Bruce to colead a group with me because of his extraordinary skill in group facilitation and his ability to help others to experience a sense of awe and magic in their transformative process. As long as his perceived successes, were recognized and acknowledged, we had an acceptable working relationship. When his work was not acknowledged, Bruce would pout and dramatically ask for praise, or set up scenarios whereby he would make a dramatic, all-encompassing intervention to draw attention to himself.

"I can't handle any criticism right now" was his standard answer to critical comments, challenges of his emotional outbursts, or requests to be on time for the group. There never was a time to review our work, because he would always have the same answer. In effect, he was protecting his shame with grandiosity.

Bruce could speak the word "shame" only while grimacing and grinding his teeth. He found it difficult to accept my criticism because he seemed to project me as his "good father." During his childhood, Bruce's father had let Bruce know that his performance was not good enough and that he had to be ultraspecial to earn his father's love.

When this pattern was pointed out to Bruce, he finally made the connection between his fear of being a failure in life and not being loved by his parents. He collapsed into deep shame, sadly requesting that he just needed a little attention. "Is this so much to ask?" As Gary could not handle grandiosity, Bruce was immobilized by shame.

As we explored his sense of shame, Bruce's grandiosity and the resultant rage became tempered. It became possible to be more ordinary in a way that others could see his humility and sense of caring. Bruce began to receive feedback from others that he was open and available to be loved. Experiencing shame unlocked the door leading away from debilitating and dysfunctional grandiosity.

The transformations of Gary and Bruce illustrate how using the opposite poles of shame and grandiosity can bring balance and wholeness to the healing process. The way out of shame leads through the passageway of grandiosity. Integrity of the self depends on resolving this tension of opposites.

## SOCIAL IMPLICATIONS

Shame can be seen as an introverted feeling and a defense to protect oneself from becoming inflated. Introverts typically prefer defenses that focus on the past rather than projecting into the future and considering ambitions to be pursued.

Present theoretical positions overemphasize the passive receptiveness of shame. Individuals tend to see themselves as passive victims of abuse, humiliation, and neglect. They resist exploring the grandiose side which lurks in their shadow. When men are confronted with their holding on to shame as a defense, their "repressed" grandiosity is awakened. The process of rebuilding a unified self (individuation) can then be enhanced by owning one's defenses and strategies to protect the shadow.

Grandiosity conversely appears to be an extroverted feeling and a defense to protect one from feeling humiliated or ashamed. Extroverts avoid introspection about their past by projecting externally and into the future. Men who exhibit grandiosity run into the same wall of self-denial as shame-bound men. Grandiose men seek external answers to internal dilemmas. This kind of man runs as fast as he can to avoid feeling the depth of despair that is required for him to embrace his shadow of shame and become a whole man.

Why is shame such a predominant emotional reaction? Why are we so indulgent with shame-bound men? Why are we so inhibited in pressing forward and risking internal inflation?

When we are individuating and moving forward, we have a sense of anxiety about how our life will unfold or our world will change. We seem to be living in a shame-based culture that restricts us from projecting into the future. Perhaps we cling to our shame because otherwise our world projections would be out of control. There is a part of us that does not want to identify with outrageousness in the world—with violence, pollution of our environment, or warring between genders, races, and nations.

We are reminded constantly of the shamefulness of our world. Public media have picked up the shaming where religion left off. Our hyperinflated commercial, materialistic world exploits our shame by bombarding our senses with messages to suggest that we are not good enough unless we purchase and consume a certain product or experience some romantic vacation. In the extreme sense, we need shame as a defense mechanism to avoid the fear of a world out of control, that is, personal inflation, ultimate disappointment, and identification with the enemy.

In our shame-based culture, we are especially ashamed of our grandiosity. As children we were punished for wanting too much, so that grandiosity never served us well. I have yet to meet a shame-bound person without an accompanying grandiose shadow. However, admitting how special and important one is can also activate shame.

Social critics of psychotherapy and of "introverted" men's work (Hillman, 1989) are wary of the possibilities of creating an improved social order with "little boys needing permission rather then taking the initiative to act." Psychotherapy in its classical style is a passive encounter that often requires long-term "sitting" on the horns of a personal dilemma before action is taken in the world. While Rome is burning, we therapists are usually fiddling with a one-sided approach that denies the "active pole" of decision making and purposive behavior.

In one way or another, we are all in a stage of recovery. We wouldn't feel alive if we weren't dealing with something. For some the battle against shame becomes a perpetual bout with an invisible shadow opponent. Shame gets recycled in a variety of guises. The struggle for recovery may become a "Sisyphus" drama, in which pushing the heavy stone to the hilltop is always followed by the fall. If only a man could glimpse how great he really is, grandiosity and shame would not be necessary.

Somehow an *ordinary* battlefield must exist where the ego and Self can reside without shame or grandiosity. Presently, these two coexist in "eternal boys" (von Franz, 1970) with their accompanying need to be special. Ordinariness is an antidote to this specialness. To be "good enough" requires finding an ordinary, down-to-earth reality testing, transcending our old ways and letting the specialness die.

## NOTES

1. Some refer to this armor as "ego." Although the ego eventually needs to be shed, at this point the ego in relationship to self is necessary to understand one's internal holding of opposites.

2. The word "decides" is used intentionally to challenge the passive mode of victimization. Certainly children *are* abused, but consciously or unconsciously they still choose their path or their poison, subsequent to being victimized.

3. I suspect that the frequency of rebellious, "hyperactive" boys has decreased. "Nice" boys have taken their place—boys who know how to please women by being "good."

# 13

## The Rescue Triangle: Shame Update

*John Everingham*

The Rescue triangle—also known as the Karpman (1968), or drama triangle—has been used for a quarter-century to untangle dysfunctional relationships and expose ulterior motives. The early authors practiced Transactional Analysis, with its emphasis on social psychology and interpersonal "transactions," and were mostly unaware of the modern understanding of shame. The continuing utility of the Rescue triangle may be enhanced by exploring some of the shame-based motives involved.

Three fundamental positions or roles dominate both literary drama and dysfunctional relationships. Figure 13.1 diagrams these basic positions and their synonyms.[1,2] The interaction of these roles in the triangle may be illustrated by a *type scenario*: an eager Boy Scout (EBS) takes a little old lady (LOL) in hand to help her across the street, unaware that she doesn't *want* to cross here. Halfway across, LOL thinks to herself, "He's such a nice young man. I won't tell him that my bus is coming." On the other side, her bus missed, LOL clouts EBS over the head with her umbrella. An essential feature of the drama triangle is that all the players shift positions: the EBS from Rescuer to Persecutor to Victim, and the LOL from Victim to Rescuer to Persecutor.

Note that the positions shift quickly, easily, almost automati-

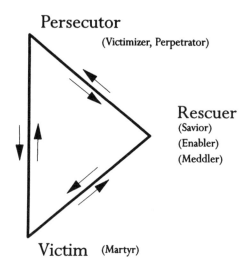

**Persecutor**
(Victimizer, Perpetrator)

**Rescuer**
(Savior)
(Enabler)
(Meddler)

**Victim**  (Martyr)

Signs of a Rescue

A. I'm doing something for you
   that you haven't **asked** me to do.
B. I'm doing something for you that
   you can do for yourself.
C. I'm putting more energy into
   **your** problem than you are.
D. I realize that I don't really **want** to
   do what I'm doing for you, and
   come to resent you.

**FIGURE 13.1**    Rescue triangle and signs of a rescue.

cally, and that each position feels uneasy and ungrounded. In real life, people enmeshed in the Rescue triangle tend to keep doing it over and over again. There's often a feeling of "Here we go again, round and round." If I continue to *Rescue*, I'll soon find myself playing *Victim* or *Persecutor*. Recognizing the triangle (or one of the roles: Victim, Rescuer, and Persecutor) often clarifies entangled relationships and makes me aware of ulterior motives, games, and disowned parts of myself (my Shadow).

Staying in the Rescue triangle reinforces codependency and internalized shame, and stepping out of it usually brings a great sense of relief (sometimes followed by a desire to grieve). But let's avoid blame and perfectionism about this. We all find ourselves in the triangle from time to time; the trick is to get out early and learn to play the drama (trauma) *lightly* (Berne, 1964, p. 64; James and Jongeward, 1971, p. 34).

**Why I Rescue (or Play Victim)    How I Can Stop Rescuing**

1. I'm not aware of doing it.

1. Read the signs, check out my feelings, and become aware. Then stop it.

2. I'm taking responsibility for *your* problem. (Gordon, 1974, pp. 38–42, 118–122).[3]

2. Let *you* own *your* problem.

3. Somebody (maybe you, society, my Critical Parent, or an unnamed fear) is telling me I *should* own *your* problem.

3. Let my Adult reject the *should*, or just consider the probable consequences. Then let go of owning *your* problem.

4. You are insisting, shaming, or seductively inviting me to Rescue you.

4. Make an I-statement (Gordon, 1974, pp. 125–155). Or simply stop whatever I'm doing "for" you. *Step out of the triangle!*

5. I'm afraid of hurting your feelings, or that you'll be lost without me, or that I'll be ashamed if you find out that I. . . .

5. Get in touch with *my* hurt, my pain, *my* shame, my fear of abandonment or rejection.

6. I want to build up credit with you, so that maybe you'll offer me something that I'm afraid—ashamed—to ask for directly, for my own sake.

6. Ask clearly for what I want. If you say "No," allow myself to feel hurt and ashamed for asking. Then ask someone else.

7. I'm involved in *your* problem because this allows me get "righteously" angry and contemptuous of those who are oppressing or abusing you.

7. Get angry at those who are oppressing or abusing *me* (or used to do so). Risk the shameful possibility that someone may think that I'm being selfish.

8. I'm focusing on *your* problem to avoid facing *my* shame.

8. Face the true source of my discomfort and dysfunction (Kaufman, 1989).

9. The Victim in me responds to the victim in you. I'm

9. Feel my own pain and shame, and let you experi-

trying to ease my pain by easing yours.[4]

ence yours. Let go of Victim.

10. I was a true victim as a child, and identify deeply with another's pain and shame.

10. This is a gateway to healing. I need to cross the threshold into my own shame and pain, rather than continuing to creep up to it, and then veering off into the triangle again.

11. I seek the moral comfort of the Victim position, which provides justification for me to play the Persecutor role "righteously."

11. Befriend my anger, jealousy, contempt, and self-righteousness. Acknowledge my Shadow (Bly, 1988).

## NOTES

1. James and Jongeward (1971, p. 86) explain the convention of capitalizing the *manipulative* roles that constitute the triangle. They also describe *true* (non-manipulative, legitimate, lowercase) victims, rescuers, and persecutors, who usually *stay out* of the triangle. I was a true rescuer when I entered Lake Michigan to aid an exhausted swimmer and asked if he wanted help as I approached him.

2. The triangle may be entered from any of the three positions. Referring to it as the Rescue triangle seems to have arisen as many therapists and clients became aware how the unbalanced ideal of "helping" led them to enter the triangle primarily from the Rescuer position. In recent years, entering the triangle from the Victim position has become more socially acceptable and even almost expected for one to be considered politically correct. Only time will tell if we shall one day refer to the Victim triangle, but the basic pattern of interaction remains unaltered.

3. It sometimes happens that both of us legitimately "own" a part of the same problem, and some meditation and discussion is required to clarify each person's piece.

4. Thanks to David Lindgren for this insight.

# 14

## Forgiving the Unforgivable: Overcoming Abusive Parents*

*John Giles*

> Silence is my shield. It crushes.
> Silence is my cloak. It smothers.
> Silence is my sword. It cuts both ways.
> Silence is the deadliest weapon.
>
> What legacy is to be found in silence?
> How many lives lost?
> So seductive its grip . . . this silence.
>
> Break it! Our silence!
> Loosen the tongue.
> Testify.
> Let's end the silence together, baby.
> Together.
> Now.
>
> —Marlon Riggs, *Tongues Untied*

I love holidays. For most of my adult life, I have loved the parades, the Sousa marches, and the fireworks on the Fourth of July.

*Based on a sermon given August 18, 1991, at the Unitarian Church of Evanston, IL, where the author is Lay Minister of Music.

But on June 30, 1986, the Supreme Court ruled in *Bowers v. Hardwick* that the U.S. Constitution afforded gay men and lesbians no legal rights to sexual privacy, and that state governments could do anything they wished with us.

Four days later, waiting for the fireworks to begin in Chicago's Grant Park, I felt completely alone, although I was surrounded by 600,000 people. When Mayor Harold Washington stepped to the platform, I had a surge of hope: Surely this liberal mayor, a man whose political career was built on championing the downtrodden, would condemn the Court for its bigotry.

Yes, he gave a speech praising the Fourth of July as a holiday all Americans could embrace: blacks, Hispanics, Poles, the handicapped, feminists, Croatians, and a hundred other constituencies were named. Yet he never mentioned the gay and lesbian people who had provided his razor-thin electoral majority. The mayor's silence spoke volumes to me. And suddenly the flag, the marches, the patriotism all seemed shallow, and I wept.

I did not realize at the time that this situation uncannily mirrored my childhood: injustice surrounded by silence. Big, strong people hurt little, weak ones. And all the while, others stood silently by, silently doing nothing to intervene.

## A RITUAL OF FORGIVENESS

In 1991, I spent my Fourth of July in a very different way. I celebrated the holiday by declaring my own independence from my abusive mother. At my mother's grave in southern Illinois, I enacted a ceremony of forgiveness culminating four years of recovery from physical and sexual abuse. No flowers or other signs of special care marked the grave, and I realized that I was probably the first person to visit since her funeral 22 years before.

The ceremony began. I read passages from her letters and other documents, all the while interjecting my own comments, expressing feelings I wanted to voice as a child but had been too afraid to utter. I shouted, whimpered, and showered sarcasm. Sentence by sentence, phrase by phrase, I exposed my mother for the fraud she was. And the whole time, I took notes for my declaration of independence and my own bill of indictment. After 45 minutes, I read my bill of particulars aloud, adding the phrase, "I forgive you" to each sentence:

For tying me up to a chair, binding my legs so tightly that they went numb . . . I forgive you.

For leaving me in the chair, for hours at a time, time after time . . . I forgive you.

For partially undressing while I was tied up in the chair and saying that I wasn't "man enough" for you . . . I forgive you.

For forcing me to help put on your undergarments, and for slapping me if I accidentally touched you while doing so . . . I forgive you.

For ruining the only birthday party I ever had by getting drunk . . . I forgive you.

For embarrassing me in front of the neighbors so many times that I was ashamed to have friends to our house . . . I forgive you.

For encouraging and forcing me to watch you while you used the bathroom or took a bath, and for never giving me any privacy, in the bathroom or elsewhere . . . I forgive you.

For turning me into your substitute husband, and for perceiving me and treating me as a sexual object . . . I forgive you.

For teaching me that sex is dirty, yet fun; for never holding me or hugging me, I forgive you. . . .

After this reading, I placed my indictment on the grave and burned it. As the flames died away, I sang my own setting of Psalm 32, a psalm of forgiveness and the transcendence of shame. I had composed the music for just this occasion. At last we departed, and I left behind much more than the ashes of my indictment.

## CHILD ABUSE

I am a human being who endured a childhood of repeated, serious abuse at the hands of my parents and older sister. I used to be an abuse victim; then I became an abuse survivor. Now I am walking the slow path of forgiveness to overcome my past. I spent several years in therapy. I have read almost every book in print on adult children of alcoholics, process addictions, child abuse, male rape, and incest. I still attend meetings of Adult Children of Alcoholics, Incest Survivors Anonymous, and Sex Compulsives Anonymous. And I live a program of recovery designed to help me become a fully healthy, completely functional, joyfully serene man. This state of being is my birthright. But for a long time, the actions of my family denied it to me.

People have asked me why I bother with this now. I was abused a long time ago. Decades have passed since I left my small home town in southern Illinois. I've achieved many successes; I have many friends and a new life. Why revisit so painful a past?

## DANGERS OF REMAINING A VICTIM

Here is my reason: the past has consequences. If you are raised by toxic parents, you may well become a toxic adult. Simply stated, untreated abused children will become either victims, victimizers, or rescuers when they grow up. All of these options have serious consequences (Everingham, 1995c).

I did not become a victimizer, although many who are abused as children do abuse their own children. I *did* occasionally flirt with rescuing others, but would abandon them when my rescuing efforts became too difficult, as I played out a process that only now do I understand. Instead, I became a victim.

I chose to be a victim by overeating, and then by losing weight inappropriately. I married a woman even though I was gay, and then gave her everything in the divorce settlement. I chose to be a victim by pursuing a PhD in a field where there were few prospects for employment when I graduated. But my self-victimization became most toxic when I passionately embraced the seductive gay-liberation beliefs that sexual license equals sexual freedom, and that promiscuity could overcome homophobia. I became sexually compulsive, just as my mother had been.

Unfortunately, I engaged in sexual activities that were not only unwise, but with the advent of AIDS, proved unsafe. I found myself in a doctor's office on December 17, 1987, faced with a diagnosis of chronic hepatitis and advanced HIV infection. My doctor gave me a life expectancy of 6 months to 2 years. Pursuing victimhood had proved the most toxic choice of all.

## THE MOST DIFFICULT CHOICE: TO FORGIVE

At this point, what were my choices? Rescuing others? Victimizing others? I had reached bottom: I had no resources to rescue someone else. I didn't have the physical energy to abuse another, even if I had wanted to. The answer had to be outside my previous experience; so I cast my eye upon the water.

And what did I see? I saw that men with "advanced HIV infection" who confronted and resolved childhood issues lived longer and coped better. I saw that even if they died, they died in the arms of a lover or surrounded by friends and family. Those who did not face the past died quickly, died hard, and died alone. Facing the past became a matter of survival: I did not want to die from AIDS.

Thus I began walking the path to health. Had I known what dangers and difficulties lay before me, I might never have begun the journey. But after following the road less traveled for 4 years, I finally reached a safe place where I could truly forgive my parents.

## Forgiveness Is Not Forgetting

I'll say it again: Forgiveness is *not* forgetting. Shame leads to denial, denial leads to forgetting, and forgetting breeds silence. Abuse thrives in an environment of denial, shame, and silence.

It's difficult to believe that when I began the healing process, I did not remember any of the abuse described. I had painted a rosy picture of my childhood: My parents were eccentric but championed rational education in the midst of their conservative fundamentalist community. They bought me a piano and encouraged me to become a musician. They supported liberal causes. I *liked* these pretend parents.

It had been too easy for me to forget a family vacation in Montana when my parents came back to the motel dead drunk and vomited all over the beds. It was so easy to forget my sister, too young for a driver's license, driving us home from St. Louis because both Mom and Dad were too drunk to drive. I didn't realize that I had lost all memory of first and second grades, when the incest and abuse was worst. As these painful memories surfaced, at first I denied that my mother had actually tied me to a chair for hours at a time, so that she could drink the day away.

As the memories resurfaced, I was grateful for my training in graduate school, where we learned how to gather documentation, even from unwilling sources, and to search out the truth behind the facade by taking a hard look at the data. As my sister and I looked through parents' and grandparents' letters, photos, diaries, and newspaper clippings, the truth gradually emerged. My family, on both sides, was toxic. Compared with other abuse victims, I was unusually fortunate. We found notes written by my mother as she lay dying. Safely hidden in a false-bottomed drawer, where my father would never find and destroy them, they were her death-bed confession—the "smoking gun" that most incest survivors never find. I will let my mother's words speak for themselves:

> When my children ran away from home, I would tie their feet, sit them on a chair, and make them stay there for a few hours. After that punishment they didn't think running away was worth it.

> The last time my son noticed my sexual charisma was in New Orleans, when the taxi driver escorted us to the door of Brennen's. Both the taxi driver and my son knew they were in the presence of one voluptuous woman.

> I once told my son: be moral, be clean, be abstinent, but isn't sex fun and dirty?

> My son has always remembered me as smelling opulently, being well groomed, and wearing the newest, sexiest fashions. Men of 70 and boys of 17 both respond to me. Even my son admits that I enchant people, and by people I don't mean men, for that is basic. I have the charm and wit to entrap even women.

These words are etched on my heart. Never again will I worship my mother and father with pretense and denial. Only by remembering them as they really were, both their positives and negatives, can I honor them. Only by honoring them in truth, not forgetting the abuse, can I ensure "my days will be long in the land which God has given me." (Exod. 20:12)

## Forgiveness Is *Not* Condoning

In her award-winning book, *For Your Own Good: Hidden Cruelty in Child Rearing and the Roots of Violence,* Alice Miller has demonstrated that our society will accept almost any argument, no matter how transparent, to condone child abuse and incest. The aphorisms, "Father knows best," "What goes on in my house is none of your business," and "Shut up or I'll really give you something to cry about" are only a few of the phrases we use to discount the needs of children. Even worse is the biblical injunction, "He who spares the rod hates his son." I constantly heard the corollary "spare the rod and spoil the child" as I grew up. And I silently watched as aunts, uncles, teachers, ministers, neighbors and policemen committed acts of violence against me and other children, all in the name of discipline.

At the same time, not everyone who quotes the Bible uses it to justify cruelty. The babysitter who confronted my mother about her behavior and helped end the most obvious forms of abuse was a devout member of the same fundamentalist church that preached, "Honor your father and your mother."

Calling violence against children "discipline" makes no more sense to me than pretending rape is "sex education." When my mother tied me to that ugly white chair, she would say "I'm doing this for your own good, so you can learn to come right away when Mommy calls." As she forced me to watch her disrobe, she said, "I'm doing this so you can learn what a woman's body looks like." Abuse done in the name of discipline or sex education is neither. Abuse is abuse and cannot be condoned.

Another insidious form of discounting abuse occurs in the name of feminism. Some militant feminists will quickly believe that fathers sexually abuse their daughters, but admit only reluctantly that some mothers abuse their sons. One woman called me a liar point blank—my memories of my mother were "patriarchal fantasies" and the "smoking gun" in her deathbed confession was either a dying woman's delusions or my own forgery.

Feminists sometimes forget that even when a woman counts for nothing in society, that same society invests her with unlimited power over her small child. The powerlessness that all too many women experience—which is correctly addressed by feminists—often sets the stage for child abuse. A woman who feels trapped, a woman whose husband offers no support, a woman who feels older than her years may act out her rage and frustration by abusing the only person weaker than she is: her child.

My own mother grew up in university communities and had lived in large cities as a young adult. Her mother was a teacher, and together they enjoyed the amenities and artistic activities that cities and university towns provide. When my father returned from World War II, he decided to take the "little lady" to his home town in the Bible Belt, so that he could work in his father's factory. My mother hated that small town almost as much as she hated my father for making so important a decision without consulting her. And she took out her rage on my sister and me. Abuse performed in the name of a woman's rage, however justified, is not feminism. Abuse is abuse and cannot be condoned.

## Forgiveness Heals Lingering Effects

The effects of abuse cannot survive once the abuse has been forgiven. One would think that my abuse must have ceased more than two decades ago, when my mother died. But the effects of abuse often linger for years after the perpetrator has died.

Touch was not allowed in my family. My parents did not sleep in the same bedroom. They did not hold hands, sit together on the couch while they watched television, hug or kiss hello or good-bye. They ridiculed couples who did touch, hug, or kiss. After I was 4 years old, my parents did not cuddle me, hold me when I skinned my knee, or comfort me when I was stung by a bee. After all, "big boys don't cry." My sister and I never dreamed of hugging. My grandmother lived next door, but saw her grandchildren only on holidays and never allowed us to touch her, lest we muss her hairdo or wrinkle her dress.

The only times I was touched as a child were when my mother tied me up or erotically touched me, when my older sister beat me, or when my father "tickled" me even after I begged him to stop. Is it any wonder that I learned to associate touch only with sexual arousal or physical abuse? No wonder I used to say, "Don't touch me unless you mean business," meaning "have sex with me."

At age 38, I learned about touch—friendly, comforting, therapeutic, playful, and sensual touch—from a book! Today I say, "Never turn down a hug from somebody you trust." Forgiveness has opened me to new and healthier ways to live. I no longer allow my mother's abusive behavior to control me.

## Forgiveness is Saying "No" to Continued Abuse

Learning to stop my father's abusive behavior is more difficult because he is still alive. He can no longer abuse me physically, but his abuse has gone underground and can still affect me if I let it.

Stopping my father's abuse means setting new boundaries between us. I no longer accept his monetary gifts at Christmas. Money may be the only way he can show love, but important as it is, money does not equal love. If he insists on sending me cash, I donate it to the AIDS Alternative Health Project. I am repaying his loans, money I used to support my addictive behavior. I no longer allow my father to play "let's show John how stupid he is" by asking me trivia questions I cannot possibly answer. No longer do I follow his practice of discounting the opinions of others by correcting their grammar. Forgiving my father has meant learning new behavior. I will not allow his abuse to live on in me.

## FINDING A PROCESS THAT WORKS

When the memories of my childhood abuse and incest first surfaced, the last thing on my mind was forgiveness. When I heard phrases like "learn to open yourself to love and forgiveness," I could only tremble with rage. I vowed that I would never forgive them for what they did. It took a long time for me to see that forgiveness is not a gift I owe my parents, but a gift long overdue to me.

In time my rational side surfaced and asked, "What are my options besides forgiveness?" I could see only two: seeking revenge or holding a grudge. Revenge . . . the word sounded so sweet. But how could I exact revenge on my mother and sister? Dig up their graves and smash their bones? And my father? No matter how hard I tried, I could not conceive of a retribution I could wreak on my father—physical, emotional, financial, or legal—that would not hurt me as much as it hurt him. I learned there are reasons why St. Paul wrote, "Vengeance is mine; I will repay, says the Lord" (Rom. 12:19).

Holding a grudge looked even less attractive. Even as I raged, I could see how addicted to anger my sister had become. I saw how anger ate away at her until she died of breast cancer at age 47. I noticed how many people in my 12-step groups simply traded one addiction for another as long as they did not face their anger and release their grudges. I saw person after person with AIDS die while nursing grudges and harboring hatred. So I was left with only one option: forgiveness.

I came to realize that revenge and grudge holding only strengthen the twisted bond which joins both perpetrator and victim like ill-formed Siamese twins. My reading taught me that only a process carefully crafted to face anger and fear (without being possessed by them) can break this bond between perpetrator and victim.

## LIVING THE PROCESS—STEP BY STEP

My first step was education. I learned that any sexual behavior between an adult and a child constitutes incest. I had to learn that just because my abuse wasn't as bad as someone else's, it was still abuse. I learned that emotional incest is as real and harmful as physical incest. I had to learn my own history, my true history.

And I learned that neither the abuse nor the incest made me gay. Although they shaped the kind of gay man I became—undoubtedly encouraged my sexual compulsion—I was gay long before the abuse started. Incest tends to confuse children on *all* sexual issues, not only sexual orientation. I finally understood why I did not discover my gay identity until I was age 29 and had been married to a woman for several years. Abuse got in the way of discovering my true sexual identity.

The second step was finding my anger. Finding it was easy enough; the trick was not letting myself take out my wrath on friends, colleagues, or lover. What worked for me was to come to church long before others arrived and descend to a basement room, where I would pound at pillows and bang a wiffle bat on the floor. At first, I could only scream. Eventually I could shout, "I hate you Mommy" or "I'm scared of you Daddy." When my words changed to "I hate it when you . . ." or "I'm scared when you . . . ," I knew I was beginning to heal. One day, after a particularly draining anger session, I became too exhausted to continue. With tears in my eyes, I plopped to the floor and thought, "I guess I'm too tuckered out to be mad anymore." I was ready to move on to the next stage of healing.

The third step was finding my sorrow. This was harder, because I couldn't summon my grief as easily as I could raise my rage. Tears came to me at the most unexpected times, and I had to learn to accept my sadness whenever it appeared. I was in a restaurant reading *Don't Hurt Lauriel* (a young adult novel by Willo Davis Roberts). Even though Lauriel's story has many differences from mine, the feelings were the same, and I was transported emotionally back to my childhood. I burst unto tears and fled to the bathroom, where I had a good 10-minute cry. Today, I let myself grieve for my lost childhood, even when it's inconvenient.

The fourth step was designing my own rituals for forgiveness. With my sister, forgiveness consisted of holding hands and forgiving each other for all past wrongs as she lay dying. For my mother, it meant the ceremony at her grave. With my father, it required several letters in which I simultaneously set new boundaries and made amends in accordance with my 12-step programs.

Along the way, I had the help of many people—in my meetings, at my church, among my circle of friends—who showed their care for me in so many ways. I also had the help of a Higher Power, whose total love and forgiveness remain beyond my comprehension.

The final step is absorbing the lessons of the past and moving on. Now I believe the old maxim: "The best revenge is living well!" My great-grandfather abused his son, who abused his daughter, who abused me. I cannot change the past, but I can learn from it. The chain of abuse that once looked endless will end with me. I will neither forget the abuse, nor condone it, nor perpetuate it. I am ready to live.

I believe this is what Jesus meant when he said, "No one who puts the hand to the plow and looks back is ready to enter the Kingdom of God" (Luke 9:62). I have put my hand to the plow of life, and am ready to sow the seeds of serenity. To paraphrase 12-step literature, I stand ready to carry this message to others and practice the principle [of forgiveness] in all my affairs. I have learned to love life more than I loved my biological mother; I no longer confuse my earthly father with a god-of-my-misunderstanding.

And when all else fails, I remember one of my own rules of life: "Everybody does the best they can with what they've got, but sometimes what they've got is *toxic*." The first half of this little saying helps me forgive; the second half reminds me to set appropriate boundaries.

## FRUITS OF RECOVERY

And the payoff for all this work? When my mother used to tie me up, she bound my feet and legs extra tight, so I could not run away. Perhaps she had abandonment issues, but all she accomplished was to make me ashamed of my legs and feet. Once I understood this relationship and worked through my feelings about it, I could comfortably wear sandals and shorts for the first time in my life. I no longer have the debilitating foot cramps that awakened me at least once every night.

But the clearest sign of healing came on the Fifth of July, the day after the graveside ceremony. I went swimming for the first time in 9 years, and after I had paddled around a bit, I suddenly realized that I was kicking my feet! How many lifeguards have tried to teach me to kick? A swimming coach in high school exclaimed, "Giles, do you have invisible chains on your legs?" Neither of us realized how close he came to the truth. I have finally broken my invisible chains.

Next Fourth of July I plan to join the rest of America: enjoy the fireworks, wave the flag (although I may wave the rainbow coalition flag of gay liberation), and listen with gusto to the marches of John Philip Sousa. I will remember that on Independence Day I found the courage to forgive my mother. And the truth of that forgiveness set my feet free, set my legs free, and set free both the scared little boy within and the brave, authentic adult gay man I am today.

If you have been wronged, I invite you to work a miracle.
    A very special miracle: forgiveness.

We perform it alone. Others can help us, but when we finally do it, we perform the miracle in the private places of our inner lives.

We do it silently. No one can record our miracle on tape.

We do it invisibly. No one can record our miracle on film.

We do it freely. No one can ever pressure or trick us into forgiving someone.

It is *outrageous*: When we do it, we commit an outrage against a strict morality that will not be satisfied with anything short of an even score.

It is *creative*: When we forgive, we come as close as any human being can to the essentially divine act of creation. For we create a new beginning out of old pain that never had the right to exist in the first place. We create healing in the future by changing a past that allowed no possibilities but sickness and death.

When we forgive we ride the crest of love's cosmic wave; we walk in stride with God.

And we heal the hurt we never deserved. Amen. Shalom.

# 15

## Inadvertent Shaming: Family Rules and Shaming Habits

*John Everingham*

Sometimes things go sour in men's organizations and support groups, or between individual men. We're floundering and feeling edgy about each other. It's especially difficult to bear because we share such strong bonds of brotherhood, affection, and respect. Maybe we're shaming each other without realizing it. This chapter explores where this unintended shaming comes from, and how to stop it.

Most of us have a shaming habit. As boys, we learned to obey certain unwritten family "rules." Today we understand how obeying these rules generates internalized shame, and keeps it going from generation to generation. To kick the shaming habit, we consciously *break the rules*!

Two recent books, Fossum and Mason (1986) and Bradshaw (1988), list nine of these rules and discuss their power to maintain family shame and dysfunction. Here we combine these lists, and add another rule, Moral Intimidation.

We can't break invisible rules. So for starters, we "call 'em out," like gunfighters in the mythical Old West. Here come 10 bad shaming rules, called out of the dimness of the saloon—into the street at high noon. Maybe you recognize some of these desperadoes.

**228**

## SHAMING RULES[1]

1. *Control.* Be in control of all behavior, interactions, and feelings. Control is basic to these rules.
2. *Blame.* If something goes wrong, blame somebody, even yourself. Don't blame the shame-generating system, or these rules.
3. *Perfectionism.* Always be, do, and feel "right." Don't try if you might make a mistake. Justify everything.
4. *Incompleteness.* Don't resolve disagreements or complete transactions. Keep feuds and resentments going. Don't confront.
5. *Denial.* Deny feelings, needs, and desires—your own and others', especially "inappropriate" ones. Deny—even the obvious.
6. *No Talk.* Hide secrets with a strict code of silence, among ourselves and others. Hold your breath, look away, and shut up.
7. *Disqualification.* Deny by disguising. Spin the shameful episode around; call it something else; distort it. Look away from the shameful part and focus attention on the positive or truthful part.
8. *Unreliability.* Don't be reliable or trustworthy, or act in a predictable way. Keep 'em guessing. Expect the same from others.
9. *Not Allowing The Five Freedoms* (Satir, 1974). Don't let folks perceive, think and interpret, feel, desire, or imagine *in their own way.* Especially not children, clients, subordinates, or yourself.
10. *Moral Intimidation.* Assume the right to decide what—and, therefore, who—is right, appropriate, humane, enlightened, professional, mature, or politically correct. Enforce moral authority with shaming threats, rhetorical questions, subtle or overt name-calling.

These . . . rules for interaction would serve as effective guidelines for developing a dehumanizing, shame-bound regime in any human system, whether a nuclear family, a staff work group, a corporation, a medical school, or an elementary classroom. The interaction flowing from these rules insidiously nullifies or voids one's experience as a person. Relationships in the system . . . inhibit the growth of a self-accepting outlook. (Fossum & Mason, 1986, p. 87)

This eloquent passage summarizes the dysfunction that habitual shaming imposes on any human group. Disobeying the rules that maintain dysfunction may look simple, but it's not always easy to do. Let's first look at the general nature of these rules.

## Rules Written in Stone?

"Rules" is used ironically and metaphorically. These are not regulations enacted by some congress or king but rather habitual patterns of human interaction that have taken on the force of unwritten law. We act like they're written in stone, and accept them like the law of gravity. Much of their potency comes from rarely being questioned.

**Our response to shaming rules is entirely natural.** If I suddenly slapped you in the face, you'd naturally feel surprised, hurt, and angry. You'd react with voice and maybe fist. Nobody's surprised when a blow generates emotional consequences; it's equally predictable for a man to feel ashamed when he's been hit with a shaming rule.

But the natural consequences of shaming acts are usually ignored or made fun of (shamed). Books, movies, and television display and decry physical violence *ad nauseam*, but say very little about shaming. Anyone but a saint is allowed to feel angry if he's punched, but the ordinary man is expected to be "mature," and rise above shame when he's being controlled, left incomplete, or morally intimidated. To *expect* to feel ashamed when hit by a shaming act—this is a giant step toward liberation.

Shame is felt and expressed in silence, so it may be difficult to recognize at first. It takes practice to learn to feel primary shame for even a part of a second. Most of us move double-time to anger or internalized shame (frozen and dull-eyed, pretending to feel okay), and this gets us in a lot of trouble (violence, addiction, etc.). But when you see the rules being applied, the shame reaction is happening somewhere, even if masked. Spotting the rules in action—recognizing patterns of shaming interaction—may help a man learn to be conscious of feeling the emotion.

All these rules involve some form of hiding and trying to disguise the true self. Incompleteness and Disqualification use particularly subtle forms of disguise, misdirection, and mystification. Subtlety bestows extra power to confound us, so extra space is devoted to these two rules.

Shame breaks, or strains, the bond between men. It may start as only a tiny tear, but the wound tends to enlarge if not repaired. If I swallow my feelings and don't admit any problem (Denial), it's tough to fix the rupturing bond (Incompleteness). We may sense that something has come between us, but not know what, or start relating in nonauthentic ways, generating more shame. Finally, we move away, sour in the throat. But there may be a silver lining to this scenario: When we finally break the rules and start telling it like it is, the restored bond tends to become stronger than before.

The cumulative effect of living by these rules is to embed toxic shame in families, men's organizations and support groups, and between individual men. If nobody sees or challenges the rules, nothing changes. Toxic internalized shame, barely noticed, accumulates its deadening effects. Feeling ashamed and alienated comes to be seen, by men especially, as normal.

But now we know that Shame—the Invisible Dragon—has an Achilles' heel. He can't handle being seen as he really is. When we take away his invisibility, call him by name, broadcast his description, expose his hideouts (obvious and subtle)—then his fire cools and his awesome power begins to drain away.

## Control

If I keep a tight rein on the situation, maybe I won't fall into a sea of treacherous self-doubt, and feel vulnerable or acutely ashamed. I often choose the short-term "fix" of control, despite knowing about long-term consequences. Fossum and Mason (1986) cover this rule well and have an additional chapter on "The Interaction of Shame and Control."

Sometimes we get into power struggles and competition for attention. A man may interrupt a lot, shut others out with long-winded or forceful talk, or crack jokes that impede the flow. "Heart talk" suffers.

Group procedure can trigger control issues. One man or faction may assume the role of lawgiver or enforcer without group consent, or may presume agreement (often based on "principles") that doesn't exist. Those who disagree feel resentful and carry internalized shame. My group often sets a time limit on the initial check-in; we're careful to *rotate* the job of timekeeper, calling him the "Asshole" for the night.

Having no single leader, we often struggle for control over who, and how, to facilitate a man's emotional "work." It's good that we know a variety of styles, but it's rarely clear at first which approach will work best for this man tonight. Sometimes it can be a real zoo. We find it essential to air our disagreements about facilitating. Usually it's best to do this after the work is done, or maybe the following week, but once in a while it's necessary to interrupt the work for two or more men to confront each other about how we're competing for control in "helping" another man.

Let's not demonize power struggles or exercising control among men. Both are essential for vitality and are part of our in-bred masculine style. But our forceful ways carry the risk of hidden shaming, and we need to appreciate and counterbalance this risk. We may feel ashamed of competing for control, but it won't harm us if we're honest and confrontive about it.

## Blame

Blaming involves a maldistribution of responsibility. Taking on too much gives us the obvious sense of violation and shame. And the man who avoids his proper share may find himself with a pocketful of "innocence," which must be defended against exposure. The blamer may feel frustrated; it's not his fault, so he's powerless to fix it. Fossum and Mason (1986, pp. 94–96) discuss cogently other aspects of the Blame rule: how it's used to avoid surprise and vulnerability, to project one's own shame onto another man, and as a backstop for any temporary breakdown of the Control rule.

Overt blaming of others doesn't look like a big problem in men's support groups today. But a man may blame himself for his sexual, angry, or competitive feelings, often calling them "macho" or "sexist." Men's socialization is a handy scapegoat. Some men take most of the blame for war, crime, "patriarchy," or troubles with their women. When a man assumes too much responsibility, I advocate calling him on it. Unwarranted self-blaming is not a virtue, but a risk factor for infection with toxic shame.

Sometimes one man becomes the group "goat," or "screwup," often with his own complicity. Humor may abound, and it's rarely noticed that the other men are projecting much of their own shame, immaturity, and irresponsibility onto him. Or the group may use him to deny the seriousness of some issues.

A good tool for breaking the Blame rule is the language of responsibility. When speaking this language, I take explicit responsibility for my own feelings, values, and opinions. Concretely, this means using lots of "I-messages" and few "You-messages" (Gordon, 1974, 1976).

## Perfectionism

Internalized shame whispers, "I don't really belong here. I'm a defective alien in disguise, who'll be banished when they find me out. My only hope is to look so good that they don't examine me carefully. Maybe—maybe—I can 'pass.'" Or perhaps a man is a touch grandiose (Lindgren, 1995), and secretly believes that the world will end if he doesn't do it all perfectly. The pretense and denial generated by such ingrained reasoning continually reinforces shame.

Perfectionism may come in with some code of masculine honor. It ruined King Arthur's court, and still plagues men today. In a group called the New Warriors, men often interact about whether the warrior "way" is being followed. In moderation, this is useful, but sometimes it moves into Perfectionism. We sometimes forget that the Warrior archetype needs to be balanced by King, Lover, and Magician (Moore & Gillette, 1990). Let's remember that "injured reserve" is both honorable and necessary among warriors (Bly & Meade, n.d.). Perfectionism and shame denied will wreck any code of honor among flesh-and-blood men.

Fossum and Mason (1986, p. 91) say that "this rule imposes a requirement and a tension on people to comply with a perfect external image, which is sometimes vaguely defined and shifting." This tension is quite different from "a morally congruent life [or] . . . pleasure in knowledge." These authors go on to describe "a competitive or comparative aspect to this rule. . . . Being right never means 'right in terms of what fits for me.' There is a better-than-others aspect to it . . . a more-right-than-others aspect." Men may exhibit this perfectionist tension in cautiously "correct" talk, exaggerated politeness, or "walking on eggs." For more on perfectionism, see Hendlin (1992, 1993).

Obeying this rule may lead to withholding honest feedback because it might be wrong. This is a serious loss among good friends and in intimate men's groups, for it increases emotional distance. A man may hesitate because "maybe I'm projecting." *Of course* he is. All feedback contains projection. Let's relax and enjoy it. A rough measure of group intimacy is willingness to risk being wrong. Usually the feedback giver has an opportunity later to own his projections. Then we see the magic of shared experience. Here's a motto for the man giving feedback: I don't have to be right; I just have to be honest.

## Incompleteness

*Type Scenario.* A man leaves his group with no warning or good-bye, and can't or won't be contacted. He's too ashamed to show up again, perhaps because he fears boundary violations.

Those who remain feel a mixture of hurt, anger, mystification, shame, and concern for the absent man. Their shameful feelings may come from abandonment, or a vague sense of "we must have done something to drive him away, but what?" Some men may speak rationally of him, but with a hard edge in their voices, denying their feelings of hurt and shame, or perhaps relief.

In one group, the men remaining felt almost as if there had been a death among them. So they had a group good-bye ritual (like a memorial service), expressed themselves, and then felt more accepting and less mystified or ashamed.

Fossum and Mason (1986, 100–102) explain that this rule masks unresolved disputes, which may reappear in unrelated issues. An unresolved dispute between adults may be projected onto a child.[2] Incompleteness may generate confusion and futile attempts to "discern the meaning of nonsense."

Incompleteness prevents interpersonal bonds from being repaired (Kaufman, 1989). There's no opportunity for amends or a makeup. Decisions are left up in the air. Resentments fester. We often don't realize how many interactions we leave incomplete, so relationships deaden, or men may drift away from each other in pained silence.[3]

If there's lots of fighting but no resolution, Incompleteness feels like guerrilla warfare, dragging out endlessly and sapping our strength. Men may wrangle over superficial matters, avoiding awareness of the real issues. But let's keep on wrangling if we're capable of honesty; the deeper issues may appear in time.

This is the rule I obey most when practicing my personal addiction to shame. Self-doubt, procrastination, and passive-aggressive bullshit can be pretty thick at times, and I get fearful of exposure and ashamed to face *anybody*. Incompleteness tends to feed on itself and snowball.

"Do I have to give up me, to be loved by you?" (Paul & Paul, 1983). Incompleteness whispers "yes" in my ear, but deep down I want to shout, "Hell no!" Completion of our transactions affirms that I'm basically okay, even when I displease or anger you. The true self is strengthened, and toxic shame recedes.

Examples of incompleteness in action
  1. In a small men's group, the guys aren't directly sharing their feelings about *each other*, especially resentment, impatience, anger, boredom, or disappointment. There's a surly, strained, low-energy atmosphere, with grumbling and put-down jokes about absent

members. Most of the men keep coming to the group because it's so unique to be able to talk about their feelings with guys.

To minimize Incompleteness, vital men's groups give support and high priority to members confronting each other—early and often. We need to air out the inevitable conflicts and irritations which arise between us. To begin the process, a man tells another of his feelings toward him. The two men address each other directly. Perhaps they move into the center of the room, so that others can surround them with support and containment, honoring the sacredness of their difficult work and its importance to the group. A man's anger or distrust is treated as a simple fact, with minimal explanation, or judgment.

Sometimes other activities are interrupted, in order to deal with what's "hot." Otherwise, emotions simmer in Incompleteness, and toxic shame begins to cover the group like a wet blanket. More on confrontation follows in a separate section later.

2. Father and son agree that son will rake leaves this morning; father returns from his golf game to find leaves unraked and son off to play soccer. He rakes the leaves himself, his anger growing. When son returns, father conveys his low opinion of his son, using rhetorical questions, dirty looks, yelling, interpretations, or blows. Son tries excuses (which don't work), and may leave with head hanging, or stay feeling frozen and resentful. Son's internalized shame is even worse if father does *not* confront him, both pretending that nothing is amiss. The eyes transmit the curse, more powerful than words. And if the eyes cannot meet, the shame is deeper still.

The son is out of integrity with both father and himself, and needs to do a makeup (make amends) to repair the interpersonal bridge. Usually a makeup can be negotiated, but if it can't, I'd advise father to impose it unilaterally. Better an authoritarian power play than lingering toxic shame generated by the Incompleteness rule.

3. In a men's organization, some leaders interact with other men in an intrusive, prodding, provocative way. They profess to be open to confrontation and certainly are at times, but they're Busy Men Doing Important Work. Time for confronting and coming to completion is limited at best. Incompleteness abounds, with attendant intimidation, gossip, and swallowed shame.

The leaders need to be more aware of the shame generated by their hit-and-run way of operating, and resolve not to start things they don't have time to finish. But time isn't the only fac-

tor; some of the men are just plain intimidated. They need to be
more aware of what's happening, and speak up sooner.

4. One night in its second month, a new support group does a trust
   exercise. Each man says which member of the group he trusts
   most and whom he trusts least; each choice is explained with
   honesty and respect. It can be a powerful experience that moves
   the group to deeper levels of intimacy.

   Sometimes one man gets the lion's share of the least-trusted
   votes. Probably his shame is intense, and nobody present may be
   prepared to deal with it effectively. This man may leave and
   never return.

   As I see it, the basic danger here is that the intensity of the
   shame evoked is far too great to be dealt with in a single evening.
   The risk of heavy-duty Incompleteness is unwittingly built into
   the exercise. After a year of bonding and some experience with
   shame work, a group might elect to try it (it's not primarily an
   exercise to build trust, but a vehicle for heavy feedback). An alternative is a simple "I don't trust you" as part of ordinary feedback or confrontation. I see this as a high-gain/high-risk exercise.
   Those who contemplate using it are advised to consider carefully the level of intimacy already present in the group, the likeli-
   hood of a "goat" emerging, and their ability to facilitate the resolution of an intense shame reaction.

## Confrontation: Pro's and Con's

Vital relationships require confrontation. Here's a man whom I've
learned to love, respect, and rely on. I feel hurt by something he's
said, or contemptuous of some action he's taking. It's never easy
to confront him, but I must, or our respect and intimacy will
suffer.

"Low tolerance for bullshit; high tolerance for imperfection"
is the motto of one group. Men's organizations and support groups
function much better when they give active blessing to confrontation, and provide time and priority for it. A periodic group inventory helps. Are there men who never confront others? Is there
someone whom nobody confronts? Leaders heavily into Control,
Incompleteness, or Disqualification need especially to be confronted, or deposed, or abandoned.

Confrontation is often loud and angry, and sometimes physical, but need not be so. A neutral adult tone of voice can be perfectly effective, as can sadness or humor. Whatever the emotional

component, it needs to be genuine. For best results, match the intensity of the emotion expressed to the confronter's feelings at the moment, with minimal under shooting or over shooting (Gordon, 1976, pp. 133–135). Avoid sarcasm and rhetorical questions. Some kind of "I-statement" is best. ("I feel bored and irritated when you take 30 minutes to check in.") Direct and genuine confrontation increases the chances of resolution and completion.

Confrontation is not control. Please don't deem it a failure if the other man refuses to change, for it is a basic expression of the true self. True, confrontation often *does* affect the man confronted, but the benefit does not depend upon controlling him.

We come to regard confrontation, scary and embarrassing as it may be, as a *gift*. One facet of this gift is that my friend sees the real me, not some caricature. We learn that love and respect survive episodes of blunt, caustic opposition. Confrontation can be educational, by revealing an unrecognized part of my Shadow. And best of all, something in our male soul craves conflict with a worthy adversary.

Deep down in our genes, we men remember how to fight vigorously without inflicting permanent damage. As with males of many species, we know that we may hurt a brother, but need not injure him. Our bonding deepens as we give and receive the gift of energized authenticity. When we show love and appreciation, it has a ring of truth tempered by the fire of conflict. We learn in our bodies that anger and love may coexist.

Pain, physical and mental, is normal and necessary to life and growth (Peck, 1978, p. 15). We become willing to inflict hurt and to receive it, to wound and be wounded (Bly & Meade, n.d.). If we're stuck in our fear of hurting, the Denial and Incompleteness rules create shameful conditions which rip off those nearest and dearest to us (Mason & Fossum, 1987). "Nice guys ruin lives" (Bach & Goldberg, 1974).

These are the pro's; what about the con's? Confrontation and anger may be overdone, or be used to avoid scarier feelings of hurt, shame, vulnerability, or tenderness. In support groups, this usually works itself out in a few months. There's a more serious problem when one or two angry men are confronting all over the place, but nobody confronts *them*. Bad news! Equality is required for confrontation to be of lasting value. The entire group should support the most timid (or intimidated) member in confronting the most overbearing. A role-reversal exercise may work wonders here.

We discern a dance of bonding and confrontation. Bond a little, confront a bit, share and trust. Bond more deeply, confront with more spontaneity and on scarier subjects, bond even more deeply . . . and the beat goes on. I realize that most of the men I feel closest to are those at whom I've been able to explode with all-out anger, and they at me.

Bonding and confrontation work best when equally balanced. How far can an imbalance go before it becomes troublesome? That's an intuitive call, but please don't wait for near perfection. And confrontation may trigger shame, so there needs to be a rough balance between the depth of the shame and the group's time and ability to deal with it.

## Denial

Denial of our emotions is almost a generic plague among American men. Fossum and Mason (1986, p. 96) show how denial of feelings can produce "a very cold system of relationships" and suggest relationships that allow us to "practice" so that we'll become more comfortable expressing our feelings honestly. This is a major theme in men's liberation, and most of our groups do good work in this area.

But there are some hitches. Some groups are safe for certain feelings—perhaps anger, sadness, or fear, but don't welcome others—often shame, competitiveness, or impatience. Feelings of dependency, hopelessness, self-pity, or self-hatred are especially likely to be denied. Once one or two men start sharing their "incorrect" feelings, many of the men discover the same feelings in themselves.

Denial, along with Disqualification and No Talk, is often supported by dismissive or machismo humor, or by changing the subject. Men may issue shaming threats using code words and warning looks, or suppressive nonverbal messages via rigid bodies, holding the breath, or averted eyes. Rational analysis may talk a man out of trusting his intuition. Soon an undercurrent of internalized shame undermines group intimacy, gathering force as denial builds.

## No Talk

Shame builds if men keep silent about personal secrets, taboo subjects, or resentments. When these are withheld even from close friends or the support group, barriers rise as anxiety about exposure drives men apart. Subjects often taboo among men are:

- Money: who has how much; jealousy about it; resentment if some men are paid by a men's organization and others aren't.
- Feelings about penis size, unusual bends, warts, etc. Lots of good humor when this taboo is broken.
- Anger at women, racial prejudice, feelings of fear or contempt for other groups of "approved" victims (Everingham, 1995c).
- Feeling superior to others, grandiose fantasies, suicidal feelings, feeling ashamed.
- Feeling intimidated by another man, especially one in the group.
- Obesity, alcohol abuse, toxic relationships, gambling, or the seriousness of these.
- Disappointment or bad feelings about the group. It's helpful to consider the Shadow of the group as a whole.

When one man finally breaks the No Talk rule on any subject, there's usually a flood of discussion, with similar feelings being acknowledged by others. A collective sigh of relief may ensue.

Breaking the No Talk rule should not be confused with invading a man's privacy or bulldozing through his boundaries (Schneider, 1977; Fossum & Mason, 1986, p. 103). When he chooses not to talk about something for reasons other than group pressure or feeling ashamed, it's unlikely that the rule is operating, and his choice deserves respect. Likewise, breaching an agreement of confidentiality is not to be seen as breaking the No Talk rule, but as a serious betrayal of trust.

### Disqualification

*Type Scenario.* Mother is consoling her 12-year old daughter, who has been sexually molested by father. "Don't be upset, dear," she says, "That's just Daddy's way of showing his love for you." Focusing on this small part obfuscates a mountain of other truth: confusion, violated trust, pain, self doubt, humiliation, lack of protection and collaboration by mother.

The scenario is both extreme and stereotypic. I chose it to counterbalance the silent massiveness of Disqualification in its ability to "sanitize" serious shaming and abuse.

Disqualification is denial by disguise and distraction. Distortion, false labels, and reframing add to the disguise. Fossum and Mason (1986, pp. 103–104) pack a lot into two paragraphs on Disqualification, but this potent and confusing rule deserves fuller treatment now.

A common form of Disqualification is to focus truthfully on one part of the picture, while not acknowledging another important part. The elephant in the living room is ignored (despite olfactory evidence), while everyone admires the colorful lights of the swinging chandelier. The type scenario illustrates how abuse (and neglect) can be "dressed up" in a clever disguise. By directing attention away from the essential part, the abuse is not denied directly, but recast as something quite different. A common distraction is the shift to a charge of impropriety ("How dare you say that" or "Such language is inappropriate") to focus attention away from the shameful content.

This technique of denial-by-distraction is widespread. It's the stock-in-trade of most advertisers, politicians, lawyers, "spin" artists, and bureaucrats. Because Disqualification is so common, we tend to think of it as normal, and lose sight of the part(s) being disguised.

When encountering this rule in any form, I usually feel a vague sense of shame in my body, sensing that "something's wrong here." But at first my mind doesn't recognize the part(s) disguised. I may mistrust my intuition, suspecting that I'm at fault for not buying the "line." I want to swallow my perception, but I still can't digest it. Confusion seems to intensify the shame and hasten its internalization, because there seems to be no way to speak my truth, even to myself. Self-doubt is magnified.

Disqualification may serve to maintain the status quo when neither party wishes to face the discomfort of confrontation. Or a man may sense that he can be outduelled on a verbal, rational level. Maybe this works when the relationship is not highly prized, but there's a price to be paid whenever I collaborate with another person to obey this rule: The extra shame creates emotional distance between us. Moderate Disqualification may not break the interpersonal bond, but it certainly strains it. Our interactions become more stylized, less real, less intimate.

### Examples of disqualification in action

1. Joe is furious at Pat. They get into the center of their group. Joe looks Pat in the eye and starts telling him off. Before he gets into it, a man asks Joe who Pat reminds him of. Premature question!

If Joe interrupts his anger to answer, he's been deflected by Disqualification, adding shame.

It's probably true that Joe's anger is intensified because Pat, or his actions, remind Joe of somebody else. George Lindall (1995) writes of the 80/20 rule, which estimates that 20% of my emotional intensity is truly directed at the person in front of me now, whereas 80% belongs to people in my past, often parents. But the 20% needs to be dealt with *first*. The Disqualification in this example comes from bad timing. The reality and validity of Joe's anger *at Pat* has been denied. Joe and Pat need to deal with what's in front of them, to restore their bond and avoid residual shame.

Even worse, there's a risk that Joe may get the idea that his anger is "inappropriate" or an "overreaction." I favor banishing these two words forever from men's support groups. Joe's likely to feel ashamed of his anger now, and may be slow to confront the next time, adding Incompleteness to Disqualification.

Later on in their work this evening, when both Joe and Pat have allowed their true selves out for exercise, the time will come to ask Joe to connect his feelings toward Pat to someone in his past. Then he'll be more able to learn something valuable from the question. How does one recognize this magic moment? Mostly by intuition and experience, and sometimes by noticing a certain calmness and deep breathing that comes over Joe when he's expressed himself with full integrity. Joe has within him the best sense of when the moment arrives, and may decline to be distracted when the time is wrong. But let's avoid Perfectionism about hitting it exactly right. Part of Pat's gift to Joe is that he's willing to take on (temporarily) the 80% of Joe's anger which is really directed at somebody else.

2. In a similar group, or at an initiation weekend, Pete is working on a heavy emotional issue, and getting bogged down. A man suggests that Pete express his anger, so he starts yelling or pounding pillows with a tennis racket. But his anger doesn't ring true, and he soon loses energy. Several men begin to insult or mock him to try to *really* get him angry. Sometimes this technique works readily and is useful.

But when prodding to anger isn't working, to continue it adds shame from Disqualification and can be downright abusive. Pete's undoubtedly suppressing some anger, but right now he's feeling much more of some other emotion: sadness or shame, hurt or fear (Fossum, 1989, pp. 77–79). Pete may be ashamed of himself because he's not performing the way many in the group want him to. Or he may be deeply frustrated and in pain because he's not being encouraged to perceive, think, feel, desire or imagine in his own way. Whatever it may be, Disqualification denies this more-important feeling, and may soon generate so much shame that Pete freezes up emotionally.

3. When they are confronted, some leaders of men's groups deflect other men's feelings about them by using Disqualification. The muttering or angry men are said to be projecting their father issues onto the leaders, or acting out of a shadow part of the King archetype, which seeks to depose the King without being willing to take up his responsibilities.

   Again, all this is probably true to a certain extent, but "explaining" the situation in this way denies the role of the provocative actions of the leaders. The use of Disqualification here just makes things worse: the "explanations" do not heal. Interaction of this kind is almost always a reciprocal dance. For the bond to be restored, each man needs to own up fully to his part in the problem.

Denial, No Talk, and Disqualification form a continuum of suppression. Why have three rules instead of one? It's easy to underestimate the shame generated by these rules. So it seems useful to distinguish between not being aware of feelings or other matters (Denial), being aware but not saying anything (No Talk), and the distraction and misdirection which is the foundation of Disqualification.

"Shadow naming" is an exercise with power to break all three rules, because it tends to bring out what's being hidden or ignored. As a ritual, it's described in greater detail in chapter 6. Otherwise, when a man takes the talking stick, or at the beginning of the meeting, or when we feel superficial or inauthentic, the man about to speak names that part of his Shadow that he's most aware of at the moment. The effects can be felt immediately—as if a clean, fresh wind circulates among us—diminishing our shame and bringing calm, honesty and new respect.

### Unreliability

When a man is erratic in keeping agreements, being on time, or attending the group, other men are likely to feel irritation, which will convert to shame if unexpressed. There may be a subliminal complaint of "How come he can get away with it, and I can't?," or identification with the elder brother in the biblical parable of the Prodigal Son. Evidently this dynamic has been with us for millennia.

More serious are situations where a man never knows when his boss will be severely critical. Or a friend will be supportive and gentle on one occasion, but harsh and pugnacious the next, without any apparent reason. Men around him learn to think twice before opening up in his presence. For many years, my family never knew whether to expect me to arrive home cheerful and loving, or withdrawn, angry, and filled with internalized shame.

Unreliability derives most of its potency from a violation of the atmosphere of trust. Trust is fundamental to healthy functioning. Erikson's (1963) first crisis is Trust vs. Mistrust (Autonomy vs. Shame and Doubt comes in second in his scheme of human emotional development.). Similarly, in Maslow's (1954) hierarchy of motivation, safety is second only to physiological needs. Part of this universal need for safety is described as the desire for "a predictable, orderly world" (Maslow, 1954, p. 86). In recent years, we've noted how many children and adults seem to cling to abusive relationships which are predictable, if not always orderly. Unpredictable behavior by those who matter to us tends to upset our emotional foundations and erode trust.

We do well to be respectful of "exaggerated" responses by adult men to unreliable behavior. They may irritate us and lead to feelings of mild contempt, but they offer unusual opportunities to heal deep wounds. Strong feelings coming from childhood may be triggered. Children often blame themselves for mistreatment by parents or other caretakers. Betrayal of trust tends to engender deep shame in the one betrayed. Unreliability deepens the wound, because a boy has no clue about "what he's doing wrong," and thus no hope of correcting his "fatal flaw." But he tries and tries to discover and correct it anyway, and his internalized shame and self-distrust deepens.

A man may come to realize that he has been an unreliable best friend *to himself*. The rule may be so deeply internalized that he can no longer trust himself to act consistently and reliably in his own behalf. If he can't count on his own friendship, he needs to give this matter high priority in his curriculum, for it adds major difficulties to his other efforts to learn and grow. Fossum (1989, p. 80) advises making "a solemn vow . . . no longer [to] give your energy to hostility against yourself. . . . Make a conscious decision to be on your own side. . . ." Few of us do this perfectly, and hopefully we forgive ourselves for occasional lapses. I personally feel more connected and calm when I become aware of the need to become more reliable to myself, and it pleases me to set aside quality time to practice this "skill" for greater proficiency. Probably we have more to learn about this aspect of unreliability.

On a surface level, avoiding ongoing shame from unreliable behavior by others is relatively simple: confront the behavior and negotiate a makeup. I regard confrontation as important whenever feelings are evoked, even if the matter looks trivial. At this level, we're not dependent little boys anymore and are much more free to choose our associates. Speaking up—man to man and eye to eye—removes a great deal of the shame, and may lead to an adult reassessment of the trustworthiness of the other man.

A variety of responses is possible from the man being confronted. He may trivialize my feelings, argue and justify, or say, "Fuck you, buddy. Get out of my face!" Shame is compounded whenever a man silently accepts the idea that his feelings are childish or trivial. Emotions never require justification. Getting caught up in argument and justifying can be frustrating and emotionally tiring, but may be seen as both men's effort to maintain their boundaries (Fossum & Mason, 1986, pp. 59–85). Personally, I much prefer the more direct and vulgar style of boundary maintenance.

In a different vein, the man confronted may be willing to move deeper into his trust or shame issues, or he may simply apologize and offer an amend. I'm not doing my friend a favor when I silently allow him to be unreliable with me. On some level, he probably knows that he's being provocative and acting out old unresolved issues. He may even be yearning for someone to take him seriously and call him on his Unreliability. The other man's response to such confrontation is usually more positive than I had feared. It's worth the risk.

### Not Allowing the Five Freedoms

John Bradshaw adds this shaming rule, "Denial of the Five Freedoms," to those previously reported. "The five freedoms, first enunciated by Virginia Satir, describe full personal functionality. Each freedom has to do with a basic human power . . . the power to perceive; to think and interpret; to feel; to want and choose;

and the power to imagine. In shame-based families, the perfectionist rule prohibits the full expression of these powers. It says you shouldn't perceive, think, feel, desire or imagine *the way you do.* You should do these the way the perfectionist ideal demands" (Bradshaw, 1988, p. 40, emphasis added). I expand this valuable concept in three additional ways.

Shamefulness arises from doubt that I'm in adequate contact with my own reality. Whether from shaming tactics (often some form of the Moral Intimidation rule) or my own uncertainty, I fear that others know me better than I do myself. I'm afraid that they can see right into me, and their penetrating eyes have the power to take command. I want to run away and hide, or fight like hell. Abrogating the Five Freedoms teaches that personal autonomy is suspect or downright sinful, and magnifies self-doubt.

Whenever a man's desires and needs are not being met, shame is likely to be part of his reaction. There may be a quick, barely conscious monologue blaming himself for wanting what he "can't have," even though "others can." This may arise from the original activation of shame in infancy. Kaufman (1989, pp. 30–35) describes the infant's need for face-to-face gazing and body contact to establish an interpersonal bond. This bond not only makes the child feel loved, wanted, and "okay to be," it lessens the shame of wants being denied. When bonding is weak or inconsistent, I think the infant's first awareness is that "something is amiss" (distress), which later becomes "something is wrong *with me*" (shame), and then "maybe they'll tolerate my being defective if I don't complain." In time, unmet needs feel shameful, neediness becomes anathema, and both needs and neediness are denied with a vengeance. Men especially are ensnared in this mordant sequence.

Restricting the Five Freedoms is a form of spiritual abuse, which may be defined as being shamed or punished for one's myths, rituals, dreams, fantasies, values, heroes and heroines, opinions, preferences, style of expression or appearance, sexual symbolism, interpretation of reality, concept of the Divine or denial thereof, form of spiritual practice, paradigm of epistemology, etc. This kind of abuse denigrates a person for the *things that (s)he values most.* It attacks that vital sense of who I am, deep down. Spiritual growth involves strengthening this vital sense, and learning to enjoy being authentic in new areas of life. The true self needs to be blessed and validated, not cursed with shame.

Abridgment of the Five Freedoms may be broken by personal

confrontation, independent of control. Group rituals or other dramatization of important values are helpful. On the social and political level, an unfortunate byproduct of regulations enforcing "political correctness" is to justify shaming with this rule. Any action or rule which denies *the freedom to be me* is to be exposed and actively disobeyed.

## Moral Intimidation

Roy Schenk and I have discussed for several years the need to recognize another shaming rule. We didn't want to clutter the concept unnecessarily, and we're aware that the original rules were never meant to be exclusive or exhaustive, but rather "a working list of recognizable patterns" (Fossum & Mason, 1986, p. 87). After much deliberation, we propose a 10th shaming rule, called Moral Intimidation.

This rule comes into play between men when one man *assumes* himself to be an authority on matters of right or righteousness. It's really good old-fashioned moral superiority redone in modern makeup. As before, tones of voice and body language are employed as powerful triggers of toxic shame. But the epithets and code words have changed to keep up with today's demonology. Most "-ist" words, when used as put-downs, carry subtle messages of moral superiority by the user, as well as threats to shame any who dare to challenge or disagree.

Expert practitioners of Moral Intimidation make extensive use of rhetorical questions, such as, "You *still* don't get it, do you?" or "Do you still believe that chauvinism?" Rhetorical questions are not questions at all, but statements recast to evade taking responsibility for one's prejudices. Misplaced responsibility usually generates shame, as well as confusion and resentment.

We may extend the Five Freedoms rule to include *valuing in my own way*. Moral Intimidation judges a man's values and opinions as inferior, and implies that the man himself is pretty depraved. Recantation is of little help, even with much groveling. As with Disqualification, the shameful feelings are magnified because the shamed man rarely realizes how he's been set up. Knowing that I've been manipulated into being ashamed is better than feeling (again) that I'm somehow inherently flawed.

Silence and defensiveness mark the man well "trained" to obey this rule. An early challenge to the posture of moral authority is very helpful. "I don't agree," "Bullshit," or "Says who?"

confronts the original topdog / underdog assumption. Refuse to answer rhetorical questions and insist that they be reframed as statements. Say, "I'm feeling defensive, for no valid reason," "I feel ashamed because of the way you're talking to me," or "I refuse to be addressed in that tone of voice." Mimicking the intimidator's voice or body language usually stops it, but you may take a parting shot as (s)he heads out the door.

Be prepared for some anger. Moral intimidators use this shaming rule on men whom they expect to be cooperative and "take it." When you don't, they tend to get panicky about losing control, and furious at you for refusing to "play by the rules." The ire of an unsuccessful moral intimidator feels a lot better than a big gob of nauseating shame, silently swallowed.

***Shaming Rules: Afterwords.***  This concludes our survey of the ten shaming rules. Disobeying them can do much to relieve dissension among us and support our work and friendship. But we all follow them at times, especially when we're under stress, so let's not get into Perfectionism and Blame about it. As with the Rescue triangle (Everingham, 1995c), the trick is to use them infrequently and lightly.

Shaming doesn't invalidate a group. Even though the rules perpetuate shame in any system, much that is healthy and valuable may reside in the same system (Mason & Fossum, 1987). Men's Lib isn't perfect, but that's no reason to condemn or trivialize it.

Inadvertent shaming among men is an unnecessary burden. Restoring a broken bond is likely to involve confrontation, mutual sharing of feelings, and some kind of mutual amend or makeup. A simple, honest statement that "I value our friendship and want it to be better" is a good start.

## SHAMING THREATS

Sometimes the shaming isn't direct, but takes the form of a threat. Moral Intimidation is likely to be policed by threats, and probably other rules too. The threat is usually delivered in code, but the message is quite clear: "If you . . . , I *will shame* you." Shaming threats today are almost as common as direct shaming, among adults at least.

Shaming threats are particularly harmful because they activate and reinforce our internalized shame, which can freeze us in our tracks to suppress anything that might lead to more primary shame. We may "require" only occasional reinforcement from without, because we have become our own oppressors. A big part of our task is to learn how to get out from under.

Shaming threats can come from expressing our feelings honestly (Kaufman, 1995). Friendships based on emotional dishonesty are indeed threatened, so expect a counterthreat. The *enormity* of our feelings may constitute a threat that comes from inside.

There's fear of being 'tarred' with a shameful reputation: "pervert," "stuck up," "off his rocker," "wimp." Code words and gestures are often more damning than the names themselves. See Baumli (1995) for shaming one-liners, which threaten more if a man doesn't cringe back to his "proper attitude."

Among straight men, shaming threats which imply homosexuality often inhibit open expression of genuine affection. If there's a code of honor (favoring such virtues as honesty and integrity, sensitivity, or activity over passivity); a man may fear being shamed for those times when his true feelings run counter to the code, and the threat may induce him to "fake it."

To deal with shaming threats, personal and group awareness is a first step. One might try naming it ("Hey, that's a shaming threat!"), but I'd use this sparingly, because the Blame rule can be activated easily. Humorously saying, "Oh, oh, here comes the threat of shame" may work wonders.

Primary shame can be shared by saying, "I'm concerned that you'll shame me," or "I want a blessing right now, not a shaming." Things may change rapidly, the shamer feeling ashamed himself or quickly changing the subject. I see both the shamer and the man being shamed are doing a kind of dance in which each bears equal responsibility. This viewpoint will minimize further shaming and blaming among honest men who care about each other.

You might try, "I don't think I'll carry your projected shame today. Carry it yourself!" (Thanks to Robert Bly for this one.) Or maybe, "I'm not buying any of your shame threats today. Go find some other sucker." If shaming intent is denied, suggest that he go to a shrink to learn emotional honesty. If he suggests that you deserve to be shamed, tell him about projection. As long as the shame threatener remains undeterred, I don't see any reason to let up my own shaming tactics. But when he turns toward honesty and humanity, I'd be quick to shift to empathy and respect. We're all in this together; shaming and threats may be a manifestation of our deep longing to confront and heal our own shame.

These last tactics carry a risk that I may overlook my own feelings of shame, which are present whenever I absorb a shaming threat or act, or whenever I see someone else being cruelly shamed. Sometimes I remember to take a deep breath and say a silent, "I'm feeling ashamed," for *nonacknowledged* shameful feelings are risky business for a "shamenik" like me. A man may be harmed more by internal denial than by the external shaming threat.

Combinations of these tactics are compatible. I'm sure you can develop some of your own, and maybe you'll tell us of your discoveries. Here's a helpful attitude toward shaming threats and acts: "Your thrust has hurt me, but I am not injured; I am not deterred; I have not quit the field. Your maneuver has wounded me, but it has failed to drive me off."

## SHAMING TACTICS AND POLITICAL CORRECTNESS

This and the following section examine how a combination of shaming rules and threats set up a shame-laden atmosphere which pollutes our lives today. Ironically, one goal of political correctness is to reduce overt shaming and restrictions of freedom and opportunity. Sanctions, countershaming, and threats thereof are instituted against speech and other symbology judged to deny equal rights of citizenship by class discrimination. My major objection to PC is that its tactics work powerfully *against* its stated goals.

But there's moral irony as well. By assigning special status to a wide variety of Victims, political correctness *de facto* directs the lion's share of its shaming attack against a single class: Able-bodied white men who aren't poor. A professor at my university, who for some time had been calling male students "rapists" for their opinions, was "busted" when a black man complained.

For several decades, we have offered members of some groups a modicum of preferential opportunity, to partially compensate for past discrimination and to increase the critical supply of mentors for each group. I support this policy. In parallel development, a new moral double-standard has arisen—one which exploits the manipulative Victim position (Everingham, 1995c). Victims now "deserve" to shame and castigate their "oppressors." This seems to come from Karl Marx's concepts of class struggle, and implies that the beneficiaries of past injustice carry full responsibility and guilt for it, as well as the obligation to make restitution. ("Correct" is almost a lexical diagnostic for American Marxism of the 1950s and 1960s). Epithets, heavy with the threat of shame, are waved in our faces to induce us to remain silent and in our "place" of moral inferiority. Disqualification disguises the shift from a reasonable social policy to an atmosphere of institutionalized shaming. The witch hunt for "oppressors" is in full cry today, complete with severe shaming threats and lots of Moral Intimidation.

The Defender of the Correct has mastered a certain body language and superior tone of voice. He will speak of this or that "-ism" in a knowing tone which implies that he has a hotline to the throne of true knowledge and Divine justice. He'll fight to maintain his position as moral "king of the hill." His weapons are an imperious demeanor or fierce readiness for verbal battle, a handy arsenal of factoids, and demonstrable prowess at being "sensitive" to the plight of victims.

Although the external consequences are much less serious, the shaming tone today reminds me of mainland China during the Cultural Revolution, and of America in the days of McCarthyism. The epithets of that era (e.g., "comsymp," "pinko," and "fellow traveler") were code words for "traitor" and had added power because their users could not be held directly accountable for charging loyal Americans with treason. Today's shamers also seek to hide behind innuendo and code words, as a kind of street fortification to shield their malice from public view and attack. Other commonalties include suppression of dissent by shaming threats, guilt by association, accusation interpreted as conviction, and widening the net of supposed oppressors to include those who call for honesty, fairness and equality.

Such tactics stockpile internalized shame and buried rage. Individual and societal Shadow is projected *en masse* onto others. Resentment toward the shamers festers, inhibiting social healing. We risk an explosion when the unknown critical mass is attained. Public shaming can no longer be dismissed as an amusing game, for we now see how deadly its political effects can be (Kaufman, 1992).

## SHAMING MEN FOR BEING MEN

There is a prevalent posture today which, subtly or blatantly, blames men ("patriarchy") for most of society's troubles. Broad hints suggest that testosterone is an evil drug, rendering men morally suspect, and requiring ever stronger legal and moral restraints for the "protection" of us all. Men's liberation operates under constant shaming threats to conduct itself in ways which women (and men enthralled with political correctness) will not find offensive.

Women use the "rights" of Victimhood to shame us as a routine matter of course, perhaps because we "deserve it." Some even appear to believe it their *duty* to shame men. Shaming threats compound the Moral Intimidation. "Patriarchy," "sexist," "macho," "deadbeat," etc., are paraded like cannon on Lenin's birthday, ready to blow away anyone who voices disagreement or demands equal treatment.

Such name-calling may be indirect, and is often nonverbal—an exaggerated sigh of exasperation, or a rolling of the eyes to imply that I'm hopelessly debauched or deficient in understanding. But if the threat is not heeded, the shaming may get more direct, even if still in code. I objected when a nationally respected psychoanalyst equated "patriarchy" with dysfunctional families, and in the ensuing discussion she advised me to join a men's group! I suppose she thought that a group might convince me that family dysfunction is mostly men's fault (some "men's" group!), and the comment certainly implied moral retardation.

Why do we put up with this shit? Disqualification may blind us to the true picture. For example: Women wield much more decision making power about sexual activity. When I first wrote that sentence, I imagined a storm of angry rebuttal focusing on men's power during rape. Despite the long-overdue emergence of male/female rape from the closet, it constitutes a small fraction of the decision making about sex. The intensity of (long pent-up) emotions about rape tempt us to believe lies which cast blame and shame upon us because we're men.

We're not yet accustomed to the idea that feeling ashamed in response to shaming tactics has an instinctive, biological component. It's natural to respond with shame to a certain tone of voice. And some of us live with the idea that it's just not honorable to pick on girls, even when they're picking on us.

Let's not blame women. We men are responsible for learning

to break the shaming rules, as an integral part of healing our own shame. Anger is useful, but staying in the Rescue triangle isn't. Initiation and bonding to men is *very* useful (Gagnon, 1995; Greenwald, 1995; Miller, 1995). Good luck!

## INTENTIONAL SHAMING

Generally, obedience to these rules is to be avoided. But occasionally there's a situation in which I may choose to apply a shaming rule, or choose to use one rule to avoid a nastier one. When this happens, it's helpful to make an open acknowledgment to the man concerned. "I understand that I'm using shaming rules on you (or name the rule); I acknowledge that you're probably feeling ashamed. So am I." Shame owned and felt is much less destructive than shame hidden and internalized.

During initiation rituals, neophytes are often shamed deliberately, or as a byproduct of the destructuring which is a necessary part of the process (Bridges, 1980). I think this is entirely appropriate, *provided that an opportunity for an amend or makeup is clearly offered.* The makeup is best mutually agreed to, as among men of integrity. It can be wonderfully educational to experience this cycle: Lack of integrity and emotional dishonesty are confronted, leading to shame and alienation from the group; then the situation is resolved via honesty and a makeup, so that both personal integrity and broken interpersonal bonds are restored. See! Nobody has to remain alienated and ashamed; there's *always* a way back for those who want to find it.

## NOTES

1. Rules 1–8 are based on Fossum and Mason (1986, pp. 86–104); rule 9 on Bradshaw (1988, pp. 39–41).

2. I once heard a woman say, "That's why men hate women. They want revenge on their mothers." I thought, "That's why women are so cruel to their sons. They're paying back their husbands." This dynamic of sexualized intergenerational abuse is underestimated even today, and shows how destructive the Incompleteness rule can be.

Maybe we're angry at women because they push our shame buttons so easily. And why shouldn't they? Women installed most of these buttons. But the more basic issue is that our fathers didn't embody the mature masculine, and we missed the experience of initiation to free us from the feminine power orbit (Greenwald, 1995).

3. Men's relationships with women too often have this quality of withdrawal into silence. The sexes typically use different styles of confrontation. Men often face the Hobson's choice of either (a) trying to use the woman's style, which places him at a substantial disadvantage; or (b) using his own style and risking the shame of being called "crude," "violent," or "insensitive;" or of picking on someone who appears weaker or more vulnerable. It's understandable that many opt for surly silence. I recommend against that choice. Stylistic equality can be negotiated with an honest and caring confronter, and perhaps knowledge of these shaming rules may strengthen a man's position (Miller, 1995). Incompleteness can be a potent weapon, but its use is often destructive to both parties (see Bly & Meade, n.d.).

4. If the response to "I feel ashamed" is "That's your problem," then it's time for serious confrontation *right now*—no changing the subject or pretending it was a joke. Failing that, you may have to kick the bastard right out of your life, for you've offered him the pearls of your honesty and vulnerability, and he's responded by spitting in your face.

# 16

## Men and Goodness*

### Andre Heuer

The harder I tried to explain the more difficult it became.
"Please!" I said to John. "Please listen. It's just not that difficult.
We just need to be ourselves. That's good enough." John, like so
many men I have worked with, wanted to be different from who
he was. I often feel the same anxiety. I have often said to myself
"Maybe if I just do this a little bit different then I'll be okay. I'll be
happy." I make the change and somehow things feel the same or
sometimes, I even feel worse. What's going on with us? What is
this discontent? Why are we so filled with self-hate that we spend
thousands of dollars on therapy, books and workshops to change
ourselves? Even worse, why is it that so many of us medicate ourselves with chemicals, sex, work, or exhaustion to forget the pain
of being?

We live in an age of self-contempt. Throughout our lives we
are told to be different than what we are. As little children we are
made to conform and to meet the expectations of parents and
teachers. We are forced to conform to their image of being human
or risk being unloved. As adults we are told to dress in the right
way, to have the correct political attitudes and to have the proper

*Based on an article by the same name in *Men Talk*, Minneapolis, MN, spring 1992. Also in
his Ph.D. Thesis, "Effects of Family, Society, and the Church on Men's Self-Image and Their
Spirituality: Approaching Ministry to Men." University of Minnesota, St. Paul, MN, 1993.
Copyright © 1992, Andre Heuer.

psychological demeanor. These expectations and the sense of being unworthy of love fill us with dread and anxiety. We believe that we don't quite measure up. In being told so often that we are wrong or not quite right we no longer have any sense of our own goodness. This sense of not being good enough affects both women and men. In this essay I will explore some of the reasons why men feel this lack of goodness and the effects on men.

We were walking into a small supper club when my father recognized an old acquaintance. My father, reaching out for the man's hand asked "Have you been behaving?" The man's reply was quick and to the point "Yeah, I have to. My wife and daughter keep me in line and my sister is staying with us right now. I have no choice." He then looked my father in the eye and asked "How about you?" My father's face lit up with a boyish smile. His eyes rolled back looking over his shoulder at my mother. He calmly recited, "Of course, can't upset the good woman here. Right, Maryan?" My mother quickly snapped back "You better not." My gut tightened.

Soon after being with my parents, I was on a walk with a woman friend. As I began to say something, she looked at me and with much indignation snarled through grinding teeth "Men!" Immediately, I looked over my shoulder at her with a sheepish grin and wondered, "What did I do wrong?" There it was again. My gut tightened. I felt a wave of anxiety come over me. I asked myself, "What is this about? Why do I feel this? Where did this come from?

When the walk was over, I went home. I sat on the couch and let myself feel the anxiety. Her statement seemed to be such a small thing. Yet, it had created such a reaction in me. As I listened to my insides, memories of being a little boy came to me. I had been out playing and gotten terribly dirty. My mom grabbed me, pointed me towards the stairs and said, "Get washed, now!" As I walked up the stairs I remembered her saying "Boys" with a tone that seemed to my ears as disgust.

I later remembered how my older sister taunted me and told me how boys were bad and that girls were good. She would tease me and often would hold me down until I couldn't breathe. When I complained to my mother, my sister would say "Mom! He was being mean to me and he's so strong. You know how mean boys are." I would sit there hurt and angry. I couldn't figure out what I had done wrong.

Many memories came to me once I remembered my sister's

behavior. My fourth grade woman teacher would give the girls treats at recess. The girls told us that the teacher said "I don't give the boys treats because they're bad." All through school we boys knew that "boys were bad, and girls were good." This, message was particularly strong around sexuality. Boys were out of control, only interested in one thing and not to be trusted when sex was involved. Girls on the other hand weren't interested because they were good. This, of course, meant I was bad. As I thought more another memory came to me. My mother was having a conversation with relatives. A young neighbor man had gotten into some trouble. He was single and a little wild. The consensus was that "What that boy needs is a good woman. She would straighten him out right away." All these memories meant one thing to me. Boys and men were bad. We needed women to point out what was bad and to straighten us out. We had no natural goodness of our own. We received goodness from women.

It was at this point that I jumped to a conclusion. It was women that made men feel bad. It was women with their sense of righteousness that made me feel not good about myself. It was not long before I realized what I was saying. As in the case of many who write and study gender issues it was easy to put the entire blame on the other sex. I quickly reconsidered the issue and asked myself "How do men participate in this process of not feeling good about themselves." I realized I had been given this message by many of the men in my life. My father by his actions had colluded in the process of helping me believe that women were better. I had heard plenty of men say how a certain woman had straightened them out. The whole culture had made it clear that women were more righteous and good. That was why we didn't hit girls, why they were allowed to go first in line, why they didn't fight in wars and why they were called innocent victims and boys and men were just casualties. Most of these rules I learned not just from women but also from men.

In facilitating groups for my clients it became clear that many men had similar experiences. They had the same feeling of moral inferiority to women as I had. Many of them felt rage and often hid their sense of inferiority with a bravado attitude. "No woman tells me what to do." I would hear often. It was a cover. As I worked with these men I found a deep sense of a lack of personal goodness. They often felt extremely fearful of abandonment. If their women left it would prove that they were not good. It would prove that they were not able to control themselves enough to earn the love of a good woman. In the fear of losing their women some men used violence. The thought of losing their women was so devastating that violence was the answer to the inner chaos they felt and a way of creating order. This was not the only way men dealt with their sense of moral deficiency.

For every man that I worked with who was violent or rageful, I found three who were depressed, passive and exhausted. Many of these men seemed burdened by the need to prove that they could do the right thing. Working hard, doing their civic duty, keeping the house up, being a good father and husband, and most of all keeping it emotionally together. Many of these men were motivated by fear of not being good enough. They feared that if they didn't do it right they would lose their family, friends and work. Most felt that if they could not maintain their lifestyle they would not be successful. Most of these men equated being good with being successful. If they weren't, their fear was that they would lose the love of the people in their lives, especially their wife or lover. After I had heard this several times I was reminded of the phrase "Behind every successful man is a good woman." These men felt without success they were worthless. They suspected that without a woman at their side, they could never be quite good enough.

As I began to equate men's feeling's of being good with being successful and having a good woman, I asked "In what ways—besides a woman being behind a man and success—does our culture give the message that men are not quite good enough?" As a boy what I often heard was "That boy needed to join the service. They would whip him into shape." The phrase "whipped into shape" gnawed at me. I remember the spankings I got as a boy. My sister was yelled at but not spanked. In school the boys received the paddle and the girls got sent to the cloak room. In sports the boys were disciplined and even hit sometimes by their coaches. The girls were protected and allowed to enjoy the few games they were allowed to play. What I learned was the way that a boy could "get it" was to receive a beating—whipped into shape.

As I interviewed other men I was consistently reminded of this attitude. Over and over again, I would hear of men as boys receiving a major beating for a minor mistake. The man would then say "I deserved it. I was out of control. You know how guys are? I wasn't ever very well behaved." If this conversation had only happened a few times I would have forgotten it. However, It happened more often then not, especially with men in prison. The example that most exemplified this attitude was described in an article in a local newspaper. The Star Tribune sports editorial piece of January 15, 1992, was about the 1966 Bills kicker Booth Lusteg. He missed a field goal during a regular season game. This was after Buffalo had beaten the same team for the American Football Championship. Buffalo instead of winning the game ended tied.

The article reads: Lusteg says some angry young Bills fans followed him through downtown Buffalo and beat him up. "Booth, why didn't you call us?" police later asked. "Because I deserved it," Booth replied.

This type of attitude prevails in our culture. Mistakes are intolerable and deserving of beatings. In schools, boys are more likely to be labeled behavior problems than girls. They are more likely to be medicated to get them under control. Boys may receive a higher rate of encouragement from teachers than girls but they also receive more punishment. Some studies indicate boys get more praise because they are considered more problematic and need praise in order to be controlled. Men receive more time on prison sentences then women for the same crime. All these attitudes arise out of the expectations that boys are out of control and that "Boys will be boys no matter what." No wonder men have feelings of being morally deficient or lack a sense of their goodness. The culture not only says that men need a woman and success to be good but also that men will probably need a good whipping in order to be good. In other words a man needs a good woman and the Marines to be good enough.

As I came to these insights I wondered what could have motivated men to continue to participate in this crippling process. It did not take much time to realize the answer. I already had it. It was my fear of not being loved. I felt that I had to continue to be successful and to find the right woman in order to be loved. I really believed that I would need to be whipped into shape so that I would be good enough to love. This fear of not being loved was the theme that was common to most of my clients and men's groups. Men wanted to be loved for who they were not for their success, image, or for the woman at their side. However, they found it difficult and sometimes impossible to let go of these conditions of their lovableness. They often chose to continue to live their lives in these images rather then take the risk of changing and losing love. Once again I saw how men were responsible for colluding in their own wounding.

As I ended my research, I found that men's sense about their personal goodness is affected in three ways. First, many men see women as being the source of their goodness. Second, men believe that they're morally and sexually out of control and the only way to get under control is to get whipped into shape. Finally, men have felt unworthy of being loved because of their lack of goodness. The way men find their goodness is through being successful.

The sad aspect is the damage this process has caused men. It has had damaging results not only for men but also for our culture. The drive for success is probably the most damaging to men. This driveness has led to denial of basic emotional and physical needs. Drugs, sex, overwork, and other self-destructive behaviors are used to meet these needs. Some men have created an inflated sense of themselves in order to feel okay about themselves. This tends to emotionally isolate them from others. Other men cannot find their sense of personal goodness and become depressed, passive and isolated. All these behaviors have caused a need for control and for perfection. The greatest effect that I have seen is that, as men, we are isolated from each other. As men we have become dependent upon women to meet needs that they are not capable of meeting. The tragedy is that our sons are denied the role models to help them discover their own goodness. This leads to the perpetuation of this cycle of hurt and pain for all men and our culture. As men, we need to discover our goodness if we are to stop this cycle. We need to be willing to heal our woundedness.

We face many obstacles in trying to heal this woundedness. It is difficult to admit to having wounds in this age of image. "Men need to have it together" we are told. Trying to be perfect causes us to want to cover up our woundedness and flaws. As we have discussed earlier, it is the fear of not being good that causes the wounding. It causes us to look for quick fixes and simple solutions to heal our wounds. It is ironic that many of the ways men try to overcome their woundedness only causes more wounding. Only when men are willing to enter into their woundedness can we hope for healing. When we bring to light our imperfections we also bring to light our goodness. It is our attempt to hide our woundedness and imperfection that cause our energy to be destructive rather than a creative and powerful blessing. It is rather paradoxical that to find their goodness men must decide to bring to light their flaws.

Each man needs to make their own decision to enter into their woundedness to reclaim their goodness. It is a journey that only he can take for himself. He cannot blame others. He must take personal responsibility for his journey. It is not an easy journey. He will experience loneliness, pain, and, most of all, grief. However, it is not a journey that a man can take alone.

In reclaiming our goodness other men will be needed. Only other men can give the full compassion that comes from the common experience of struggling with this woundedness. We will have to be willing to allow men to see and hear our struggle. We will have to ask men to accompany us on our journey. We will need to let men nurture and guide us. As men journey together they will experience a deep and abiding love with each other. This love will be the sign of men's goodness. It is then that men's goodness will permeate and change our lives, culture, and world.

# 17

## Men and Intimacy*

### Patrick Dougherty

Men are different from women. We know that the sexes have different bodies, view and experience life differently, and are raised and treated differently. Yet we are often trying to make what works for one gender work for the other.

Alcoholics Anonymous and similar 12-step programs are examples. From the structure and origins of AA, we can see that it is a program developed by men out of an understanding that men often prefer clear rules and guidelines, especially when working with something as vulnerable and elusive as addiction. Psychotherapy offers a contrasting example. The whole process and environment of therapy is much more geared to what women find comfortable and safe.

Gender differences are also being blurred in the area of intimacy, a situation that continues to confuse men and frustrate women.

If asked about the components of intimacy, many of us would list self disclosure, talking face-to-face, expressing feelings, listening empathically, sharing vulnerability, and being direct and honest. But these components fit women's style of intimacy much better than men's. While many men may feel intimate under these

*Adapted from *The PHOENIX*, March 1989 issue. Copyright © Patrick Dougherty, 1989.

circumstances, others do not, because much of what men understand and experience as intimacy is missing from this list.

Women do not, as is often said, know *more* about intimacy than men. They only know more about what works *for them*.

Many of the current theories of intimacy begin by looking at childhood. We see that girls tend to be concerned with cooperation and fairness in their relationships, whereas boys focus on rules and competition. We don't find much face-to-face disclosure among boys—just the opposite. Most boys are taught to deny and repress any desire to show vulnerability, and to toughen up because someday they'll "be a man." The conclusion drawn is that intimacy has been socialized out of males by the time they become adults.

These observations and theories certainly point out some of the struggles that boys experience growing up, and have implications for issues which men wrestle with when trying to be intimate, especially with women. But the conclusion drawn is simply wrong.


## A DIFFERENT INTIMACY


Boys learn *different* ways of being intimate. Boys become friends or buddies, hang out together, play sports together, use their imaginations together in play or to fantasize about the future. They joke around together, drive around together, and explore the world together. Recognizing these typical aspects of boyhood, I cannot imagine anyone concluding that boys do not have intimacy in their lives.

Theorists often overlook the substantial change in the male world brought on by the industrial revolution. Before the industrial revolution, most boys worked at their father's side, or were apprenticed to another adult male. A boy learned to be a man by spending most of his day in a close relationship with a mature and productive male. After the revolution, the father and other adult males went off to factories and offices for most of the day. The men often came home spent and empty. Both at home and at school, a boy's world came to be filled with women and other boys. Boys lost their fathers and male teachers, and fathers began to be alienated from their sons and families.

How boys are initiated into manhood has changed forever.

The father often brings home a distant and seemingly uninterested presence, or one of intolerance and domination. More and more, boys came to be born into a masculine void. The void becomes a lifelong wound—a wound of spiritual neglect, which a man must confront to make sense of his life.

Men today are speaking out about their isolation, about feeling like they are living in an empty world, about the lack of meaning in their lives. They speak of their desire for true intimacy to combat the emptiness. These men are drawn to people who are willing to listen to them, willing to let them articulate the pain inside. They are being drawn toward people who *have* a form of intimacy and are willing to teach them how to be intimate. These people are usually women.

So men learned, by default, to imitate what women call intimacy. It has been very helpful, and perhaps the only way in modern society that this search for deeper intimacy could have begun for us. And the face-to-face style of intimacy certainly has an important place in living a full masculine life.

## SEARCH FOR MASCULINITY

But most men after a time begin to sense that there is something missing. We now can share our feelings and communicate, and are getting lots of strokes for doing so, but we come away not feeling grounded in our maleness. Today, what often connects us to our maleness is the pain of being deprived of masculine models in childhood.

We have an important need that is rarely talked about. Men need to connect with their memories of the vibrant and creative *boy,* the one that knew plenty about being intimate and close to other boys. This boy is the one who will help us remember what it's like for a man to be intimate.

More and more men are claiming and affirming our style of getting together and interacting with each other as men, enjoying doing things the way men do them. The word "buddy," long derided as implying a superficial relationship, is being used again with pride and affection. We're remembering how to be intimate while competing with other men—playing football with a group of guys, racquetball with a friend or tennis with a business partner. Although task orientation is often derided by those using the limited definition of intimacy, men are rediscovering how good it feels to help a man move his furniture, to paint a house with a group of friends, to lay sod and get dirty together. Doing these masculine things *together* can powerfully affirm our friendships and our sense of grounded masculinity.

Hunting, fishing, and other outdoor sports are also typical male modes of affirming masculinity and facilitating intimacy. Many men tell of the pleasure they feel sitting beside a friend for hours in a duck slough. Or of the tenderness a man can feel toward a friend after a cold weekend of ice fishing, staring down their ice holes and hardly saying a word about anything serious.

There is a resurgence of storytelling in the male world. Men for centuries have found pleasure in listening to myths and stories, and reflecting on what they have to say about a man's life. To some, this may seem to be indirect and unclear, lacking the precision of declarative statements and the directness of face-to-face interaction. Yet men take great pleasure in just listening, and in sitting and allowing the story to sink into our consciousness. A man's way of intimacy does not need to be direct and articulate. Sometimes these qualities actually ruin the experience of being together for men.

Making fun of each another and joking around together is also finding its way back into the world of men. After sorting out the shaming and wounding ways of making fun of someone, men are seeing the affection that is often behind a joke. Native Americans have long believed that making fun of a person is an admission of affection and an acknowledgment of friendship. Some may criticize this style as indirect, but many men say that it feels very good to be on the receiving end of this sort of kidding around.

In current media, from television sitcoms to the printed word, these ways of male bonding are often portrayed as primitive or unevolved, and often pathetic. Such portrayals are just attempts to shame men away from masculine intimacy. The message from these sources seems to be that unless men master the feminine style of intimacy we are to be looked down upon and pitied. In reality, until men come to terms and accept who they are, they will always feel shame at their inability to be more authentic and intimate.

To be truly intimate with either men or women, a man must establish the deep foundation of his masculinity. This can be discovered only in the company of other men. It should be obvious that we cannot learn it from women, or from men who practice only a feminine style of intimacy.

As he continues to experience his deep masculinity, a man's capacity for intimacy becomes infinite. Grounded men can choose when to share their feelings, when to joke around, when to listen to stories and grunt, when to compete and when to be gentle.

This journey to intimacy leads men on a long adventure, often painful but usually exciting. It means revisiting childhood to find both the wounded and the vibrant boy; it means learning about sharing feelings and being vulnerable; it means remembering what we already know about being intimate. And it leads men back to being with other men.

# 18
## Shame, Initiation, and the Culture of Initiated Masculinity

*Michael P. Greenwald*

The mature Masculine must be reclaimed by the modern world. Its virtual absence from technologically advanced societies has, in the author's view, resulted in one of the more serious moral crises ever to face Western civilization. Earth's population has in its grasp the means to create a virtual Utopia. Yet we lack the collective will even to ensure against the annihilation of entire cultures through starvation and disease. In our world, genocide is barely noticed. Rape is used as an instrument of both pathological male self-expression and ethnic war. We are willing to enhance performance chemically (with antidepressants or steroids, for example) at the expense of accepting our human limitations. We tolerate planetary pollution and disgracefully high infant mortality rates. Violence is becoming the preferred solution to interpersonal disputes. In all this, we see evidence that mature Masculinity, in its fullness, has all but been forgotten, and that "Boy Psychology" (Moore & Gillette, 1990) is prevalent.

To reclaim the mature Masculine, we begin where the young men of traditional societies invariably began—by remembering initiation.

**266**

## INITIATION REMEMBERED

A boy lies safe in the arms of his mother. He does not fit quite as comfortably against her body as he used to. But he is perfectly happy to be cuddled by her, bonded to the warm, nourishing sensuality of her body and the light of love in her eyes.

Suddenly, the door of the hut bursts inward. Men, painted and disguised, storm into the room. Mother wails and clutches at him, trying vainly to offer protection from the demons who have invaded their safe and private world. The boy is seized by rough hands and screams in terror. Reaching for his mother, he is ripped from her grasp and dragged out into the night. Throughout the village, his playmates are being carried off by large, frightening figures. Mothers follow the parade crying, praying, beating their breasts and tearing their hair. The fires of the village now seem wicked and diabolical, no longer warm and familiar. The boy feels the terror of separation from his anchors to comfort and reality.

As the men leave carrying off the boys, mothers collect in groups to congratulate each other on their fine performances and the grandness of the show that they have just presented. They are sad, yes, to lose their little boys. But they are proud and pleased by their work of nurturing another generation of young men to readiness.

The boys, meanwhile, are taken far into the darkness. They are lost, disoriented, perhaps blindfolded. They have no idea how to get back home, to Mother. Terror, fear of a death they cannot yet conceive, perhaps panic—all roil in their bodies. Soon an overwhelming sense of loss will envelop their fright.

They are carried to a place of isolation, used only at sacred times for sacred purposes. No women are allowed in this place—and no woman would care to go there. It is a place of masculine energy, where the very air is pregnant with the memory of ancient ritual. The earth seems to be stained with the afterbirths of earlier labors—labors of initiation, about to begin again.

Here is ritual space; with no sense of time or other place. This is liminal space, the threshold where that which was is no more, and that which will be is not yet.

Here, the men have made preparation. They have gathered the sacred materials, the necessary food. They have tested themselves, cleansed themselves, determined their tasks. Individually and as a group, they have reconsecrated themselves to the spirits of the village, or to something or someone greater than all and of which each is a part.

In this place, for a timeless period, the boys are subjected to physical, spiritual, and emotional processes handed down as sacred tradition. Among such ordeals may be scarification, circumcision, the breaking of teeth, the piercing of flesh. The boys may be buried in mock graves, each face-to-face with his own unimagined death. They may be tricked and taunted by their elders. Discipline is strict, and perhaps they are beaten for transgressing the most minute regulation. Soon, they realize that there is no Mother here to comfort them in their pain. They confront the need to care for themselves, lest they perish. They face tasks that bring them to the edge of their own mortality. Once in a while a boy dies.

But they also are trained. Mentors teach them. They learn the essential values, customs and culture of their society. Their curriculum includes the skills and burdens, the rights and privileges, the responsibilities and authority of being a man in the life stream of the village. Each boy will emerge knowing deeply that he is unconditionally a member of the tribe of Men. "All for one, and one for all," may be no exaggeration. He comes to know and trust the initiates within his cohort and the men who have acted as his initiators. Each boy learns by experience who is to be entrusted with which responsibilities, who can be relied upon to exercise communal or civic authority, and who is destined to act as priest or shaman. At last he assimilates the understanding that his individual future is bound up in a masculine collectivity, a masculine interdependence, essential to the survival of the village.

The boys also receive healing: physical healing from the rigors and wounds of their ordeal, and emotional healing from the pain of separation from their mothers. Healing comes in part through the ministrations of the initiators. The boys experience at first hand the power of men to heal men's wounds. They realize that their initiators suffered identical wounding and scarring; the initiators once were boys themselves who endured the same rite of passage. This recognition opens a door deep in the psyche—a door both to the power of self-healing and to a deep bonding with men.

Finally, the boys discover the healing reintegration inherent in their own evolving spirituality. They are introduced to the communal sense of the sacred. They learn songs and myths of origin, explanations of nature, and the mysteries of their own existence in a universe infinitely large. Ritual elders invite them to surrender themselves spiritually to the right order of things. As they learned that they are unconditionally members of the tribe of Men within the village, so they now learn that the village has its place in the natural order of the world, which has its place in the natural order of the cosmos. They begin to know that all life draws on a larger energy, necessary for the universe to survive.

At last the time of separation is ended and the initiates return home. They are different now. No longer are they tied to their mothers, looking to them for nurturance. Rather they have become young men growing toward the prime of their physical strength. Not yet mature enough to be entrusted with command, they are nevertheless clearly separated from the world and the work of women. They know that they are men and they know who and what men are in the world. These initiated young men hold the future of the hunt and the future of the physical life of the village. They hold also the future of the continuing initiation of men into the spiritual life of village, world, and cosmos.

## THREE ENERGIES OF INITIATION

My thesis is that initiation is essential to a man's cohesive sense of himself as Masculine. Through initiation, the Masculine becomes enlivened and empowered, so that a boy may become a mature man.[1] Without initiation, Boy Psychology maintains its grip upon the boy's self and he is never fully able to take his place in the world of men.

Three specific energies of initiation can be identified.[2] The first of these is the wounding-testing-separating energy, the energy of the ordeal. This is a dark, confrontive and threatening energy; through it the boy comes to know and tolerate different kinds of pain: physical pain of an intensity he could not have imagined before; emotional pain of separation from his mother and from reliance on external nurturing; and a deeper psychic pain of uncertainty and fear. This latter pain is not merely that he has been set adrift without a paddle but the awful realization that he may well die, alone, bereft of all which has been familiar to him—unknown, unseen, and unblessed.

Teaching-bonding is the second specific energy of initiation. This is a lighter energy, although not always less confrontive.

Through it, the boy comes to discriminate, identify and participate in both the manual skills and cultural rules which mark him both as a member of the village and as a man. He is taught how men are to behave among themselves, with women, and in relation to the world. He bonds to a male cohort—his fellow initiates—and identifies himself as a member of that cohort, sharing its pride, its achievements, its failures, its responsibilities, and its reputation. Now he belongs to a group in which he may continue to test himself and share the learning of life lessons. Now he can experiment, try his wings, experience ungainliness, practice speaking in a deeper voice, share his dreams of himself as a man—all within the protective cover of other initiates who are experiencing a similar adolescence. Bonds formed here are lifelong, supporting his sense of manhood until death.

Initiation's third specific energy is the healing-spiritual energy. Through it, the surviving initiate enters into the other world, where all things are pure spirit; a world where magic is ordinary, expected, unremarkable, and death is merely the completion of whatever was to be accomplished at this turn of the wheel. This energy welcomes the initiate to a place of surrender, to a place of paradox, to the wonderful place of understanding that he is absolutely *not* in control of the events that shape his life, while he is yet entirely responsible for his own being. This energy is the province of the spiritual elder entrusted to embody the divine connectedness of each to all.

The young man who has been shaped by these energies is ready for the tasks of manhood, and equipped to face the further stages of initiation which he will encounter later in life.


## THE MATURE MASCULINE


For most men in Western society, exposure to the energies of initiation is, at best, haphazard and chaotic. Lacking a cohesive experience of initiation, we have to ask—because our bodies, culture, and spirits cannot tell us—"What *is* the mature Masculine?"

The Masculine is not the same as either "male" or "man." Confusion on this point easily derails productive exploration of deeper fundamental structures within all men and women. Each living human being is a potential expression of the Masculine—as well as the Feminine. Another roadblock to deeper insight is to be found in the current entrancement with a cramped and confining "political correctness" that heavily shames and attacks politically anyone who states the obvious: Men are fundamentally different from women. Meaningful understanding of our deeper selves requires that both men and women explore honestly how we differ socially, psychologically, and spiritually.

The Masculine is ancient, deep and powerful. Following Moore and Gillette (1990), I view the mature Masculine as a balanced gathering of archetypal energies. These archetypes are the King, the Warrior, the Magician, and the Lover. The King presides over right order, fulfillment, definition of boundaries and values, fertility, communal abundance and prosperity, blessing, sacredness. The Warrior's function is action, strategy, aggression in service of the King, forward leaping or thrusting, loyalty, discipline, and individual prosperity. He is master of the hunt, guardian of the boundaries, executor of the King's orders. The Magician's domain is transformation, healing, and teaching, to which he brings awareness, insight, manipulation, reflection, and judgment. The Magician confronts the King's power and reminds the other archetypes of their responsibilities. The Lover enjoys play and display, the arts, sensation, aliveness, passion, appetite, and physical and spiritual satisfaction. He embodies an empathic sense of the world, a boundary-less connection to the universe, aesthetics, mysticism, and spirituality.

The mature Masculine is not without its dark Shadow. Moore and Gillette (1992a, 1992b, 1993a, 1993b) illustrate their important concept that the Shadow of each archetype is bipolar. Thus, the Shadow King may manifest as Tyrant or Weakling Abdicator; Shadow Warrior as Sadist or Masochist; Shadow Magician as Detached Manipulator or Denying Pseudoinnocent; Shadow Lover as Addicted (Don Juan) or Impotent.

It is important to differentiate conceptually between the Shadow of the mature Masculine, on the one hand, and the immature Masculine or Boy Psychology, on the other. A tangible—though admittedly subjective—distinction can be detected between the Tyrant and the High-chair Tyrant; between the Sadist and the Grandstander Bully. My hypothesis is that initiation is integral to the "death" of Boy Psychology and emboldens the flesh-and-blood man to face his Shadow. Unless and until initiated, the boy has no competence or reason to confront candidly the parts of himself that he does not wish to know. Facing the Shadow is a job for the *mature* Masculine.

Most boys in our society have no access to initiatory process. In the early and middle parts of this century, male school teachers and coaches, the clergy, extended family and even scout leaders were able to fill, at least to some extent, the role of initiator. It is important to recognize the singular contribution the military traditionally made in the initiation of young men. Indeed, it is probably no accident that the military experience tracked traditional models of initiation fairly closely. The separation of young men from their homes, the isolation and ordeal of boot camp, the perceived universality of service, the availability of training and education in technical skills and leadership, the uniquely male identity of the institution, the overwhelming importance of loyalty to one's unit and the indoctrination of the ethic of service to the nation—in all these we can see the energies of male initiation .

Today all of these initiatory efforts have pretty much disintegrated. Without the availability of conscious initiation, boys age only to act out caricatures of the mature archetypes and their shadow parts. There is danger in the current prevalence of Boy Psychology, which manifests as

> abusive and violent acting out behaviors against others, both men and women; passivity and weakness, the inability to act effectively and creatively in one's own life and to engender life and creativity in others (both men and women); and, often, an oscillation between the two—abuse/weakness, abuse/weakness (Moore & Gillette, 1990, p. xvi).

We have forgotten that, like all energy, the Masculine demands acknowledgment and integrated expression. Without legitimate avenues of expression, the Masculine becomes regressive, and seeks outlet in destructive ways—acting out in violence, crime, abuse of self and others. When a society no longer knows how to initiate, nor even how to recognize and acknowledge the mature Masculine, there is no consensual way for Everyman to experience the constructive nature of Masculinity in its fullness. As a consequence of this ignorance of the mature Masculine, all the deep archetypal Masculine energies begin to seek their expression in distorted ways. Thus, it is not surprising that today's world associates "masculinity" with such things as rigidly hierarchical devaluation of both the Feminine and women, sadomasochistic pornography, exaggerated machismo, growing levels of violence, material acquisitiveness, and pseudo-initiatory gang and college rituals. The more the Masculine is shamed, the more shamefully the Masculine shows up. The more shamefully the Masculine shows up, the more ashamed it deserves to be.

When the Masculine is shamed, it is not enough for flesh-and-blood men simply to be human. To be "real" men we must become something more. We must now metamorphose into supercreatures: sports heroes with multimillion dollar contracts, soulless political candidates saying what will get them elected rather than the truth, financial tycoons. These men are the "winners," our televisions tell us so. The rest of us, losers by definition, are invited to redeem ourselves from this double dose of shame by further burying our true masculine selves so as to emulate the winners. Where such emulation is clearly not possible, we make a profession out of our shame, joining the ranks of those who see the feminization of our society as the answer (see Zubaty, 1993).

Thus, many American men live lives in which their Masculinity is shamed or cursed. It is essentially shaming to impose on anyone a task or a role which is beyond his ability to fulfill—to ask a boy to do a man's job in any realm (e.g., emotional, physical, or spiritual). Yet we do it to ourselves and each other all the time. Similarly shaming is exposure to the ridicule and the ignominy of public failure. Listen to the laugh tracks of sitcoms where men are portrayed as silly wimps who have never "gotten it" and will never "get it." Even more deeply shaming is to hear "You are no man" from a woman and to believe that she speaks the truth. Such scorn for that uninitiated part of a man of which he already feels significantly ashamed can be painfully and enduringly emasculating. The airwaves teem with messages suggesting that deep Masculinity is wrong, an anachronism, dangerous, and no longer welcome or even tolerable in modern society.

When the mature Masculine becomes so deeply buried in a society, the available models of masculinity are mere shades, ephemeral and untrustworthy. Some essential element is missing from the fabric of society, from the very life-energy of the culture. Chaos, violence, wantonness and denial are predictable outcomes.

## MALE INITIATION HEALS MASCULINE SHAME

Male initiation operates in many ways as an antidote to masculine shame. One of the functions of initiation is to separate a boy from his mother's way of being and feeling. In the face of the initiatory ordeal, a boy cannot remain passive and retiring, or helplessly long for rescue by Mother. He cannot continue to be enamored of his own piteous suffering, or hide behind his own immaturity.

Through initiation, a young man discovers that his pain must be—and can be—carried, that it is a part of his growth. Acknowledgment and containment (neither suppression nor expression) of his feelings become his allies. He can feel the grief and rage of his separation, or the joy and relief of his survival, and learn to embrace the power of that emotional energy, and be strengthened by it. He does not need to "stuff" the energy or to dissipate it through undirected flailing or unfocused outburst. Thus, initiation awakens a man's mature emotional body, and so provides him a powerful antidote to the deadening impact of internalized shame on the Masculine.

The ordeal aspect of initiation also awakens the physical body to an awareness of the great potential of its own physical strength and determination. An initiated man can protect his own integrity against onslaughts from without and within. It is my belief that the boy's confrontation with his own physical fear, and his body's deep discovery that he can go forward "with the fear on the tip of his sword," leave the young man with an extraordinary weapon for vanquishing shame. The bodily experience of discovering his physical boundaries is more than a metaphor. Especially where shame has been derived from physical, sexual or emotional invasion, or from athletic failures, the newly awakened physical sense of self—of the "I am"—sends an unmistakable message of empowerment to the spirit. The sense of being able physically to define boundaries and then to protect them is, in my view, essential to the healing of internalized shame. As the initiate learns to differentiate from the Feminine and to defend against its seductive and regressive pull, he is empowered against the malignant wounds inflicted by the shaming of the Masculine.

A significant manifestation of internalized shame is a certain general confusion, or ignorance, about everything—especially about everything that might be helpful in healing shame. Shame tends to freeze a man in place because he cannot be assured that what he thinks he might want to do is correct, acceptable, productive, or healing. In this respect, the teaching/bonding energy of initiation teaches the boy what is *right*. This energy teaches him what the right things are for the young man to do, and it teaches a boy about what is *right* about masculinity.

Archetypally speaking, initiation teaches that it is part of a man's job, for example, to protect, to hunt, to provide governance, to love his mate, to participate in ritual, pursue a mission in the world. The initiated young man knows not only what he is supposed to do, but knows that his tasks serve, and are honored by, the society. In this way, a male's role *as a man* is defined and supported by his culture. He knows without asking that his activities will sustain his society as well as his own sense of mission and self-esteem. Society blesses his maturing masculinity and his manhood.

Such knowledge is significantly reinforced by the fact that *all* the young men share the experience of initiation. They have a common sense of doing and being "right" *as a man*. The cohort of former playmates now collectively embodies culturally sanctioned maturing masculinity. It is a group to which each man can turn for continuing reassurance that he is "okay." The bonded initiated cohort provides a psychological space where it is safe to experiment with and express his emerging manhood and masculinity. It also provides a socializing influence, imposing appropriate limits against behaviors that would pose an unacceptable threat to communal norms.

Thus initiation confronts shame through the provision of mentoring, of cultural guidance and wisdom, and through the bonding of each man to a cohort—all of which enliven a man's sense of the rightness of the Masculine in the world.'

Finally, initiation heals shame through its invocation and evocation of the spiritual. In this respect, a man surrenders to a higher sense of order as culturally defined; he surrenders to the secular King and accepts his place as a man in the world. And, through the spiritual aspect of initiation, a man surrenders to his place in the cosmos: he submits to the Sacred King and accepts his place as merely human, merely a man. This sense of self-acceptance, of humility, is the very opposite of toxic, internalized shame. I do not think the two can coexist, for the moment one accepts that he feels ashamed, the shame itself tends to dissolve. It is critical to recognize that this sense of surrender is by no means a surrender *to* the wound. It is certainly not a retreat into an embrace of Boy Psychology or childish preinitiatory helplessness. It is rather an acknowledgment of fallibility, a sense of acceptance that life is imperfect, that life both bruises and blesses. The power of paradox, the power of the joke, the sense of wonder—all of these convey the message to the initiated man: "Lighten up!"

Thus we see how the process of initiation, by invoking spe-

cific energies, can provide both healing and antidote for the shaming of the Masculine that infects our modern social and personal
environment.[3]

## A SUBCULTURE OF INITIATED
## MASCULINITY[4]

Over the last 10 years, hundreds of men have invested a great deal
of energy to provide male initiatory experience through the New
Warrior Training Adventure.[5] The New Warrior program demonstrates that it is possible to expose today's men to the energies of
initiation, and to continue the process through the development
of a bonded cohort. The program is consciously and intentionally
initiatory, and provides ongoing group experience to help integrate initiation into daily life.

Such experience, as with other programs of similar intent, is
necessarily quite different from traditional tribal initiation. Our society as a whole no longer agrees that initiation is important, so
there is little cultural support for the returning initiates. Moreover,
we are heterogeneous and mobile, intensely educated in secular
matters, and exposed to conflicting values, traditions and mores. It
becomes almost impossible to imagine, much less define and in-
culcate, consensus about how boys should be taught. Although
some would suggest that Western consciousness may now be ex-
panding to include wider recognition of the validity of spiritual
experience (Redfield, 1993), we are ending a century in which scientific thinking about human development and education has
made little room for transformative processes such as initiation.

At its inception, the New Warrior Training Adventure was neither consciously initiatory nor concerned with having any particular cultural significance. But after a decade of experience, we
may begin to discern an emerging subculture. Cultural change is
rarely the result of conscious effort, but emerges as a response to
human need. One similarity between tribal initiation and the New
Warrior program is that both somehow meet a need deeply felt in
our culture.

New Warriors and men who are pursuing initiation in other
ways, appear to be developing a common set of rituals. A common
jargon has arisen, as well as an approach to solving problems and
resolving disputes. A set of recognized values has emerged about

how men of integrity behave, at least towards other men (Everingham, 1995d; Kauth, 1992). Groups actively define what is required of men who would leaders, and provide an organized leadership training program. Perhaps most important, these men express pride in their manhood, and tend to be unashamedly committed to realizing the potential inherent in the mature Masculine.

These phenomena look like benchmarks for what may be called a subculture. My purpose here is not to stir up debate about nomenclature, so "subculture" is used tentatively to denote the *direction* of cultural change, and to help make the distinction from a cult or movement. It strikes me that we are witnessing the emergence of a transmissible subculture of initiated masculinity.

Men in our society have been starved for something that will somehow connect to their own deep Masculinity, and encourage its expression. This explains the phenomenon known as the "Men's Movement." Great teachers such as Robert Bly, Michael Meade, Joseph Hillman, Kenneth Druck, Warren Farrell, and Robert Moore have awakened many thousands of us to our yearning to know ourselves as men. The author's experience belies the premature obituaries for the Men's Movement which sometimes appear in the popular press. All over the United States—and in Canada, Great Britain, New Zealand, Australia—men continue to attend and develop New Warrior training programs. Throughout America, men's councils and other men's groups are continuing to explore what it means to be male in this society, and how the Masculine will manifest in the new millennium.

Where men have been consciously and intentionally exposed to initiatory process, and experienced the empowerment available in an initiated cohort, they are drawn further into unembarrassed exploration and expression of their manhood. Once men have a vision of what they *can* be, and sense that this potential is welcomed by some portion of society, they continue to broaden and deepen their masculinity. This is not merely an introspective, self-absorbed exercise. The initiated man understands that his life must be of service to his family, community, and world. In such service lies his ultimate sense of self-esteem as a man.

At the moment, a subculture of initiated Masculinity is more a vision than something susceptible to ethnographic measurement. But as we awaken collectively to our social task of initiating young men of all classes and races, I predict that we will see further evidence of the emerging subculture, and come to view its consolidation as essential to the realization of the mature Masculine. One vital function of the mature Masculine is nothing less than to cohere much of what is now disintegrating in our society.

## SUMMARY

Tribal initiation is described. Initiation is conceived as essential to a male's cohesive sense of being a man in the world. This sense develops as the ultimate result of the interaction of three separate and synergistic energies: ordeal energy; teaching-bonding energy; and healing-spiritual energy. Initiation involves separation of a boy from the mother's orbit and his bonding with a male cohort, and the integration of his emotional identity as a man and with a secure position as a member of the community. One source of toxic shame is the failure our society to initiate men into a "Subculture of Initiated Masculinity." As the essential process of masculine emotional, social and spiritual development (i.e. integration with self, community and cosmos), initiation is both a powerful healer of internalized shame and a defense against its destructive effects.

## NOTES

1. Initiation is best thought of as a process which opens the door to a new stage of further growth, or marks a change in direction in a man's life. Transformation does not fully manifest overnight. Further initiation must occur as a maturing man individuates. For example, at some point a man must grow beyond his exclusive identification with the male group (Bernstein, 1987).

2. I acknowledge with honor Larry Hall, PhD, for birthing this concept.

3. Additional examples of the impact of initiation may be found in chapter 10, where Christopher Miller discusses "Male Initiation: Filling a Gap in Therapy," and in chapter 6, where John Everingham discusses the Shadow, masculine archetypes, and the New Warrior training as part of his overview of "Men Facing Shame: A Healing Process."

4. I thank John Everingham for valuable discussions that helped me to clarify my thinking on this topic.

5. Other programs, such as Men's Councils, are also notable in the effort to revive initiatory process.

# 19

## From Shame to Self-Esteem*

*Philip M. Powell*

Shame occurs because we have been taught that something about ourselves is deeply flawed. We just don't have the right equipment to be the right kind of human being. The only antidote for shaming yourself and others is a permanent dose of higher self-esteem. Not the usual bubba like braggadocio. I mean real self-esteem. The kind that involves self-forgetting because you know you are all right, because you are both real and good as a human being. As Jewish people say, you're a mensch—a real human being. So, I am going to tell you how to grow into a real human being—one whom you can take to the bank of life with confidence.

To raise your self-esteem permanently, you must be willing to change, really change your approach to life. I'll show you how to do it. First, you need to understand yourself and there are certain tools to use for this. The most basic tool is William James's theory of the self and self-esteem (James, 1910), supplemented by the ideas of folks like Maslow (1955), Mayeroff (1990), and Sullivan (1953).

---

*This chapter reflects ideas based on 20 years of teaching and studying self-esteem. Some of these ideas have been presented in workshops at two International Men's Conferences held in Austin, TX (1992), and in New Braunfels, TX (1993).

## WILLIAM JAMES'S THEORY OF
## SELF-ESTEEM

James believed that the self had two basic ways of experiencing the world with two different modes of consciousness. These he called the "I" and the "me." The "I" refers to thinking which is automatic or spontaneous but which occurs without reflecting on what you are doing. One example of "I" thinking is when you drive down a familiar road that you travel all the time. You just drove home while thinking about a thousand different things, all of which involved topics other than driving. This is the automatic "I" thinking. An example of spontaneous "I" thinking can be shown using the same example. Suppose something happened that was surprising while you were driving home, something like a gargoyle falling off one high building next to the road and landing right in front of you while you were driving. Assuming you survived this, the swerving you did to avoid the accident is an example of the spontaneous "I" thinking. You did not know the exact movements you would make to avoid hitting the falling gargoyle. The movements you made were spontaneous.

Interestingly enough, this also provides an example of the second form of thinking, called the "me." The moment you became conscious of the fact that you were in a situation which required evasive maneuvering to avoid the gargoyle, you were functioning in the "me" mode of thinking. Now let's be careful here. The "I" part of this car driving example includes the spontaneous movements you made to avoid the gargoyle. The "me" part of this involves you becoming aware that the situation of driving home this particular time is radically different from the usual trips home. If you did not become aware of this difference you would have died or been badly hurt. *The "me" then involves all moments of thinking when you are aware of what you are doing in order to modify your actions as needed.* It typically is induced by being surprised. You think you are going to have something happen one way but it happens another.

So being surprised leads to becoming aware that things in life don't have to happen like you expect them to. The result of "me" awareness is that you learn to be flexible, to take things on the fly, to take things with enough openness that you can change in even a familiar situation if something odd happens. Change does not have to involve bad outcomes. It can also involve good ones. How many a man has thought that he was not good looking in the eyes of a woman he was interested in, and one day he discovered that the woman not only liked him, but saw him as good looking too? So you can be very pleasantly surprised by life, and start seeing yourself as better than you thought you were.

Next, James said that the "me" was divided into three parts: material, social, and spiritual. "Material me" refers to your body and all physical objects you identify with, such as your car or favorite suit. "Social me" refers to all the prestige and recognition you receive. "Spiritual me" refers to all the deep, personal thoughts you think, and related actions you perform, as well as all the psychological faculties that allow you to act this way (memory, intelligence, character, morality, ideology, etc.). The catch is that these three me's are developmental, with the material being first, followed by the social and lastly by the spiritual. So we are one of these types of selves, more or less.

Depending on how we are treated, we develop certain feelings about ourselves. We strive to retain the status quo if we like our treatment, or we act to change our situation. Suppose we are ashamed of ourselves because we feel we are too fat. Then we will engage in what James called material self seeking. We might diet or we might continually make jokes to distract others from looking at our terrible bodies. Or we might become shy to avoid being "seen" by others. Suppose again, we are ashamed of ourselves socially—we just don't fit in. We don't have enough money to buy the right clothes, we don't get enough social attention, we never get promoted in our jobs, etc. What we will do, according to James, is seek ways to get social attention. We might dress in ways which dramatize our need for attention, even negative attention.

I once knew a woman who wore long black oversized dresses because she feared sexual attention. Once she started wearing stylish clothes, it became obvious that she was the finest looking woman around. But first she had to be encouraged by her friends, so that she would want the new attention.

Lastly, there is spiritual self seeking. This refers to a person who feels that everything he does has to be deep and important. He rarely just has fun or looks at cartoons or stops reading the *New York Times*. He's obsessed with deep thoughts.

The overall point of self seeking is that we all try to correct ourselves when we feel we lack something. And this is all right as long as such acts are temporary, but if they are permanent or chronic, they reflect serious self-esteem problems. I know a man who can only talk about his ideas and *his* problems. He has serious spiritual self seeking behavior and has low self-esteem. He is trapped inside his own crap.

## TYPES OF SELF-ESTEEM

James offered the first definition of self-esteem that was accepted in our culture. He defined self-esteem as equal to a high ratio of successes over pretensions (i.e. expectations). This leads to three basic levels of self-esteem: high, medium, and low.

High self-esteem means that you have a wide range of expectations or life goals you want to achieve and that you are achieving or have achieved. High self-esteem people are low in anxiety; they are risk takers. They are confident, popular, able folks who define who can hurt them and are rated as generally successful in what they do (Coopersmith, 1967). Low self-esteem people are anxious, take no risks, have little confidence, are unpopular, and tend to have or show less ability. Anyone can hurt them, and they are relatively unsuccessful.

Persons medium in self-esteem fall in the middle between high and low in these characteristics. Subtly, James' formula suggests some other types of self-esteem. One is defensive high self-esteem. This is a person who maintains a high level of self-esteem by focusing his attention and efforts to being successful in just a few areas of life. This is the so-called big fish in a little pond. We have all seen people who are hot stuff as long as they stay in their home town and work for their rich father or play basketball as the home town star. But if these people tried to move out into the big time they would fail—if they left their town, left their job, left the rich father, left their town to play ball in the pros.

There is a fifth type of self-esteem called the uncertain low. This is a person high in ability, but who is doing the wrong type of work or is associating with the wrong type of people to support him or her and feels bad about himself accordingly. So, you see, we have five types of self-esteem categories, which are from highest to lowest: high, defensive high, medium, uncertain low, and low.

Only the first type of high, the true high, needs no self-esteem enhancement. All other self-esteem types need self-esteem improvement. Another thing, if you know your self-esteem is low, truly low, you need the help of a trained psychologist, psychiatrist, pastoral counselor, other mental health professional, or a transformational group process to help you work on your self-esteem. The procedures offered herein will help you and indeed you will have to do these too if you want to raise your self-esteem, but the anxieties and demons you will have to face will be much more difficult to handle alone than would be true for any of the higher self-esteem levels. I call the low just mentioned "true low" to distinguish it from uncertain low.

## EIGHT STEPS TO IMPROVE SELF-ESTEEM

Here are eight steps to improve self-esteem. Follow these and self esteem is bound to rise. If any step becomes too difficult for you, seek the help of a counselor to help you examine the issues and feelings involved.

1. *Measure your level of self-esteem.* This can be done two basic ways: cognitively and emotionally. Here is the cognitive approach. First, list all of the important goals you want to achieve in your life. Second, decide honestly whether or not you are achieving these goals. If you are not, your self-esteem is low. If you are achieving some of your personal goals, your self-esteem is medium and if you are achieving all of them, your self-esteem is high. Next, decide if you have few goals or many. If your self-esteem is high with few goals you are probably a defensive high. If your goals are many and you are achieving them, you are a true high. If you are a true high, you do not need this process at all, although it may interest you. Most likely, you are somewhere between true high and true low.

   The emotional approach to measuring self-esteem involves assessing your feeling tone. Are you pessimistic in your attitude toward life? Or are you realistically optimistic, a person who smiles when he can? Is life a glass which is half empty or half full? Are you depressed much of the time like some sad sack or are you generally optimistic? If you tend to be pessimistic, depressed, and nonenthusiastic about life, then you have a low(er) self-esteem. If you are realistically optimistic about your life and its many interactions and experiences, not denying bad things that occur to us all, but either always expecting the good stuff to happen to you, or at least trying to see the positive even in the negative, then you have higher self-esteem. Higher self-esteem people are more energized and fun to be around. They tend to stimulate others to be excited about life, too.

2. *See yourself clearly.* This is tough. You may need another honest person to help you here. The goal is to see what type of self you are. Are you a material self, a social self, or a spiritual one? To do this we will use a question inspired by a test devised by Kuhn and McPartland (1954) and scored by measures using James' theory. Write down 20 answers to the question, "What kind of person am I?" Rate each of your answers as "material me," "social me," or "spiritual me." An answer is material if it refers to your physical body or to a physical object you own or respect. Examples: I am 6'4" tall and am a homeowner.

A social answer refers to a role you play. I am a father, a lover (yes, lover is a role—you are expected to act a certain way if you are someone's lover) or a friend. An answer is spiritual when it refers to a psychological characteristic that is peculiar to you as a person such as thoughtfulness or high morality. (Note that James said spiritual when we would say psychological.)

If most of your answers are material ones then you are that type; if most are social, you are this type and so on. This gives you a key to the type of self seeking you are likely to be doing. If you rate yourself as social, you can bet that when you self seek it is done in the area of getting social attention. It tells you what you feel you lack in life!!!!

3. *Change your behavior.* There are eight changes you must undergo in a certain spirit.

a. Stop engaging in *either-thinking*. Nothing is either-or. Everything in this world is shades of gray. People mired in either/or thinking see life as a grand vaudevillian stage, where someone like God is waiting for them to make a mistake before He will take a big Broadway hook and pull them off the stage for a bad performance. This just ain't so. We ain't angels or saints down here on earth. But you might get pulled off the stage of life for *not trying*, not doing the best you can, mistakes and all.

Learn from your mistakes. Learn to give a better performance next time by getting feedback now. So many folks hunger for perfection, rather than strive to be excellent. Perfection is not your destiny. Excellence is. Learn to pat yourself on the back when you are on the road to being better, when you take one step towards your goal. It's like learning to pat yourself on the back for playing the game of life at all. It's tough to be alive.

It's hard to be human. It's a thankless job. Guy goes to work every day making a living to support his family. That's good. Guy goes to a school play after working 10 hours to see poor acting from his kid. That's good. Guy goes to the hospital because his wife is sick. That's good. Learn to keep track of your own goodness, which is the greatest good. Your goodness will never be based on the great things you have done, but on the little things you do daily to sustain yourself and others. You can't be an either/or thinker to act this way. You will damn yourself before you even try.

b. Pay attention to how you dress. It is a truism that the lower the self-esteem, the poorer the dress. If you do not think well of yourself, then why dress nicely? When self-esteem rises, dress improves. This is because you honor yourself, so you start treating yourself better. As self-esteem truly rises, a man will start improving in small ways. This may be the only improvement noticeable at first, but it signals a deeper change within.

c. Present yourself like a winner. If you want to be promoted, act like you are promoted already. Act like those who are promotable. Do what they do. People with self-esteem problems act defeated. People "smell" this and use it against them. Sometimes people are like wolves, tracking a weaker wolf. So dress better, smile, work harder, respect yourself, pray, and people will think more of you.

d. Change your friends. If you want to improve your self-esteem, move away from your old network of friends who have been supporting your lower self-esteem. Find other friends, positive people, who will support your improvement. Get a new job where you are valued, where you can create a new social history. Old friends and colleagues tried to treat you as you were—not as you are now. Screw them! Let someone new get the benefit of your new self. This is tough language, but our problems are tough. Tell certain people to screw off, because you have better things to do. One of ten first steps in change is to learn to say NO to anyone and everyone who needs you to do stuff that keeps you down.

e. Take feedback about your behavior but *never* about your essence. This is a subtle step. Never let anyone define who you are, but listen when an honest and accurate person tells you about how you are coming across to him. People in low self-esteem let everyone tell them how to be. They try to please even strangers. Forget this. Let people earn your ear by their deeds. Evaluate the source of feedback. Value accurate feedback even if it hurts, but never let someone tell you what you are.

f. Reflect about yourself and others. Learn to think about what you need, and act accordingly. Figure out what others need from you, and why. Then you can decide what you are going to do and whom you are going to please. Establish yourself as the author of your own existence. Become free.

g. Be consistent with who you are. To do this, you must have some idea of who you are and where you are going in life. If you decide to be a good person, this means you will not gossip about people, you will avoid hurting them even if they hurt you sometimes, you will walk an extra mile to do right as you understand it. Being consistent allows you to take responsibility and authority for your actions and decisions in peace.

h. Be genuinely concerned about yourself and others. This teaches you how to know and to care for yourself and for others (Mayeroff 1990). You need to take care of your needs first before you can help anyone else. Without this, you have only narcissistic, misguided meddling in the lives of others. There is nothing more annoying or boring than being the village narcissist. Also, no matter who you are you have got to learn some social skills to care for others. Here are five that are absolutely necessary:

- Learn how to speak to meet others with respect. Make eye contact, Smile more than you frown if the person is halfway interesting. Otherwise avoid them.
- Never talk down to anyone—treat them like they can raise as much hell or heaven as you.
- Follow the law of reciprocity—if someone helps you, repay them.
- Find folks that interest you so you can stop talking about yourself.
- Work hard, be honest and contribute to your family and society in any way you can.

Following these social rules guarantees that you will be a social success with genuine friends. You will die happy, and a crowd of folks will attend your funeral.

4. *Show your true self.* This has three parts:

a. Handle pain and view it different. Pain is always a sign that something is wrong with the way we are living. It is always positive information. So listen to your body. Take a moment now while you are reading this to calm down and notice any pain in your body or your mind. Now promise yourself to take care of whatever the problem is. Notice that this involves correcting your thinking as well as your actions. When you do this, the pain improves, even if it is cancer! I firmly believe that you can heal yourself if you change your thoughts, actions and feelings.

When you change your thoughts and actions, your feelings must change because you are creating different experiences for yourself. Most importantly, start to notice that your pain is always connected to your negative thoughts. This is true for bodily pains, but most true for thoughts you have, painful expectations. I often notice soreness in my joints because I have gout. This reminds me to consume less wine and red meat. I can simply modify my diet to lose weight, without putting myself down for being overweight, which never helps. Correct the problem, but never blame the self, because it is the only tool we have for living.

b. Take vacations. Going on a vacation does not mean planning everything like you do at work, accounting for your time. "Vacation" means to leave what you normally do and do something relaxing. Workaholics don't take vacations. They arrange field trips and activities to occupy every waking moment. They even create activities for the whole family and make everyone feel guilty when they don't want to participate. Take a real vacation to gather new perspectives and relax the body to alleviate pent-up stress and prolong life. Stay away from workaholic, type A personalities on vacations. Leave them home.

c. Accept responsibility for yourself. This involves three related aspects: (a) Explore what you want to do in your life and do it, and explore what you want to become; (b) blame your life on no one; and (c) do things for yourself. Exploring what you want to do and become is important as it keeps you on the path of self-actualization. Never con yourself. I once knew a person who always talked about how her life would be different if she had been a painter. So I asked to see her work. Lo and behold, it was good stuff, but she had never tried to market it. So I told her that I knew some artists connected with well known galleries who might be able to help her. She never took me up on this suggestion! Some people are just afraid to change the way they live. You've got to lose this fear. You've got to put up or shut up.

Blame your life on no one. Everybody has had bad things and good things happen to them and theirs. There is always someone with an even worse life. Also, some of the negative, hell all of the negative and all of the positive, experiences created your self in the first place. You can't be you and blame your life too. That's contradictory.

5. *Meet your basic needs first so you can grow.* Maslow's (1955) theory of self actualization tells us that deficiency motivation must be taken care of before growth motivation can begin life. Deficiency motivation refers to a set of needs being met strictly in this order: 1) physical needs (food, clothing, housing); 2) a safe environment; 3) acceptance by others; and 4) self-esteem. Deficiency motivation operates differently from growth motivation. Once you get deficiency needs met, you stop needing to think about them. Growth needs always involve you wanting them more and more. There are two growth needs, the need to self-actualize and the need to understand existence fully. These needs become evident only as self-esteem problems decrease in your life. This leads to our next big step.

6. *Recontruct your self-concept.* People with self-esteem problems always have the basic problem of a dysfunctional self-concept. We have already measured self-concept with the "kind of person" test described earlier. You have to take your list and throw away any "I am" statement that does not reflect what you want to do with your life. Junk any component which is what someone else wants, not you.

I learned an important theory when I was drinking one night. My friend, name of Rufus, is rough, tough and very intelligent. He's a decent guy who drove tanks in the war. He calls his theory the "crap" theory of human development, although crap isn't exactly the name he used. When a guy's bag gets too heavy, he sidles up to another guy, sort of friendly like, and puts some of his crap in the guy's bag. You've got to watch your bag to see that it contains your crap and no one else's. If you don't you will be living out the implications of someone else's crap and not your own. This sounds funny, but it ain't. It's worth remembering.

Pick new roles you want to play in life and play them with all your heart. Personally, I discovered quite by accident that I like to talk to men's groups, to the gifted, to kids and to any folks who are trying to grow and figure that I can help them. I don't like real formal meetings because "I ain't much for airs and such." I like Texas because a lot of people here are the same as me—earthy, proud, reasonably hard working, and God fearing. I figure the world is full enough of highfalutin folks so it doesn't need me as an extra one. I got to live the way I know is best for me and I am ruthlessly pursuing my life from this viewpoint.

Learn new work. By new work, I mean that you will find that by being real about who you are, you will naturally do things that feel right. You will place yourself in the best position to discover what God wants you to do with your life. You will start doing it with a zeal that can be scary. And once you live this new way you will find yourself rising in Maslow's hierarchy of needs—your deficiencies will be corrected and folks will know that when they deal with you, they are dealing with the real megallah, the real thing. That's rare. It may be totally different work, or the same work with your personal groove in it, your emphasis stamped all over it. Find this one groove and you are home free.

Never derogate yourself. We all have a ton of negative thoughts. Keep a diary of these thoughts and make every attempt to stamp them out. I call this the "killing the roaches" substep of self-concept change. Don't keep putting yourself down. There are plenty of cynics and bastards who will bad-mouth you. You simply can't afford to do it to yourself. As Winston Churchill might have said, "Never, never, never, never, never give up on yourself".

The biggest roach you have to kill is the ideal self—all those fancy goals you have. All you've got is yourself now. Don't wait to live. Live now. Do your best now. Put all that fancy crap in the fireplace where it belongs, if you can stand the stench. God accepts you in heaven if you start right now, so don't postpone living right. What about the negatives that still come into your life after you have purged yourself of the tendency to put yourself down? I've got an answer for this, too. Analyze negatives for useful information. If there is nothing useful being said, blow it off.

Leave all bad environments. A bad environment is any place or social situation which is dangerous to your growth. This includes marriages, family relationships, ideological beliefs, jobs, even towns, where you do not fit. Drop them as soon as you can, but be practical as you go. Finally, expect shakeups of energies as you grow and explosions too as you give up unnecessary defenses. What is happening is that all selves have what Harry Stack Sullivan (1953, pp. 158–171), an Irish-American psychiatrist, once called "good me, bad me and not me" experiences in life.

"Good me" experiences are those where somebody told you you were good and you felt good as a result. You remember your "good me" experiences. You can remember "bad me" experiences with anxiety. "Not me" experiences are those where you broke some taboo and were punished or shamed so badly that you actually repressed and denied these experiences. They are unconscious roaches.

Often when you start working on self-esteem, you will remember instances of childhood abuse which lie at the base of your low self-esteem. How could you learn self-esteem when your true self was rejected in such a painful way? How can you trust that anyone could ever truly love you if your family rejected you? You are permanently ashamed. In severe cases, you feel you are better off dead. Once your self-esteem raises though, you release these fears. Fears bind energy. So expect outbursts of energy which will allow you to both work and play harder!

Finally, meditate and relax whenever you need to. This clears the mind and body and will prolong your life. I recommend *How to Meditate* by Lawrence LeShan (1975).

7. *Be realistic in trusting yourself and others.* Accurately examine yourself to see where you are trustworthy. If you are a blabbermouth, ask others not to tell you their deeper secrets because you talk too much. I actually heard a person say this once. Or if a friend talks too much you will be careful about what you say around them. You just accept some personal limitations and the limitations of others.

8. *Be honest yet merciful with yourself.* Give yourself credit for your intentions and behavior as long as you are being productive in the way you personally define it. After all, it's your life, not your family's or society's. You have to live and die for yourself. At this point, your self-esteem is permanently on the rise. Shame is not a part of your vocabulary, although you will have a new type of guilt. You will feel guilty any time you are not true to yourself.

Life is like a bank. It's filled with money, pleasure, love, grace, opportunity, growth, and a whole host of God-given experiences. Self-esteem is the way out of shame and despair, a way to get your piece of the action, your share of the bank of life. Interested?

# 20

## Beyond Shame: Transforming Our World

*Roy U. Schenk*

### OUR PRESENT WORLD VIEW

Many of our authors have shown how internalized shame is the primary cause of war, environmental destruction and interpersonal violence. Shame is so prevalent in our world that it is difficult to visualize what human life will be like when we move beyond its domination. We have some hints, and we will look at these later in this chapter.

In Chapter 2, I presented a schematic representation of our current plane of existence (see Figure 2.1). This visualization is reproduced in a modified form in Figure 20.2. It represents an existence created by judging others and ourselves. Judgments divide people on the basis of superiority and inferiority, good and evil, better than and not as good as, victims and perpetrators, angels and beasts, and countless other ways—all to compensate for our own shame-induced feelings of inferiority and inadequacy. Running through this plane is a fine line of equality that marks the intersection separating the superior from the inferior and good from evil.

I believe this accurately depicts our world view or present mind-set, and shows how precarious equality is. We cannot achieve equality among human beings as long as we accept this world view. There is simply not room on the line for everybody and even when we stand astride the line, we overlap into one or both of the divided categories.

We could just shrug off this situation with a remark like: "This is the way things have always been and will always be." This is a defeatist attitude which might have been acceptable in the past. But today we are confronted with our own power to destroy life on earth either dramatically by nuclear war or more gradually by mindless pollution. We see an epidemic of water, air and soil pollution all over the world. Acid rain is destroying both fish and forests.

The average human sperm count has already decreased 50% worldwide, evidently as a result of estrogen-like pollutants (Hileman, 1994). In addition, wars continue their deadly toll, and are becoming increasingly deadly and vicious as the world powers develop more effective military hardware and supply it to smaller nations. The social fabric of nation after nation is rapidly deteriorating as people lose hope and strike out in despair, focusing solely on their own short term interests.

It is time to recognize that we have other options. We need not continue down the same path. As human beings *we choose* to judge and divide people. These are shame-based habits learned from childhood, habits that can be unlearned and replaced with different habits. In this chapter we will examine some of the immense benefits to be gained by developing new habits of relating to each other. But first we need to understand the nature of these new habits.


## A NEW WORLD VIEW


The present world view divides people into categories (good and evil, inferior and superior, etc.), and this division arises and is maintained by our habits of judging ourselves and others. Equality is reduced to a fine line separating superior from inferior, good from evil. It is only at this dividing line that we are able to suspend judgment of others and ourselves. Now envision a new plane of existence, a new world view, which passes through our present plane at the line of equality. This new plane of existence is

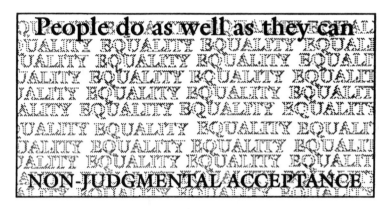

**FIGURE 20.1** The equality plane of existence.

based on equality: equality is present everywhere and is taken as the norm. This new plane is depicted in Figure 20.1, and its intersection with our current plane is illustrated in Figure 20.2.

How can we get onto that plane? All that is required is to move from our habits of judging ourselves and others to a new habit of accepting ourselves and other people. This includes accepting ourself and others *even when we do judge ourself or others*. Access to this new plane of existence comes through establishing nonjudgmental acceptance as the norm for ourselves and others. Nonjudgmental acceptance does not mean "anything goes," nor does it mean that we must accept being hurt without challenging a person whose behavior hurts us. It means that we have clear boundaries, and we confront and challenge invasions of our boundaries, while we continue to accept the person who is invading them.

Some people use the term "unconditional love" to describe this new behavior pattern or habit. Perhaps we need to use a term that unites the aspects of love and acceptance. In time, it will be helpful to develop positive language and move beyond negative terms like "nonjudgmental" and "unconditional," because what ever we oppose we keep alive. But for now the negative terms may be useful to remind us of where we are coming from.

Prophets and spiritual leaders throughout history have articulated themes of love and acceptance. Because these ideas have been advocated so often and so long, and with little apparent ef-

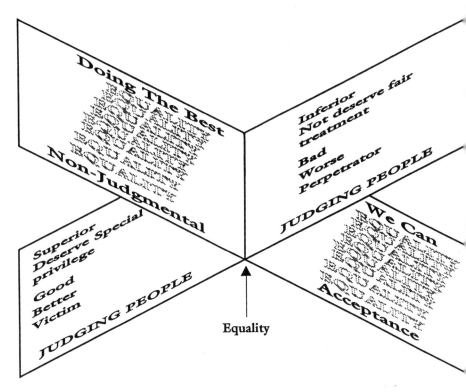

**FIGURE 20.2**   Future plane intersecting our present plane.

fect, it may seem hopeless. The goal of a world based on love and acceptance may seem unattainable simply because it has not yet been achieved. That attitude leads only to despair.

## POWER OF TRANSFORMATION

Today, as we approach the close of the twentieth century, we have the awesome capacity to destroy human life on earth. At the same time, we have a growing understanding of the transformative power of loving and acceptance.

My awareness of this power came from participating in transformational weekends conducted by two different groups, the New Warrior Network[1] and Landmark Education Corporation[2] The physical experiences of these weekends were dramatically different. The first was very physical and openly confrontational. The second was very sedentary and intellectually challenging. Yet both experiences created awe-inspiring transformations in most of the participants. Shy wallflowers became outgoing; belligerent bullies became delighted and excited sharers. People broke out of protective walls they had lived behind for decades.

Amazed that experiences so different could produce such similar results, I looked for their common elements and I found several. The first is a predominant attitude of nonjudgmental acceptance. This does not mean pretending that people are perfect, but rather choosing to accept ourselves and each other *as we are,* with all of our defects and failings. None of us is infallible, so we cannot create a milieu of *total* acceptance. Fortunately perfection is not necessary. Our present milieu is so unaccepting and judgmental that we can create a dramatically different environment simply by establishing acceptance as the norm. The powerful ways people respond to this environment demonstrates that we share an intense desire for wholeness and health.

A second commonality involves acting together in community. An accepting community is a "safe container" that gives us permission to let go of the repressions and inhibitions we have developed over the years as shields against shaming.

A third commonality is challenge. Each person is challenged to take a look at his or her life, and to choose to let go of repressions and inhibitions. Because our shields against shame are deeply internalized lifelong habits, it is not feasible to break them down completely in one brief weekend. This is why both groups incorporate ongoing programs for people to reinforce the new belief system and to practice the new habits.

A fourth commonality is confidentiality. Most people will not expose their shadow parts unless they are confident that their revelations will remain within the confines of the group.

These weekends have shown me that we can break out of our old shaming habits and transform our lives. However we have been so deeply and repeatedly wounded it is unlikely that people of our generation will completely transform our lives. We will continue to carry scars from the wounds of the past just as fifty years later my knee still bears a scar from a childhood bicycle accident. But we can go far. We can create an environment characterized by love and acceptance, a society in which love and acceptance are the norm, a society in which new generations will learn the habits of acceptance and love from birth.

What will this world be like? How will it be to no longer judge each other on the basis of superiority or inferiority, good or evil, right or wrong? In an environment where acceptance and love are the norm, we gain control of our lives. We no longer have the need nor the ability to pass the buck or to blame others. Each of us has responsibility for our own life. When challenged and supported to do so, we can take charge of our lives, and live happier and more fulfilling lives as a result.

This is both liberating and scary. It is scary because we have not been trained to assume control of our lives. But we can learn the skills we need. I observe men in the New Warrior Network who are committed to developing the process and are growing in skill. There is a lot of experimentation, fumbling, and error; however, we are learning. One crucial task is learning to make necessary judgments and discernments without letting these become judgments about ourselves or others.

I was raised a Christian, and I believe that acceptance and unconditional love is the world view that Jesus embodied. For example, when Jesus confronted the woman about to be executed by stoning for adultery, he refused to pass judgment on her (John 8:11). On several occasions, he advised his disciples to "judge not, lest you be judged." (Matt. 7:1; Luke 6:37). His warning that we will not enter the Kingdom of Heaven until we become "like little children" (Matt. 18:3) conveys a vision of a world based on acceptance and love, and beyond good and evil. Jesus knew that love is the most powerful force on earth. Other prophets and spiritual leaders have brought similar messages.

I find that I have trouble giving up judging good from evil. How can good and evil become irrelevant or even meaningless? In many conflicts and especially in war, each side defines itself as good and defines its opponents as bad. This indicates that good and bad are only creations of our minds. Learning that Socrates developed the concept of good and evil was helpful. But without good and evil, on what basis do we confront and challenge people when they do things we think are inappropriate? The early Christians and Quakers experimented with working out this question in everyday life, and many people are engaged in similar experiments today. It is frustrating to leave this question unanswered, but I don't know the answer at this time. Because we sustain what we oppose it seems we need to avoid duality. Perhaps self-interest, meeting needs or embracing our shadow will provide the basis for a new system.

I have found that one highly effective way to change my habit of judging people is to respond to my judging internal voice with the message that people are doing the best they can. An amazing change of attitude comes from accepting that belief. I still am tempted to return to the judgmental plane by thinking, "But I am doing better than that person is, so I am better." However, I can choose not to accept that judgment. Accepting that a person is doing the best s/he can does not mean we must accept harmful behavior. Rather it opens the possibility for effectively confronting and challenging such behavior.

I have come to believe that it is only by accepting and loving men as they are that we can effectively challenge them to transform their lives. I think this powerful paradox is the fundamental understanding that Jesus and other religious prophets and leaders have identified in the past. And I believe that the New Warriors have developed an effective way to help make this concept work with men.

I am also experimenting with and observing the effects of visualizing each person I encounter as magnificent. In fact, each of us is magnificent, even if we only consider our physical beings. We are truly awesome when we also consider our brains, our minds, our spirits and their complex interactions with which we are only vaguely familiar. Visualizing oneself and others as magnificent is actually being honest about ourselves.

There is a part of me that does not want to give up judging. I believe this is because I still carry residual shame and inferiority feelings, so I still feel an urge to compensate. The scars from past wounds are unlikely to ever be completely lost. But that is okay. To be human is to be imperfect, to make mistakes, to learn by trial and error. We do not need to feel shame for this.

## A VISION OF THE FUTURE

Let's turn now to the future, and begin to develop a vision of how life will be when acceptance and love become our habitual ways of relating to each other. We will look at how this would be likely to affect four areas: the development of our human potential, our relationships with others, our relations with the spiritual, and the socialization process. Most of my thoughts in these areas are very tentative and subject to change. Prognostication is risky business.

One can feel ashamed of being proven wrong by events. But as John Everingham tells me, I don't have to be right, I only have to be honest.

## HUMAN POTENTIAL

When we internalize shame, the experience is so painful that we generally choose almost anything which we believe will reduce further shaming. We tend to inhibit and repress whatever parts of ourselves we believe will induce shaming. When we learn to remove the shaming messages and stop internalizing shame from messages we receive, we will no longer inhibit or repress our spontaneous and exuberant feelings and actions. For an idea of unrepressed spontaneity, look at the behavior of young children who have not been completely squelched.

I anticipate that children and adults will develop far more extensive areas in which they are creative. For example, if you are not put down because "You can't sing!" you are more likely to sing. A lot more people will discover that they can sing well. The same is true for other creative areas. As people become more creative, they will be more interesting, less sedentary and more involved in joyful living.

Play and sports will be less competitive, but no less exciting and challenging; and they will involve far more people as participants. Alcoholism, and other drug addictions, which appear to be shame based, will all but vanish. Prisons as we know them will be abandoned as relics of a barbarous past. Crime will be minimal and people who commit crimes will be challenged to make amends and lead exemplary lives. People needing incarceration will be treated with care, respect, and dignity. We will understand the observation of Kalil Gibran (1923) that "the righteous is not innocent of the deeds of the wicked, the guilty is oftentimes the victim of the injured, and the condemned is often the burden bearer for the guiltless and unblamed."

## RELATIONSHIPS WITH OTHERS

Early in life people will develop much clearer boundaries, and will learn to protect those boundaries. It is quite normal for us to encroach on other people's boundaries because we are not omniscient. What is important is that people are able to identify and protect their own boundaries. This need not be an occasion for shame. One can be respectful of the encroaching person and simply make clear what one's boundaries are. In this way, we will achieve more honest and caring relationships.

When shame is no longer used to coerce people into conforming, our motives will change. The standards we live by will change to integrity, commitment, discretion , caring, compassion, and respect for others. We already know that a self-motivated person is more likely to live up to standards than is a person upon whom someone else's standards are forced. This does not mean that we will live in a perfect world. We will still learn by trial and error. But our learning will be accelerated, so less wounding will occur. People will be more sensitive and considerate of the needs of others because their own needs are being met more effectively.

When we no longer suffer a serious deficit of caring and acceptance, our urgent drive to find one person who can meet all of our needs will no longer exist. We will be able to choose our relationships with others on a less needy basis. We will certainly not lack relationships, and perhaps we will have even more relationships. Some of these will be more intense and deeply caring relationships than we are now capable of. We will be more spontaneous because we will be unafraid of being shamed. In part this will result from a reduced emphasis on achievement, particularly for men, which will free up time to develop and nurture relationships. With less urgency and neediness in relationships, we will choose more carefully the person(s) we want to be close to, and we will feel safer in allowing them to be close to us. Gender will become less important as we reduce the pressure to conform to restrictive gender roles. A child's gender may become irrelevant during the first ten years of life.

Social progress will be far easier to achieve. As people come to peace with themselves and feel less pain from extensive wounding, they will be less resistant to reducing the pain of other people. Life will become even more interesting and more exciting. It will be a delight to develop our physical, emotional, and spiritual potentials. In fact, I believe the world will become more exciting, delightful, and fascinating than we can presently begin to imagine. People in this future will look back on today's world and wonder how we were able to survive the rage and hatred, the violence and brutality, and the animosity and shaming which are so prevalent today.

## RELATION TO THE SPIRITUAL

Our response to shaming tends to inhibit and repress us, and we become fearful of whatever is different. This is particularly true of the spiritual, which many regard as foreign, subtle or mysterious. Today, religious groups claim a monopoly on spirituality, but I propose that spirituality will blossom as we move beyond shame. People will feel freer to talk about their religious and mystical experiences, and our understanding of spiritual phenomena will expand dramatically. Earlier prophets and visionaries will not be discredited; instead their messages will become clearer and will make more sense to us.

There appears to be a power, which is often called God, permeating the universe. Our present knowledge of this power is attained as if "looking through a glass darkly." Many people, groups and religions have found ways to access that power through a wide variety of prayer and meditation techniques. The striking differences in the ways this power is approached suggest that we have not yet learned to access this power in its fullness. More effective access to this power is likely to be achieved in the new plane of acceptance and love.

There are faint hints that mental telepathy, psychic healing, and other forms of psychic phenomena may become more fully understood and developed. Some alleged psychic phenomena may be found to be fakery. However, I anticipate that we will find many of these phenomena are genuine, and that many of us will learn to use them when we are no longer inhibited by fears of being shamed for being gullible.

## SOCIALIZATION

Infants and children need to learn the rules of their society in order to function effectively in it. For example, agreement about which side of the road to drive on is rather important to automobile-using societies. The right and the left hand side of the road work equally well, as long as everyone agrees which to drive on.

For this and other social conventions, the fact of universal agreement may be more important than the substance of what is agreed to.

If we do not use shame to enforce society's behavioral standards, how will we teach these conventions? We find clues in Montessori schools and other programs designed to reduce shaming in socialization and education. Perhaps the most important thing is simply being conscious that our goal is to avoid shaming and to create non judgmental acceptance.

Our socialization process needs to include the message that as human beings we make mistakes. If we can accept our fallibility as normal and acceptable, we can learn that it is not something to be ashamed of. We need to teach this important message to members of future generations, while we struggle to learn the same message ourselves.

To summarize, when we heal our shame and replace it with self-esteem, acceptance, and caring, we have the potential to dramatically transform human life on earth, creating a world filled with wonder and delight.

Let's get on with the task.

## NOTES

1. New Warrior Network, P.O. Box 844, Wendell, MA 01379. (508) 544-0001.

2. Landmark Education Corp., 250 Mission St., Suite 403, San Francisco, CA 94105. (415) 882-6300.

# Appendix
## Toward Epistemology Functional for the 21st Century

When I was a freshman at U.C.L.A., I overheard a sophomore ask, "How do you know, that what you know, is valid knowledge?"[1] Later I learned that this is the central question of epistemology—the study of how one gathers and evaluates knowledge.[2]

As a scientist, I'm disturbed that so many of my colleagues seem to pay little attention to the foundations of our work. Much heated argument and misunderstanding is based upon differing, but unstated, assumptions about epistemology and the methodology derived from it. And much important knowledge is dismissed or ignored for being based upon unfamiliar or devalued epistemology. This is especially true for the human sciences.

We need to adopt the idea that *all* paradigms of epistemology have both strengths and limitations. One area of limitation frequently left unconsidered is how well the knowledge-gathering methods are suited to the questions being asked. To say it more directly: We have to match the paradigm to the problem.

Recall that there are two equally valid ways to predict the behavior of light. But in designing a camera, we must use particulate equations for the light meter, and wave theory for the lens. If the paradigm/problem match is wrong, no functional camera will result.

When we take a global view, it seems clear that the "hard" sciences are well suited to the easy problems, but the "soft" sciences are required for the difficult ones. "Hard" sciences are those that test hypotheses by rigorous adherence to the protocol of con-

**302**

trol, measure, and reproduce (CMR). This protocol is often called *The* Scientific Method; I consider it to be *a* scientific method, and will refer to it as "CMR Science."

The difficult problems are mostly those involving the behavior of members of our own species, and include those covered in this book, as well as broader aspects of men's liberation, human behavioral/emotional/spiritual healing in general, and most approaches to the preservation of our planet. I judge CMR Science to be thoroughly inadequate for solving these problems, even though it is clearly the epistemology of choice in other areas. There's an urgent need for us to develop the "soft" sciences, and to employ with honor those already developed. The first step is to cease expecting CMR to be the *only* valid scientific method at our disposal, and to restrict its use to appropriate applications.[3]

So—how do we know that 'what we know' is valid knowledge? I've made a start toward improved paradigms of epistemology for the human sciences. Science is broadly defined as ways of being honest about the natural world. If it isn't honest, it isn't science. Testing protocols (such as CMR) have great value in exposing error and bias, but the protocol should not be allowed to substitute for the *sine qua non* of honesty.

Four criteria are proposed for a successful scientific method. It should work well for its specific applications, and also be communicable, rigorously honest, and humane.

Where do we look for better methods to facilitate human healing? One source is the method of exemplars, pioneered by Maslow (1954) and by Bandler and Grinder (1975). Choose the most successful method, or practitioner, you can find for some reasonably specific problem. Analyze the elements of the total exemplary program, and then try them out, singly or in bunches, on other problems. Gather experience about what works well where, and how often. A variant is to examine several exemplars, looking for common elements, which can be tested first.

I've made a preliminary analysis of the 12-step program of Alcoholics Anonymous, which appears to me to be the best program overall for the problem of alcoholism. The exemplar chosen is not critical to the method, and readers are invited to choose their own. The point is that an exemplar be chosen and followed up, rather than just throwing up one's hands with complaints of "too many variables" or "You can't change human nature."

An important characteristic of the 12-step program is that the "investigator" is inside the phenomenon, not allegedly standing outside observing from the sidelines, as in CMR Science. This gives him more proximate access to information, and substantially enhances his understanding of what he observes. The ability to be an inside investigator/participant makes information more directly applicable to each individual, not only to a group. Individual change is the focus of the "action." Statistical analysis recedes in importance.

In CMR Science, the assumption that the scientist is an objective observer—disinterested in the outcome—is mostly fictional. To be sure, chemists do not personally enter orbitals to rearrange electrons. They remain outside by physical necessity, and alter variables by changing experimental conditions—influencing trillions of molecules simultaneously but never touching a single one of them—and by measuring a statistical effect. Kuhn (1970) and Barbour (1974) describe the paradigm-dependency of observations even in physical science, and this effect is greatly magnified in the human sciences.

The advantage of having an "insider" investigate human change is threefold: the investigator experiences the process directly, individuals are more easily observed, and the pseudo-objective posture of the investigator is no longer upheld, facilitating honesty.

In AA epistemology, the alcoholic/investigator takes responsibility for his own recovery. No physician or shaman is assigned his case; if he wants their help, it's his job to seek them out. Beginners are encouraged to start practicing the program in small ways at first, but willingness to begin is an essential ingredient.

Twelve-step groups acquire members by self-selection, so that self-acceptance is enhanced by meeting with people who share common experiences, as well as similar failings and forms of addiction. This "magic of shared experience" is an encouragement to honesty in expressing emotions and recounting personal material. Honesty is further upheld by exemplars within the group, and by the tradition of anonymity, which creates a safe "container" for practice in breaking Denial, No Talk, and other shaming rules. Honesty blesses the true self.

Anecdotal communication is the norm in 12-step programs. The major portion of *Alcoholics Anonymous* (1976) is devoted to publishing the "stories" of individual alcoholics. Today, "anecdotal" is usually spoken with a slight sneer, or other pejorative intonation; we need to rescue it from its present imprisonment in the lexicon of shaming threats. I view anecdotal communication as the style of choice for human behavioral and emotional healing. The effectiveness of "telling my story" is difficult to overemphasize (see Everingham, 1995b, under Talk About It.)

Communication is usually face to face in AA, or over the telephone. "I-statements" are the norm (Gordon, 1976, pp. 115–171), and members who use other forms are often gently reminded. Intuition and other activities of the nondominant cerebral cortex are not greeted with suspicion.

*Alcoholics Anonymous* (1976, p. 164) states that "Our book is meant to be suggestive only" and predicts that further inspiration is to be expected. The "suggestive only" point is occasionally infringed by some members, but anyone can read the "Big Book" for clarification. "Take what you want, and leave the rest" is the usual position.

Twelve-step programs consciously and explicitly include a "necessary vital spiritual experience" (*Alcoholics Anonymous*, 1976, p. 27 and throughout the book). Surrender to a power "greater than ourselves" is integral to the program. Religious controversy is minimized by having the alcoholic choose his own conception of God, Goddess, Higher Power, or whatever name fits his concept. This device encourages 12-steppers to make a serious investigation of their *own* values, assumptions, and beliefs, and rework or discard those no longer judged to be functional. An entire chapter is devoted to "We Agnostics" (*Alcoholics Anonymous*, 1976, pp. 44–57).

Service to others is part of the twelfth step, and is seen to be primarily for the benefit of the server, not the recipient. I see this as having the effect of reducing the self-surveillance of shame-bound addicts, and forcing them (us) to relax for a while and enjoy attending to others.

Kurtz (1982) has analyzed the intellectual and philosophical basis of AA. He concludes that AA works because it comes to terms with the reality of essential human limitation, and incorporates essential limitation into an effective therapy for shame. His point about shame is extended by Fossum and Mason (1986) to other addictions.

Taken together, these features constitute an epistemological paradigm in which formal reproducibility is sacrificed, but offset by gains in immediacy, honesty, individual responsibility and freedom, and direct access to information. However, there is a kind of functional reproducibility, which never yields a perfect copy, and is not in any sense guaranteed. The precision possible in CMR Science cannot even be approached by an AA-based paradigm. The question becomes: What price, precise?

Communicability is excellent, personal, and does not require a college degree. The style of communication is quite different from that of CMR Science, but I submit that it is equally effective. There is a moderate gain in humaneness, in that CMR Science always faces a conflict of interest over the immediate benefit of individual subjects being subsidiary to the benefit of a larger group, via knowledge gained. Twelve-step "subjects" rarely face this conflict.

Is AA effective in healing alcoholism? It's not effective all the time, or for everybody, but it's rarely doubted that it is the best overall approach we have for alcoholism, especially when its 50-year record is considered. Assessing generalizability of this paradigm to other problems requires further study.

Readers are encouraged to make their own analysis/synthesis of paradigms of epistemology for the human sciences. Produce your own definition and criteria for valid science, look around for examplars (or devise an alternative method for finding paradigms), and evaluate them in the light of your criteria. I wish you godspeed, for this is serious business that we can little afford to postpone.

## NOTES

1. In an absolute sense, one never *does* know. But personally and as a society, we continually rely on incomplete knowledge to make important decisions. I assume that better functional epistemology leads to better, albeit imperfect, choices.

2. I use "epistemology" in a broadly inclusive way, certainly *not* limiting it to logic, cognition, certainty, or constraint. Conversely, my position is not to deconstruct Western philosophy or traditional scientific reasoning (see Rabinow, 1986; Rorty, 1979), but to point out areas of knowledge in which I see these disciplines as deficient, and to suggest improvements *for these areas*. I agree with those who point out that acceptable "truth" is often influenced by historical practices and systems of power (Forcault, 1982; Hacking,1984). Above all, my goal is

*functional* epistemology, not that which reinforces perfectionism, control, or moral intimidation.

3. Gould (1989, pp. 277–285) argues cogently for the value of historical aspects of natural science, and for equal validity and status for the methods and epistemology necessary to historical inquiry.

# References

Abbott, Franklin (1987). *New men, new minds*. Freedom, CA: Crossing Press.

*Alcoholics Anonymous* (3rd ed.). (1976). New York: A A World Services.

Ansbacher, Heinz L., & Rowena R. Ansbacher, eds. (1956). *The individual psychology of Alfred Adler*. New York: Harper.

Astrachan, Anthony (1988). *How men feel*. New York: Doubleday.

Baber, Asa (1989, May). The little orphan girl. *Playboy*, 36, 39.

Bach, George R., & Goldberg, Herb (1974). *Creative aggression*. Garden City, NY: Doubleday.

Baker, Russell (1987). *About men*. New York: Poseidon Press.

Bandler, Richard, & Grinder, John (1975). *The structure of magic* (Vol. 1). Palo Alto, CA: Science and Behavior Books.

Barasch, Marc Ian (1993). *The healing path: A soul approach to illness*. New York: Putnam.

Barbour, Ian G. (1974). *Myths, models, and paradigms: A comparative study in science and religion*. New York: Harper.

Baumli, Francis (1985). *Men freeing men*. Jersey City, NJ: New Atlantis Press.

Baumli, Francis (1995). On men, guilt, and shame. In Roy U. Schenk & John Everingham (Eds.), *Men healing shame*. New York: Springer.

Berne, Eric (1964). *Games people play*. New York: Grove Press.

Bernstein, Jerome S. (1987). The decline of rites of passage in our culture: The impact on masculine individuation. In Louise Carus Mahdi, Steven Foster, & Meredith Little (Eds.), *Betwixt and between: Patterns of masculine and feminine initiation* (pp. 135–158). La Salle, IL: Open Court.

Bernstein, Jerome S. (1991). The U.S.-Soviet mirror. In Jeremiah Abrams & Connie Zweig (Eds.), *Meeting the Shadow* (pp. 214–218). Los Angeles: Tarcher.

Bly, Robert (1985). *Men and the wound* (audiotape). St. Paul, MN: Ally Press.

Bly, Robert (1987). The erosion of male confidence. In Louise Carus Mahdi,

Steven Foster, & Meredith Little (Eds.), *Betwixt and Between* (pp. 189–197). La Salle, IL: Open Court.

Bly, Robert (1988). *A Little book on the human shadow.* San Francisco: Harper.

Bly, Robert (1990). *Iron John: A book about men.* Reading, MA: Addison-Wesley.

Bly, Robert (1995a). Seven sources of men's shame. In Roy U. Schenk & John Everingham (Eds.), *Men healing shame.* New York: Springer.

Bly, Robert (1995b). Healing internalized shame. In Roy U. Schenk & John Everingham (Eds.), *Men healing shame.* New York: Springer.

Bly, Robert, & Meade, Michael (N.d.). *The male mode of feeling* (audiotape). Vashon, WA: Limbus

Bradshaw, John (1988). *Healing the shame that binds you.* Deerfield Beach, FL: Health Communications.

Bridges, William (1980). Transitions: Making sense of life's changes. Reading, MA: Addison-Wesley.

Broughton, James (1990). "Shaman Psalm." In *Special Deliveries* (p. 170). Seattle: Broken Moon Press.

Campbell, Joseph (1988). *The power of myth.* New York: Doubleday.

Clark, Thomas (1975). Institutional and individual views of male involvement in family planning. In *The male role in family planning conference proceedings* (pp. 12–21). Office of Family Planning, California Department of Health.

Coopersmith, Stanley (1967). *The antecedents of self-esteem.* San Francisco: Freeman.

Darwin, Charles (1955). *The expression of the emotions in man and animals.* New York: Philosophical Library. (Original work published 1872)

Diamond, Jed (1985). What good are men? In Francis Baumli (Ed.), *Men freeing men* (p. 105). Jersey City, NJ: New Atlantis Press.

Dougherty, Patrick (1988a). Men and shame (audiotape). St. Paul, MN: Patrick Dougherty.

Dougherty, Patrick. (1988b). Shame: An audio workshop (2 audiocassettes, plus workbook). St. Paul, MN: Patrick Dougherty.

Eliot, T. S. (1952). "The Love Song of J. Alfred Prufrock." In *Complete poems and plays.* New York: Harcourt, Brace & Co.

Erikson, Eric H. (1963). *Childhood and society* (2nd ed.). New York: Norton.

Everingham, John (1995a). Some basics about shame. In Roy U. Schenk & John Everingham (Eds.), *Mean healing shame.* New York: Springer.

Everingham, John. (1995b) Men Facing Shame: A Healing Process. In Roy U. Schenk & John Everingham (Eds.), *Men healing shame.* New York: Springer.

Everingham, John. (1995c). The Rescue Triangle: Shame Update. In Roy U. Schenk & John Everingham (Eds.), *Men healing shame. New York: Springer.*

Everingham, John. (1995d). Inadvertent Shaming: Family Rules and Shaming Habits. In Roy U. Schenk & John Everingham (Eds.), *Men healing shame.* New York: Springer.

Everingham, John. (1995e). Toward Epistemology Functional for the 21st Century. In Roy U. Schenk & John Everingham (Eds.), *Men healing shame*. New York: Springer.

Farrell, Warren (1990). Society's "Disposable Sex." *Transitions*, 10, 1, 4–5, 15.

Foucault, Michel (1982). The subject and power. In Hubert Dreyfuss & Paul Rabinow (Eds.), *Michel Foucault: Beyond structuralism and hermeneutics* (pp. 208–228). Chicago: University of Chicago Press.

Forward, Susan, & Buck, Craig (1989). *Toxic parents*. New York: Bantam.

Fossum, Merle A., & Mason, Marilyn J. (1986). *Facing shame: Families in recovery*. New York: Norton.

Fossum, Merle (1989). *Catching fire: Men coming alive in recovery*. San Francisco: Harper.

Frost, Robert (1939). "A Servant to Servants." In *Collected poems*. New York: Halcyon House.

Gagnon, John (1995). Basic male shame. In Roy U. Schenk & John Everingham (Eds.), *Men healing shame*. New York: Springer.

Gibran, Kahlil (1923). *The prophet*. New York: Alfred Knopf.

Giles, John (1995). Forgiving the unforgivable: Overcoming abusive parents. In Roy U. Schenk & John Everingham (Eds.), *Men healing shame*. New York: Springer.

Gilkey, Langdon (1966). *Shantung compound*. New York: Harper.

Gilligan, Carol (1981). *In a different voice: Psychological theory and women's development*. Cambridge, MA: Harvard University Press.

Gordon, Thomas (1974). *T.E.T.: Teacher effectiveness training*. New York: Wyden.

Gordon, Thomas (1976). *P.E.T. in action*. New York: Bantam.

Gottlieb, Paul (1987). The reunion. In Russell Baker (Ed.), *About Men* (pp. 141–144). New York: Poseidon Press.

Gould, Stephen Jay (1989). *Wonderful life: The Burgess shale and the nature of history*. New York: Norton.

Greenwald, Michael P. (1995) Shame, initiation, and the culture of initiated Masculinity. In Roy U. Schenk & John Everingham (Eds.), *Men healing shame*. New York: Springer.

Hacking, Ian (1984). Five parables. In Richard Rorty, J. B. Scheewind, & Quentin Skinner (Eds.), *Philosophy in history* (pp. 103–124). Cambridge: Cambridge University Press.

Henderson, Joseph L. (1964). Ancient myths and modern man. In Carl G. Jung and Marie-Louise von Franz, *Man and his Symbols* (pp. 104–157). New York: Anchor.

Hendlin, Steven J. (1992). *When good enough is never enough: Escaping the perfection trap*. Los Angeles: Tarcher.

Hendlin, Steven J. (1993, spring). Looking God in the eye: The religious and spiritual roots of perfectionism. *The Quest*, 40–48.

Hetherington, William (1990). A warning to all who value justice in the American judicial system. *Transitions 10*(3), 4–11.

Hillman, James (1989). *Blue fire*. New York: Harper Perennial.

Hovey, Frances (1989). Five life sentences—for nothing. *Transitions 9*(6), 1–2.

Jacoby, Mario (1990) *Individuation and narcissism: The psychology of self in Jung and Kohut*. London: Routledge.

James, Muriel, & Jongeward, Dorothy (1971). *Born to win: Transactional analysis with Gestalt experiments*. Reading, MA: Addison-Wesley.

James, William (1910) The self. In William James (Ed.), *Psychology. The briefer course*. New York: Henry Holt.

Jesser, Clinton (1987). Oh my loving brother. In Franklin Abbott (Ed.), *New men, new minds* (pp. 104–106). Freedom, CA: Crossing Press.

Jung, Carl G. (1928). The relations between the ego and the unconscious. *Collected Works* (Vol 7). Quoted in Jacoby, Mario. (1990). *Individuation and narcissism: The psychology of self in Jung and Kohut (pp. 85–86)*. London: Routledge.

Jung, Carl G. (1964). Approaching the unconscious. In Carl G. Jung & Marie-Louise von Franz (Eds.), *Man and his symbols* (pp. 18–103). New York: Anchor.

Jung, Carl G. (1983). *The essential Jung*. Selected & introduced by Anthony Storr. Princeton, NJ: Princeton University Press.

Karpman, Stephen B. (1968). Fairy tales and script drama analysis. *Transactional Analysis Bulletin*, 7, 39–43.

Kaufman, Gershen (1980). *Shame: The power of caring*. Cambridge, MA: Schenkman.

Kaufman, Gershen (1989). *The psychology of shame: Theory and treatment of shame-based syndromes*. New York: Springer.

Kaufman, Gershen (1992). *Shame: The power of caring* (3rd ed., rev. & expanded). Rochester, VT: Schenkman.

Kaufman, Gershen (1995). Men's shame. In Roy U. Schenk & John Everingham (Eds.), *Men healing shame*. New York: Springer.

Kaufman, Gershen, & Bly, Robert (1995). Healing internalized shame. In Roy U. Schenk & John Everingham (Eds.), *Men healing shame*. New York: Springer.

Kaufman, Gershen, & Raphael, Lev (1991). *Dynamics of power: Fighting shame and building self-esteem* (Rev. ed.). Rochester, VT: Schenkman.

Kauth, Bill (1992). *A circle of men*. New York: St. Martin's Press.

Keen, Sam (1991). The enemy maker. In Jeremiah Abrams & Connie Zweig (Eds.), *Meeting the shadow* (pp. 197–202). Los Angeles: Tarcher.

Kimmel, Michael, & Messner, Michael (1989). *Men's lives*. New York: MacMillan.

Klein, Lucille (1990). The psychology of the orphan archetype (audiotapes). Evanston, IL: C. G. Jung Institute of Chicago.

Kohut, Heinz (1971). *The analysis of the self.* New York: International Universities Press.

Kohut, Heinz (1977). *The restoration of the self.* New York: International Universities Press.

Kubler-Ross, Elisabeth (1969). *On death and dying.* New York: Macmillan.

Kuhn, Manford, & McPartland, Thomas (1954). Empirical investigation of self attitudes. *American Sociological Review, 19,* 68–76.

Kuhn, Thomas S. (1970). *The structure of scientific revolutions* (2nd ed., enlarged). Chicago: University of Chicago Press.

Kurtz, Ernest (1981). *Shame and guilt: Characteristics of the dependency cycle.* Center City, MN: Hazelden.

Kurtz, Ernest (1982). Why A.A. works: The intellectual significance of Alcoholics Anonymous. *Journal of Studies on Alcohol, 43,* 38–80.

Lee, Ronald R., & Martin, Colby J. (1991). *Psychotherapy after Kohut: A textbook of self psychology.* Hillsdale, NJ: Analytic Press.

LeShan, Lawrence (1975). *How to meditate.* New York: Little, Brown.

Ley, Dorothy C. H., & Corless, Inge B. (1988). Spirituality and hospice care. *Death Studies, 12,* 101–110.

Lindall, George (1995). A shame-based model for recovery from addiction. In Roy U. Schenk & John Everingham (Eds.), *Men healing shame.* New York: Springer.

Lindgren, David L. (1995). Grandiosity: The shadow of shame. In Roy U. Schenk & John Everingham (Eds.), *Men healing shame.* New York: Springer.

Lyman, Peter (1987). The fraternal bond as a joking relationship. In Michael Kimmel (Ed.), *Changing Men* (pp. 148–163). Newbury Park, CA: Sage.

Macchietto, John (1992). Aspects of male victimization and female aggression: Implications for counseling men. *Journal of Mental Health and Counseling, 14,* 375–392.

Machado, Antonio (1984). *Selected poems of Antonio Machado.* Chosen & translated by Robert Bly. Middletown, CT: Wesleyan University Press.

Maslow, Abraham (1954). *Motivation and personality.* New York: Harper.

Maslow, Abraham (1955). Deficiency and growth motivation. In Marshall R. Jones (Ed.), *Nebraska Symposium on Motivation.* Lincoln: University of Nebraska Press.

Mason, Marilyn, & Fossum, Merle (1987). Facing the space between: Shame, the invisible dragon (audiotape). Workshop, American Association of Marriage and Family Therapists, Chicago. Highland, IN: Creative Audio.

Masson, Jeffrey M. (1984). *The assault on truth: Freud's suppression of the seduction theory.* New York: Farrar, Straus & Giroux.

Mayeroff, Milton (1990). *On caring.* New York: Harper.

Mendelson, Eric (1990). How relevant an issue is "anti-male sexism? *Standing*

*Committee for Men Newsletter, 9,* 3–5. Alexandria, VA: Amer. Coll. Personnel Assoc.

Mickel, Andy (1988). Death-in-living and Twin Cities men. *Men Talk, 12,* 1–9.

Middleton-Moz, Jane (1990). *Shame and guilt: The masters of disguise.* Deerfield Beach, FL: Health Communications.

Miller, Alice (1981). *The drama of the gifted child.* New York: Basic Books. (Translated by Ruth Ward from *Das Drama des begabten Kindes.* [1979] Frankfurt am Main: Suhrkamp Verlag. Also published in English as *Prisoners of Childhood.*)

Miller, Alice (1984). *For your own good: Hidden cruelty in child-rearing and the roots of violence* (2nd ed.). New York: Farrar, Straus, & Giroux. (Translated by H. and H. Hannum from *Am Anfang war Erziehung.* [1980]. Frankfurt am Main: Suhrkamp Verlag.)

Miller, Alice (1986). *Thou shalt not be aware: Society's betrayal of the child.* New York: New American Library/Meridian. [Translated by H. and H. Hannum from *Du sollst nicht merken.* [1981]. Frankfurt am Main: Suhrkamp Verlag.)

Miller, Christopher (1995). Male initiation: Filling a gap in therapy. In Roy U. Schenk & John Everingham (Eds.), *Men healing shame.* New York: Springer.

Moore, Robert (N.d.). Rediscovering masculine potentials (audiotapes). Evanston, IL: C. G. Jung Institute of Chicago.

Moore, Robert, & Gillette, Douglas (1990). *King, Warrior, Magician, Lover: Rediscovering the archetypes of the mature masculine.* San Francisco: Harper.

Moore, Robert, & Gillette, Douglas (1992a). *The King within.* New York: William Morrow.

Moore, Robert, & Gillette, Douglas (1992b). *The Warrior within.* New York: William Morrow.

Moore, Robert, & Gillette, Douglas (1993a). *The Magician within.* New York: William Morrow.

Moore, Robert, & Gillette, Douglas (1993b). *The Lover within.* New York: William Morrow.

Moyers, Bill, with Bly, Robert (1990). *A gathering of men* (videotape). New York: Mystic Fire Video.

Nathanson, Donald L. (1987). Shaming systems in couples, families, and institutions. In D. L. Nathanson (Ed.), *The Many Faces of Shame* (pp. 246–270). New York: Guilford.

Osherson, Samuel (1986). *Finding our fathers.* New York: Fawcette Columbine.

Paul, Jordan, & Paul, Margaret (1983). *Do I have to give up me to be loved by you?* Minneapolis: CompCare Publications.

Pearson, Carol S. (1986). *The hero within: Six archetypes we live by.* San Francisco: Harper.

Pearson, Carol S. (1991). *Awakening the heroes within: Twelve archetypes to help us find ourselves and transform our world.* San Francisco: Harper.

Peck, M. Scott (1978). *The road less traveled: A new psychology of love, traditional values and spiritual growth.* New York: Simon & Schuster.

Perls, Frederick S. (1969). *In and out the garbage pail.* New York: Bantam.

Perry, Danaan (1985). We're not ready yet, but soon: Exploring the edge of maleness. *In Context, #10,* 47–49.

Potter-Efron, Ronald, & Potter-Efron, Patricia (1989). *Letting go of shame.* Center City, MN: Hazelden.

Pynchon, Thomas (1973). *Gravity's rainbow.* New York: Bantam.

Rabinow, Paul (1986). Representations are social facts: Modernity and post-modernity in anthropology. In James Clifford & George C. Marcus (Eds.), *Writing culture: The poetics and politics of ethnography* (pp. 234–261). Berkeley: University of California Press.

Redfield, James (1993). *The celestine prophecy.* New York: Warner.

Robertson, John, & Fitzgerald, Louise (1990). The (mis) treatment of men: Effects of client gender role and life-style on diagnosis and attribution of pathology. *Journal of Counseling Psychology, 37,* 3–9.

Rorty, Richard (1979). *Philosophy and the mirror of nature.* Princeton, N.J.: Princeton University Press.

Sartre, Jean-Paul (1966). *Being and nothingness.* New York: Washington Square Press. (Original work published 1943.)

Satir, Virginia (1974). *Conjoint family therapy.* Palo Alto, CA: Science and Behavior Books.

Schenk, Roy U. (1982). *The other side of the coin: Causes and consequences of men's oppression.* Madison, WI: Bioenergetics Press.

Schenk, Roy U. (1989). *We've been had: Writings on men's issues.* Madison, WI: Bioenergetics Press.

Schenk, Roy U. (1991). *On sex and gender: Thoughts of Dr. Schenk.* Madison, WI: Bioenergetics Press.

Schenk, Roy U. (1995a). Shame in men's lives. In Roy U. Schenk & John Everingham (Eds.), *Men healing shame.* New York: Springer.

Schenk, Roy U. (1995b). Beyond shame: Transforming our lives. In Roy U. Schenk & John Everingham (Eds.), *Men healing shame.* New York: Springer.

Schneider, Carl D. (1977). *Shame, exposure, and privacy.* Boston: Beacon Press. (Reprinted 1992, New York: Norton)

Schneider, Carl D. (1987). A mature sense of shame. In Donald L. Nathanson (Ed.), *The many faces of shame* (pp. 192–213). New York: Guilford.

Schneir, Miriam (1972) *Feminism: The essential historical writings.* New York: Vintage.

Schoenbeck, Lorilee (1992, November). Yoga: On and off the mat. *Poor Joe's Metrozine* (now *The Portland Metrozine*), 20–21.

Smalley, Gary, & Trent, John (1986). *The blessing.* New York: Pocket Books.

Smith, Cyprian (1987). *The way of paradox: Spiritual life as taught by Meister Eckhart*. New York: Paulist Press.

Stevens, Anthony (1983). *Archetypes: A natural history of the self*. New York: Quill.

Straus, Murray, (1993). Physical assaults by wives: A major social problem. In Richard J. Gelles & Donileen Robert Loseke (Eds.), *Current Controversies on Family Violence* (pp. 67–87). Newbury Park, CA: Sage.

Sullivan, Harry Stack (1953) *The interpersonal theory of psychiatry*. New York: Norton.

*The twelve steps: A healing journey*. (1986). Center City, MN: Hazelden. Anonymous.

Tomkins, Sylvan S. (1987). Shame. In Donald L. Nathanson (Ed.), *The many faces of shame* (pp. 133–161). New York: Guilford.

*Twelve steps and twelve traditions*. (1950). New York: A A World Services. Anonymous.

von Franz, Marie-Louise. (1964). The process of individuation. In Carl G. Jung and Marie-Louise von Franz, (Eds.), *Man and his symbols* (pp. 158–229). New York: Anchor.

von Franz, Marie-Louise. (1980). *Puer Aeternus*. New York: Harcourt Brace Jovanovich.

Zubaty, Rich (1993). *Surviving the feminization of America*. Tinley Park, IL: Panther Press.

# Index

*Springer Publishing Company*

## SELF-ESTEEM
### *Research, Theory, and Practice*

**Chris Mruk,** PhD

Low self-esteem is frequently an underlying factor in a range of psychological disorders, including depression, suicide, and certain personality disorders. The recent explosion of research and literature on self-esteem only emphasizes the need for a comprehensive examination of what we know and do not know about this complicated issue. Dr. Mruk provides a thorough analysis of the vast literature, from which he derives the most practical and effective methods available for the enhancement of self-esteem. His recommendations are based on both qualitative and quantitative findings, and take into account both individual and societal factors. This book should be required reading for all advanced students, researchers, and academics, as well as clinicians, who are concerned with the enhancement of self-esteem.

### Contents:

*1995   240pp   0-8261-8750-1   hardcover*

536 Broadway, New York, NY 10012-3955 • (212) 431-4370 • Fax (212) 941-7842

**Springer Publishing Company**

# BECOMING A FATHER
## Contemporary Perspectives

**Jerrold Lee Shapiro,** PhD, **Michael J. Diamond,** PhD, and **Martin Greenberg,** MD, Editors

One of the most important events in men's lives is becoming a father. This transition has life long psychological, social, and emotional effects. In this volume, the editors and contributors explore both the dramatic increase in the involvement of fathers in pregnancy, childbirth, and early parenting, as well as the implications of fatherhood from a sociocultural, psychodynamic, and personal perspective.

*Springer Series: Focus on Men*
1995   384pp   0-8261-8400-6   hardcover

536 Broadway, New York, NY 10012-3955 • (212) 431-4370 • Fax (212) 941-7842

**⑤** *Springer Publishing Company*

# THE PSYCHOLOGY OF SHAME
## Theory and Treatment of Shame-Based Syndromes

**Gershen Kaufman,** PhD

Foreword by **Silvan S. Tomkins,** PhD

*"This is an extremely thoughtful, creative and ambitious book...virtually any psychologist who practices or studies psychotherapy will find this volume useful, enjoyable and provocative...it works from a theory of human development and experience to create a comprehensive approach to psychopathology and psychotherapy."*
—Contemporary Psychology

### Contents:

**Part I: A Developmental Theory of Shame, Identity, and the Self.** Phenomenology and Facial Signs of Shame • The Face of Shame over the Life Cycle • Internalization of Shame • Psychological Magnification of Shame Scenes • Reformulating Psychopathology.

**Part II: Psychotherapeutic Intervention.** Restoring the Interpersonal Bridge • Returning Internalized Shame to its Interpersonal Origins • Identity Regrowth and Healing Shame • Developing Equal Power in Current Relationships and the Family of Origin • Time-Limited Group-Focused Treatment for Shame-Based Syndromes.

**Epilogue: A Language of the Self.**

*Behavioral Science Book Service Selection*
*1989   320pp   0-8261-6670-9   hardcover*

536 Broadway, New York, NY 10012-3955 • (212) 431-4370 • Fax (212) 941-7842